Conditionality Revisited

Conditionality Revisited

Concepts, Experiences, and Lessons

Edited by

**Stefan Koeberle, Harold Bedoya,
Peter Silarsky, and Gero Verheyen**

THE WORLD BANK
Washington, D.C.

ISBN 0-8213-6013-2   978-0-8213-6013-2
e-ISBN 0-8213-6014-0

Library of Congress Cataloging-in-Publication Data

Conditionality revisited : concepts, experiences, and lessons learned / edited by Stefan Koeberle,
   Peter Silarszky, Gero Verheyen.
       p. cm.
   "This book originated in the Development Policy Forum 'Conditionality Revisited' hosted
by the World Bank's OPCS Country Economics Group in Paris on July 5, 2004"—P.
   Includes index.
   ISBN 0-8213-6013-2 (pbk.)
     1. Economic assistance—Congresses. 2. Conditionality (International Relations)—Congresses.
   3. Economic assistance—Political aspects—Congresses. 4. Loans, Foreign—Political Aspects—
   Congresses. 5. Economic development—Finance—Congresses.
   I. Koeberle, Stefan, 1965- II. Silarszky, Peter. III. Verheyen, Gero. IV. World Bank.

HC60.C62486 2005
338.91—dc22
                                                                    2004062945

Contents

Part IV Toward Country-Owned Approaches: Do We Still Need Conditionality?

Part V Partnerships in Policy-Based Lending

Part VI Conclusions

Foreword

Why do we need to revisit conditionality? Conditionality became a controversial concept after international financial institutions, particularly the International Monetary Fund and the World Bank, provided policy-based lending to help developing countries adjust to the debt crisis of the 1980s. Since then, the tension between country ownership and conditionality has emerged as a central issue in the debates about policy-based lending. Over the past quarter century, the development community has learned from the experience with policy-based lending around the world: Among the most important lessons are that conditionality cannot substitute for ownership, general blueprints do not (always) work, and principles matter more than policy prescriptions. Many critics of traditional conditionality have also asserted that some of the past practices were either too intrusive or ineffective, and in some cases undermined government ownership and implementation of sustainable economic policies in developing countries.

The approach to conditionality has shifted away from the old model of the 1980s, but has not yet settled on a new one. While there is now generally more recognition of the importance of ownership, a stronger focus on development results, and greater selectivity based on country performance, there are still different views and approaches among the international financial institutions, bilateral development partners, recipient governments, and critical observers. Some, including the World Bank and the International Monetary Fund, have embarked on the task of streamlining conditionality, greater selectivity, and new approaches such as programmatic lending. Others, including the European Commission, are seeking to reconcile the objectives of predictable budget support for low-income countries with performance orientation by basing disbursements on outcomes. And there are also those who remain unconvinced by these efforts and advocate a partnership between donors and recipients that could forsake conditionality altogether.

This book takes stock of recent experience with these new approaches to conditionality over the past few years, and discusses a number of key questions. Is there still a useful role for conditionality? What is the right balance between ownership and conditionality? How has conditionality changed with the streamlining efforts of the

World Bank and the International Monetary Fund? How have the content and focus of conditionality evolved? What has been the experience with different types of conditionality, and do they matter—be it ex ante, programmatic, process-oriented, or outcome-based conditionality? How can we make partnerships in conditionality more effective? Although this can only be the beginning of a dialogue, we hope that this volume of contributions by authors from a wide variety of backgrounds will make a contribution to the ongoing debate on development effectiveness and the future shape of conditionality.

James W. Adams
Vice President
Operations Policy and Country Services
World Bank

Acknowledgments

This book was made possible by the authors of the papers, who freely shared their insights and shared a common interest in advancing the development dialogue beyond institutional boundaries. We are particularly grateful to the policy makers from low- and middle-income countries for sharing their firsthand experience with conditionality. Contributions from development practitioners from international and bilateral development agencies, leading scholars, and experts from civil societies enabled us to review the past experience with conditionality from multiple viewpoints and present what we hope is a balanced study of this complex issue. The input and active involvement in the discussion of all participants of the Development Policy Forum "Conditionality Revisited" in Paris on July 5, 2004, was also essential.

We especially appreciate the support, interest, and cooperation of James W. Adams, Vice President, Operations Policy and Country Services, and John M. Underwood, Director, Operations Policy and Country Services, World Bank. We are grateful to Sabine Hader, who in addition to helping to draft the agenda of the Forum was instrumental in organizing the event. The administrative support of Pansy V. Chintha was also critical. We acknowledge with appreciation the support of the staff of the Paris Conference Center of the World Bank.

The Editors

List of Participants

Adams, Jim	Vice President Operations Policy and Country Services World Bank
Ahmed, Masood	Director General Department for International Development (DFID) United Kingdom
Allen, Mark	Director Policy Development & Review Department International Monetary Fund
Ansu, Yaw	Sector Director Poverty Reduction and Economic Management World Bank
Arce, Marcelo Barron	Viceministerio De Inversion Publica Y Financiamiento Externo Ministerio De Hacienda Bolivia
Baile, Stephanie	Principal Administrator Aid Effectiveness & Donor Practices Policy Co-ordination Department Organisation for Economic Co-operation and Development, Development Assistance Committee
Bedoya, Harold	Senior Economist Operations Policy and Country Services World Bank
Bhattacharya, Amar	Senior Adviser Poverty Reduction and Economic Management World Bank

Bruce, Colin
Senior Manager
Operations Policy and Country Services
World Bank

Buiter, Willem
Chief Economist
European Bank for Reconstruction
and Development

Burton, John
Deputy Chief Economist
Department for International Development
(DFID)
United Kingdom

Bus, Riny
Head of Division
International Financial Institutions,
UN and IFIs Department
Ministry of Foreign Affairs
Netherlands

Chhibber, Ajay
Director
Operations Evaluation Department
World Bank

Collier, Paul
Professor
Oxford University
United Kingdom

Dervis, Kemal
Former Minister of the Economy
Turkey

Edwards, David
Director
Operations Evaluation Division
Asian Development Bank

Gillies, Alison
Adviser
Operations Policy and Country Services
World Bank

Gillsater, Björn
Senior Advisor to Executive Director—Nordic
and Baltic Countries
World Bank

Gomez, Mauricio
Vice Minister of Economic Relations
and Cooperation
Ministry of External Relations
Nicaragua

Greenhill, Romilly
Policy Officer—Aid and Accountability
ActionAid International
United Kingdom

Hader, Sabine
Senior Operations Officer
Operations Policy and Country Services
World Bank

Hall, Chris	Program Coordinator Operations Policy and Country Services World Bank
Hervio, Gilles	Head Economic Cooperation and PRSP Process European Commission
Isenman, Paul	Head Policy Co-ordination Department Organisation for Economic Co-operation and Development, Development Assistance Committee
Jaramillo-Vallejo, Jaime	Adviser Operations Policy and Country Services World Bank
Jones, John	Director Institute for Global Networking, Information and Studies Oslo, Norway
Jones, Terence	Group Leader Capacity Development Group Bureau for Development Policy, United Nations Development Programme
Kabbaj, Mohamed	Head of Division Ministry of Finance and Privatization Morocco
Ketsela, Mulu	Minister of State Ministry of Finance and Economic Development Ethiopia
Killick, Tony	Senior Research Associate Overseas Development Institute London, United Kingdom
Koeberle, Stefan	Adviser Operations Policy and Country Services World Bank
Kurowski, Per	Executive Director for Central America, Spain, Mexico and Venezuela World Bank
Ladd, Paul	Economic Advisor International Poverty Unit HM Treasury United Kingdom

Levy, Joaquim   Secretary of the Treasury
                                  Ministry of Finance
                                  Brazil

Lin, Soe   Advisor
                                  Policy Co-ordination Department
                                  Organisation for Economic Co-operation
                                  and Development, Development Assistance
                                  Committee

Malesa, Thaddeus   Consultant
                                  Operations Policy and Country Services
                                  World Bank

Manh Cuong, Cao   Head of General Division
                                  Foreign Economic Relations Department
                                  Ministry of Planning and Investment
                                  Vietnam

Manning, Richard   Chairman
                                  Development Cooperation Directorate
                                  Organisation for Economic Co-operation
                                  and Development

Mizrahi, Simon   Policy Co-ordination Department
                                  Organisation for Economic Co-operation
                                  and Development, Development Assistance
                                  Committee

Montador, Bruce   Vice President
                                  Multilateral Programs Branch
                                  Canadian International Development Agency
                                  Canada

Morrissey, Oliver   Professor
                                  University of Nottingham
                                  United Kingdom

Mukanbetov, Sanjar   Director Investment Policy Department
                                  Ministry of Finance
                                  Kyrgyz Republic

Nankani, Gobind   Vice President
                                  Poverty Reduction and Economic Management
                                  World Bank

Nduke, Felix Orah   Manager
                                  Policy and Performance Review
                                  African Development Bank

Niane, Thierno Seydo   Coordonnateur
                                  Ministère de l'Economie et des Finances
                                  Senegal

Page, John	Chief Economist African Region World Bank
Paulson, Sara	Director Office of International Development Policy Department of the Treasury United States
Quesnel, Brice	Head Multilateral Development Banks Division Ministry of Finance France
Roeskau, Michael	Director Development Cooperation Directorate Organisation for Economic Co-operation and Development, Development Assistance Committee
Sani, Yakoubou Mamane	Commissaire Chargé du Développement Ministère des Finances et de l'Économie Niger
Silarszky, Peter	Economist Operations Policy and Country Services World Bank
Thann An, Pham Thi	Ministry of Planning and Investment Foreign Economic Relations Department Vietnam
Tumusiime-Mutebile, Emmanuel	Governor Bank of Uganda Uganda
Ung, Duong Duc	Director General Foreign Economic Relations Department Ministry of Planning and Investment Vietnam
van der Ven, Ad	Coordinator Multilateral Bank Affairs Ministry of Finance Netherlands
Watt, Patrick	Policy Officer Policy and Campaigns Department ActionAid International
Westman, Bo	Senior Policy Adviser Department for Global Development Ministry of Foreign Affairs Sweden

Williamson, John	Senior Fellow Institute for International Economics United States
Wolff, Peter	Head of Department German Development Institute Germany
Yanara, Chhieng	Secretary General Cambodian Rehabilitation and Development Board Cambodia

Part I
Introduction

Overview

Conditionality has been a controversial topic ever since policy-based lending gained prominence in the early 1980s. It has become a renewed topic of interest with the emergence of a new international aid architecture that is converging around a number of trends. Some bilateral donors are emphasizing budget support as a way of financing development to complement or substitute for their traditional reliance on project-based aid. The international consensus around the importance of the Millennium Development Goals is providing a greater results orientation for development. Country-driven development strategies such as the Poverty Reduction Strategy Papers (PRSPs) increasingly serve as the coordinating framework for prioritizing development aid. The recognition of country ownership as a central determinant of aid effectiveness raises the question of how conditionality should be designed, how it should be coordinated among different donors, and whether it is still needed. At the same time, a variety of efforts have been undertaken to streamline conditionality and explore new approaches to its design.

Objectives

The objective of this collection of articles is to share some of these experiences to date and to contribute to a better mutual understanding and greater convergence within the development community on when and how conditionality might still play a useful role in supporting countries' development efforts. This book originated in the Development Policy Forum "Conditionality Revisited" hosted by the World Bank's Operations Policy and Country Services Country Economics group in Paris on July 5, 2004. About 60 leading political decision makers from low- and middle-income countries, development practitioners from international and bilateral development agencies, and leading scholars and experts from civil societies reflected on the recent experience with conditionality with a goal of developing a better understanding of concerns with conditionality and helping to guide future trends in policy-based lending. The opinions they express here are not intended to represent an official statement of the institutions with which they are affiliated. This publication makes the results of the research in the area and the discussion at the forum accessible to a wider audience.

Most of the contributors to this book argue that donors should approach the design of conditionality with a degree of humility, recognizing that the problems faced by developing countries are complex in nature and often do not lend themselves to a single solution. Their acknowledgment that not all of the development approaches and advice of the past turned out to be as appropriate or effective as it could have been only serves to underscore the importance of approaching development with blueprint or general prescription in mind. Some would nuance this conclusion by emphasizing that principles such as the rule of law, sustainable public finances, and a favorable investment climate have nonetheless emerged as broadly accepted ingredients of successful development—even though each country has to find its own specific development path.

Many critics have pointed to the potentially corrosive effect of conditionality, and there is an increasing recognition of the limitations of the traditional approach. Although some have gone as far as suggesting giving up conditionality altogether, most observers would probably agree that some conditions are needed to ensure mutual accountability and due diligence. There is less agreement on how explicit such conditions should be and what form they should take.

More conditionality cannot compensate for weak government commitment or implementation capacity—a key lesson of the past two decades from which different conclusions can be drawn:

- Selectivity in favor of countries with favorable policy environments and commitment to a viable development strategy may be more effective than attempts to cajole and persuade reluctant reformers.

- A country's track record is a better indicator of its determination and effectiveness in implementing a viable development strategy than elaborate promises for future efforts. Turnaround cases, new governments, and crisis situations may provide windows of opportunity for reform, although the timing and ability of donors to properly assess such situations remains questionable.

- The quality and impact of policy-based lending or budget support tend to be greater with fewer, more focused, and streamlined conditions that are critical to the success of the program. As long as there is adequate commitment to reform, conditionality for good performers can be less prescriptive.

Ownership is an elusive concept. It does not imply or even require full consensus—as several observers point out in this book, some form of conditionality can sometimes play a useful role in helping champions of reform push through effective measures against the determined resistance of vested interests. At the same time, effective policy reform not only requires domestic capacities, but also is best achieved through a broad policy dialogue. There seems to be an emerging consensus on the importance of analytical and diagnostic work as a critical contribution of international donors to help countries evaluate different options and formulate their own development strategies.

Conditionality has traditionally been associated with policy-based lending, primarily provided by the International Monetary Fund (IMF), the World Bank, and regional development banks. As other donors have increasingly shifted part of their development aid to budget support, there has been an increased recognition of the need to harmonize donor approaches to conditionality. It is probably fair to say that it is less clear on what framework to harmonize around. Part of the issue is that few countries have come close to the vision of a clearly articulated and prioritized strategy with realistic expected results and a robust monitoring framework that would guide donor support. To the extent that reality falls short of such a country-driven policy matrix, donors will mostly still find it necessary to operationalize their support and harmonize their efforts through a more specific bilateral understanding that risks not being fully aligned with the country's own strategy.

As the contributions in this volume illustrate, many questions around the different donor approaches to conditionality remain controversial. How relevant is the number of conditions? Is ex ante or ex post conditionality more conducive as a mutual commitment device? How can budget support be more predictable—by focusing conditions on specific policy actions or on outcomes? How can risks be managed, and what is the optimal risk and failure rate of conditions and programs?

Ex post conditionality based on completed actions provides an alternative to traditional ex ante conditionality that promises to be more flexible and more supportive of government ownership. It is at the core of the programmatic approach to policy-based lending that has increasingly become the World Bank's choice to support medium-term reforms.

Another possible design option involves conditionality that bases disbursement of aid on the achievement of outcomes. The European Commission has espoused this approach as an alternative to move away from intrusive micromanagement through policy matrices and action plans to allow countries greater flexibility in choosing their specific paths toward reaching their stated goals. Potential drawbacks of this approach, which are discussed in this book, include the limited accountability of the governments for determining the actual outcomes, unclear results chains, and the limited availability of relevant data. In addition, there is a question as to whether basing disbursements of aid on outcomes might jeopardize the predictability of resource flows.

Some observers support the idea of using international minimum standards and codes (similar to the Basel requirements in the banking sector) to determine countries' eligibility for support from developing agencies. Others caution that using a set of standards as a reference point quickly risks becoming a one-size-fits-all approach. To ensure accountability of international development institutions toward their clients, a few advocate the idea that international development institutions should provide insurance policies for the failure of reforms based on their advice.

In addition, there is also a question of terminology; the term "conditionality" is not being used by the various observers with the same meaning. For some, it has become synonymous with the alleged attempt of the Bretton Woods institutions to impose the Washington consensus around the world. Others use it as a summary concept to mean all the explicit and implicit requirements for lending, including covenants for project-based aid, environmental safeguards, and performance-based aid allocations. To be consistent, this book uses the term conditionality as the specific set of conditions attached to the disbursement of policy-based lending or budget support—which of course can take different forms, ranging from explicit agreements to implicit understandings and from traditional ex ante conditions based on promises to ex post conditions based on actual completed measures.

Most of these discussions are relevant for developing countries that have the capacity and commitment to provide a credible basis for budget support. But there is also a question of the most appropriate approach in countries with inadequate policy performance, particularly fragile low-income countries with weak policies and institutions. Possible responses can range from disengagement and limiting aid to policy dialogue, technical assistance, and focused policy-based lending. Process conditionality and ex post conditionality are possible options when issues of weak track record and credibility arise. The use of grants instead of loans and credits could be more appropriate in high-risk environments where policy reforms are more likely to fail.

The collection of papers in this book will contribute to this ongoing debate. Although some of the issues discussed may not be fully resolved in the near future, mutual understanding of differing views and approaches is important for successful cooperation and development of future thinking on conditionality in the modern aid architecture.

Organization

The book is structured as follows. The remainder of part 1 provides a brief overview of the main sections of the book. To set the stage for the subsequent contributions, Mr. Tumusiime-Mutebile, governor of the Bank of Uganda, summarizes the experience with conditionality in Africa from the perspective of a policy maker in an aid-recipient country. Part 2 focuses on changes in the approach to conditionality in both World Bank and IMF programs and recent experiences with streamlining conditionality. Part 3 discusses how the content of policy-based lending has evolved over the past decade and what lessons emerge for the use of conditionality. Part 4 presents the debate on practical design questions of conditionality, including the issues of conditionality versus country ownership and ex ante versus ex post conditionality. Part 5 examines how cooperation among development partners—nongovernmental organizations, international financial institutions, bilateral donors, civil society, and governments—can make policy-based lending and budget support a more effective tool of development policy. Part 6 offers concluding observations.

Part 2. Conditionality Revisited: What Has Changed?

This section focuses on how the World Bank and IMF are currently approaching conditionality. Both institutions have changed their understanding and practice of conditionality over the past few years, especially through a thorough review of their own practices, renewed efforts at streamlining, and an openness to new design approaches.

Mark Allen, director of the Policy Development and Review Department at the IMF, summarizes the IMF's own analysis of conditionality and its experience with implementing new guidelines. The IMF's extensive review covered all aspects of conditionality in IMF programs, in particular the role of structural conditionality and issues of ownership. Allen concludes that the IMF has appropriately adapted conditionality to country circumstances as well as streamlined conditionality to a more acceptable level. At the same time, he acknowledges that the role of loan conditionality is not always effective when used as a tool for leverage, and should instead be used to give the country authorities a framework to take appropriate measures based on strong policy dialogue.

Stefan Koeberle, manager of the Country Economics Unit at the World Bank, summarizes trends in World Bank adjustment lending over the past 25 years. He sketches the evolution of lending instruments that were initially introduced to provide short-term balance-of payments support for adjustments that aim to reduce economic distortions, correct their external and internal imbalances and liberalize their economies. Over time, however, the World Bank's policy-based lending increasingly focused on social sectors and more medium-term structural and institutional reforms that require a sustained engagement. He suggests that the World Bank has not only reduced the number of conditions attached to policy-based lending but also has adapted its design approaches toward greater customization and flexibility. In particular, programmatic lending involving a series of operations based on prior actions has emerged as a promising approach to reconcile predictability of resource flows with a focus on results.

Tony Killick, senior research associate at the Overseas Development Institute, examines the changing attitudes toward conditionality by both the World Bank and IMF. He acknowledges that over the years, both institutions have moved away from seeing conditionality as a tool for financial leverage. While conditionality has been streamlined in recent years, Killick remains skeptical as to exactly how much staff buy-in there is in practice. He points to various debt reduction schemes, such as the Highly Indebted Poor Countries (HIPC) Initiative, in which the development institutions have started to avoid past defensive lending practices that tended to reduce the development impact. Taking into account the move toward more country ownership and partnerships through policy dialogue, Killick finds that a constructive way forward seems to have been found, although a significant risk remains that new approaches will also increase the amount of aggregate conditionality placed upon the client countries.

The contributions and discussion in part 2 of the book highlight a number of issues, questions, and suggestions for the World Bank and the IMF's approach to conditionality:

- **The role of conditionality.** The concept of conditionality itself has moved from one of financial leverage to one of mutual accountability and due diligence. Both the IMF and the World Bank perceive their support as being more an aid to help remove the constraints for policy actions than a reward for particular policy actions. The support is also meant to tip the balance between reformers and non-reformers in borrowing countries, creating a more accommodating environment for the adoption of country-owned policy reforms.

- **Conditionality and ownership.** A consensus seems to exist that country ownership is a necessary condition for the successful and sustained implementation of policy reforms. In this context, both institutions have a role to play in helping to forge ownership through analytical work and dialogue. Nevertheless, respecting full ownership may create some tensions with the due diligence obligation of these institutions as lenders, especially when independence in policy advice is compromised by extreme interpretations of ownership.

- **Quality of policies and conditionality.** There is a tension between ownership and conditionality that cannot be fully resolved and should instead be frankly acknowledged. However, some observers suggest that the tension can be addressed in part by expecting borrowing countries to follow some minimum standards on fundamental policies to gain access to financing from donors, leaving space for any additional country-grown policies beyond those minimum standards. This approach is facilitated by the improvements in the policy environment that have taken place in almost all countries in the past decade. It would also be consistent with the drive to ease the debt burden through the HIPC Initiative and could perhaps prevent corrosive defensive lending. A critical component for further improvements in the policy framework is to continue efforts to build local capacity and institutions, especially in low-income countries.

- **Policy failure and conditionality.** When expected results are not achieved, it is difficult to ascertain the underlying reason. Were the relevant conditions wrong, or did exogenous developments overcome the positive effects of the right policies? Failure may be the result of inappropriate or inconsistent policies, or insufficient recognition of capacity constraints. However, development takes place in an inherently uncertain environment where not all risks can or should be avoided. If the optimal rate of failure is not zero, a key question is: Which conditions are the appropriate ones?

- **Results focus and conditionality.** A greater results focus in the use of conditionality is warranted to enhance aid effectiveness and provide fiduciary assurances to aid donors. This will require a better understanding of the links between specific policy actions and expected medium-term outcomes. Outcome-based conditionality may provide a possible approach that minimizes interference in the choice of policy actions and thus promises greater ownership. However, its potential drawbacks include uncertainties about the results chain between actions and outcomes in many sectors, an inappropriate focus on outcomes that are beyond the control of the authorities, difficulties associated with measuring results where no prior indicators exist, and a bias toward policy areas that are more amenable to quantifiable indicators (education, health).

- **Streamlining conditionality.** Both the World Bank and the IMF have increased their efforts to streamline conditionality and the number of conditions. Nevertheless, continued progress in this area hinges on having effective buy-in of these objectives by the respective staffs of both institutions. Although the absolute number of conditions says little about effectiveness or relevance, a focus on conditions that are critical to the success of the program and owned by the country seems appropriate.

Part 3. Policy Approaches and Policy-Based Lending: What Have We Learned?

Part 3 discusses the critical factors for the success of policy-based lending, drawing on the lessons of aid effectiveness over the past decade that general blueprints do not (always) work and that principles matter more than policy prescriptions. This section addresses the following questions:

- Given the importance of the country policy environment as a determinant of development effectiveness, what contribution can the design and content of conditionality make?

- How has the content of conditionality changed in light of the development experiences of the 1990s?

John Williamson from the Institute for International Economics describes the reasons for the introduction of policy-based lending by the World Bank in the early 1980s, its goals, and its evolution over time.

Ajay Chhibber, director of the Operations Evaluation Department (OED) of the World Bank, bases his conclusions on OED's evaluation of the effectiveness of policy-based lending. He shows that developing countries' policies improved in roughly two-thirds of all countries, in all regions, and in almost all areas between 1999 and 2003; countries with good/improving policies grew more rapidly than countries with bad/deteriorating policies; and growth is a major factor in poverty reduction. According to these findings, World Bank lending has been concentrated in countries with improving policy environments. Operations typically fail owing to insufficient knowledge, no track record, lack of country ownership, and overoptimism. Chhibber concludes that conditionality has some impact on implementation of reforms but little impact on long-term adoption of reforms and outcomes.

Paul Collier of Oxford University focuses on conditionality in poor-performing, low-income African countries, where policies are deteriorating and poverty is getting worse. He attributes the failure of conditionality in these countries to the lack of ability to enforce agreements. The key issues associated with conditionality include psychological reactions of country stakeholders to imposed conditions, credibility, the importance of favorable learning experiences (often from crises), and the distinction between consequences of bad policies and of external shocks. Collier favors ex post conditionality (selectivity) given past credibility problems and process conditionality resulting from lack of domestic accountability in poor-performing countries. He also strongly advocates the introduction of general international minimum standards and codes—similar to the Basel requirements for the financial sector—that could be used to determine countries' eligibility for support from developing agencies.

Joaquim Levy from Brazil's Ministry of Finance addresses conditionality from the perspective of a middle-income country. He stresses the importance of country ownership for success of reforms and describes the positive experience Brazil has had with programmatic lending, the flexibility provided through a sectorwide approach modality, and the experience with subnational loans. Levy speaks in favor of developing a new, flexible World Bank approach to middle-income countries (similar to the PRSP for low-income countries), reducing the cost of doing business with the World Bank, enhancing the World Bank's effort to facilitate public-private partnerships, and relying more on a country's national fiduciary and safeguard systems.

The contributions and discussion in part 3 of the book highlight a number of issues, questions, and suggestions regarding the link between a country's policy environment and the content of conditionality:

- **Selectivity.** Countries with good governance may have external financing requirements due to exogenous shocks; more frequently, however, these requirements are the result of inapproriate policies, fragile institutions, and poor leadership. At the same time, civil society tends to be weak in the countries where aid is most needed; this is further compounded when the implementing institutions are corrupt or incompetent. Consequently, it has been suggested that development agencies should work largely with the private sector and civil society. Moreover, selectivity amplifies role models for countries at the lower level of the spectrum.

- **Minimal international standards.** Establishing standards in development policy lending, similar to the Basel accords, might result in punishing high-risk reformers (for example, new governments) and might be difficult in some areas (fiduciary arrangements). There is a need to balance international benchmarks and tailor-made approaches. It was argued that many recipient countries could define these standards themselves.

- **Accountability.** Domestic accountability should be supported and enforced through donor conditionality. Some argue that upward accountability (conditionality) is often at the expense of downward accountability. Others argue that international standards have a positive role in achieving mutual accountability.

- **Fragile countries.** Donors should focus their support on reforms promising short-term payoffs, rather than providing significant financing. Given that fragile countries generally suffer from lack of capacity, weak institutions, and feeble policy-making capacity, there tends to be a strong assymetry between donor and borrower. Consequently, operations risk being overburdened with overdefined and intrusive step-by-step process conditions—even though the commitments are lower. It is recommended that capacity building should always be linked to the reform program in these countries, in order for them to become more equal partners in the process.

- **Middle-income countries.** Maintaining consistent lending to middle-income countries is important for the World Bank, not only for financial reasons, but also in order to be able to transfer knowledge to low-income countries. One possible approach to middle-income countries could be based on the following four-step process: (1) the government announces a reform program for about three years, (2) it organizes a donor conference, (3) donors commit resources for the three-year period, and (4) a joint review is conducted.

Implicit conditionality. Some observers voice concern that the PRSP approach for low-income countries has involved an increase in "process" conditionality that may be construed as a one-size-fits-all intervention in the borrowing country's political process. In addition, some observers express concern that the World Bank's practice to allocate aid to low-income countries through a formula that involves a judgment of country policies through the Country Performance and Institutional Assessment introduces implicit conditionality based on standardized criteria. Critics point to the inclusion of potentially controversial components, such as privatization and assessments of the investment climate, as an indication that the spirit of the Washington consensus blueprint-based approach to development remains embedded even if it is no longer explicitly included in loan conditionality.

Part 4. Toward Country-Owned Approaches: Do We Still Need Conditionality?

Part 4 encompasses the complex relationship between conditionality and country ownership. A variety of approaches and their merits are discussed, including the advantages and drawbacks of ex ante and ex post conditionality. The experience with outcome-based conditionality is of particular interest.

Kemal Dervis, former Minister of Economics for Turkey, reflects upon the usefulness of conditionality to support policy reform in his country. While arguing for fewer conditions, he suggests that a fine balance needs to be struck in order to recognize linkages among different segments of the economy. According to Dervis, a comprehensive and well-thought-out program is necessary to successfully tackle macroeconomic issues. That being said, he cautions against an approach to conditionality and policy advice where ideology dominates over the actual substance of policy choices. He also makes a case to move toward a system of binding international codes and standards.

Gilles Hervio, head of the Macroeconomic Division of the Development Directorate of the European Commission, presents the case for a multiyear system of outcome-based conditionality. This approach has been used by the European Commission for 10 years and aims to avoids the adverse consequences resulting from nonfulfillment of specific conditions. The objective of this approach is to empower the country to take ownership of reforms, and leave the choice of policy options to the country itself. Hervio argues that this modus operandi allows the client countries more freedom and allows the governments to proceed in a way acceptable to the various stakeholders in the process. Other benefits include a reduction in volatility and subjectivity that was inherent in old-style conditionality. However, this approach is not without problems, including the difficulty of setting target indicators when data are not readily available.

The contributions and discussion in part 4 of the book highlight a number of issues, questions, and suggestions on the tension between ownership and conditionality:

- **Conditionality and aid delivery.** It has been recognized that there is a case for conditionality as long as there are limited resources and a need to formulate allocation rules. It is critical, however, that conditionality be driven by developmental considerations that conform to the needs of the country, rather than by political or geostrategic interests. Rather than being prescriptive, conditionality should be based on good diagnostic and analytical work and focused on local country contexts.

- **Streamlining conditionality.** In their efforts to streamline conditionality, donors should be careful not to ignore critical policy areas. One important lesson is that while prescriptive development models are mostly inappropriate, donor programs should adequately reflect the breadth and interdependence of sectoral and cross-sectoral policies. Careful consideration should also be given to the complexities of the nature of state and nonstate actors. Some observers claim that the development community is still too focused on the "nation state," without much consideration of the breadth of stakeholders that shape and are affected by various policies.

- **Ownership and results.** The donor community has been criticized by some for not doing enough to measure results, with the argument that subjective policy actions still predominate conditionality, without sufficient linkage to medium-term outcomes. Not only does this make it more difficult to arrive at a more objective assessment of performance, but it also tends to undermine country ownership. This may be exacerbated when a multitude of donors influence the approach and content of conditionality and establish parallel processes for monitoring and reporting country performance.

- **Donor coordination.** Coordination of processes and frameworks should allow room for diverging opinions and approaches. At the same time, it should ensure that borrowing countries are not overwhelmed by redundant or overlapping conditions that exceed their capacity to implement programs and monitor results. Several principles should be respected, including the use of existing country arrangements, a greater focus on results, shifting away from micromanagement, improving resource predictability, enhancing transparency, and reducing volatility. It is a subject of considerable debate to what extent it is useful to address political governance issues as part of conditionality.

- **Pooling of donor budget support and conditionality.** As many bilateral donors have been providing a sizable share of their aid allocations through budget support, the importance of harmonization among donors and with the international financial institutions has increased. There are concerns that lack of coordination may result in more conditionality and greater micromanagement that is insufficiently aligned with the country's own priorities. Questions have also arisen as to whether financial flows might become more volatile when several donors make their financing contingent on the same set of conditions. Also, it remains to be seen whether coordination among a wider number of donor participants in budget support could contribute to compromises with less clarity and specificity in the conditions. Indeed, some observers suggest that greater diversification of donor conditionality might be in the interest of recipient countries as a way to lessen the risk of aid flow disruption and increase predictability of aid flows.

Part 5. Partnerships in Policy-Based Lending

Part 5 focuses on how best to foster effective partnerships as part of policy-based lending or budget support. Among the ingredients of successful partnerships among development partners, this section highlights the importance of a strong ex ante policy dialogue. A key operational question is how to align donor support where country performance is inadequate.

Richard Manning, chairman of the Organisation for Economic Co-operation and Development's Development Cooperation Directorate, directs attention to the assessment of partnerships in policy-based lending. He stresses the need to answer how partnerships can help to improve the use of conditionality in policy-based lending and how different approaches to collaboration can enhance predictability of aid. According to Manning, the real challenge in the context of partnership is what to do with the category of countries where a policy dialogue is currently difficult but where persistent poverty calls for donor support. He suggests that such countries require even greater harmonization, donor alignment, and a functioning partnership model.

Dr. Duong Duc Ung, director general, Foreign Economic Relations Department of the Ministry of Planning and Investment of Vietnam, presents Vietnam's experience with policy-based lending and conditionality. He mentions a number of benefits resulting from well-designed policy-based lending, including its important catalytic role and source of fast disbursement funds and capacity building during the country's transition period. However, he points out that, at times, conditionality from strong donors tied the recipient government to an accelerated reform roadmap that was not always fully adapted to country circumstances. He further suggests that at times conditionality was found to be overly broad and scattered, involving too great a number of implementing agencies, reducing the loan focus while excessively increasing the time spent on negotiations. He suggests that policy measures are often designed in a fixed manner, leaving little room for modifications during the implementation stage. Among the lessons learned, Ung mentions the need for governments to take full ownership of the design of policy measures as well as exercising strong leadership role during implementation. He concludes that a frank and open consultative process between the government and donors is a must for a successful implementation of policy-based loans.

Oliver Morrissey of the University of Nottingham focuses on policy dialogue as a way of describing partnerships. He suggests that policy reform is a slow and difficult process. Consequently, donors can be more effective agents of policy change if they support policy dialogue rather than attempt to force this process through conditionality. He contends that conditionality, within its role of supporting the reform process, is most likely to be effective if used to support policy reform dialogue. Morrissey believes that ownership is not what ultimately matters, but the belief that a particular policy is the best policy for that country; in his view, policy dialogue facilitates this transmission of information. He supports the need for conditionality, but proposes two principles to guide conditionality: (a) that conditions be related to observable and verifiable policy inputs, not outcomes; and (b) that conditions be independent of each other (unless the policy actions are known to be complementary).

Patrick Watt, policy officer at Action Aid, is mostly concerned about the rather loose way in which partnership is used in the development discourse. He defines partnership in more detail and examines what sorts of conditionality would be appropriate under a true partnership approach. He contends that one cannot really have a partnership unless there are some basic shared objectives and goals, and that accountability and learning flows both ways. In Watt's opinion, a true partnership approach would involve a country-donor relationship without economic policy conditions, no technical assistance to control the budget process because donors believe in the government's intentions, and greater transparency about how compliance is judged—in essence a relationship of mutual trust and respect for the domestic decision-making processes.

The contributions and discussion in part 5 of the book highlight a number of issues, questions, and suggestions on partnerships and conditionality:

- **Current state of partnerships.** Donor money continues to be seen as an inducement for policy reforms rather than as a tool for partnerships. Donor partnerships in many countries are considered to be uncoordinated, fragmented, and lacking direction, and the donor processes continue to be overly complex. Most observers agree that there is a case for greater order and simplification in these relationships. Some commentators criticize donors for not taking responsibility or the required accountability when they have faltered in the development process. The U.S. Millennium Challenge Account promises to be innovative in developing partnerships by selecting countries based on clearly defined eligibility criteria—one of which is an adequate donor coordination arrangement.

- **Toward true partnerships.** True partnerships imply a donor-recipient relationship that is based on mutually agreed objectives and transparent responsibility and accountability, rather than one that is based on a paternalistic model. The challenge for the donor community will be to establish such relationships, especially in situations where some objectives and interests are not fully determined. Additional challenges arise in those cases where the culture and incentives differ between donor and recipient, or where the country environment is in disarray to the extent that mutual partnerships are not possible. It has been suggested that the various approaches to conditionality—from the European Union's focus on results and outcomes, to the predominant reliance on policy inputs in World Bank and IMF programs—too narrowly define conditionality and targets in crisis situations. However, more recently donors have increasingly recognized the importance of avoiding a one-size-fits-all approach to conditionality and resisting micromanagement of reform programs. Donors are also subscribing to greater transparency on how compliance with conditionality is judged, to be held accountable for the quality of the development assistance, and to respect domestic decision-making processes.

- **Policy dialogue as a form of partnership.** There is a general acknowledgment that donor approaches have increasingly shifted from coercion to persuasion in recognition that policy reform is a slow and difficult process. However, to be effective agents of policy change, donors must offer support rather than attempt to force this process through strong ex ante policy dialogue. Effective policy dialogue can lead to stronger country ownership and improved donor coordination. Policy dialogue is of particular importance if it helps to raise the PRSP and poverty reduction issues higher on the development agenda. It should be a two-way street where both parties learn and share viewpoints, as well as agree to disagree on some issues. In the end, a developing country government official concluded that partnership is about discussion, dialogue, and coordination—not always about reaching a consensus.

- **Partnerships in poor performers**. There is a belief that conditionality is ineffective in poor policy environments and that the donor community needs to approach these cases differently. While conditionality tends to be less extensive and less prescriptive for good performers, donors have in the past tended to ask poor performers and fragile countries for a greater number of conditions—perhaps in the expectation that compliance and reform implementation may be weaker. In countries where there is simply no policy dialogue and no way of engaging in a mutual and transparent relationship with the authorities, several academics proposed that donors rely more on grants, instead of lending as the preferred aid modality, while at the same time increasing the emphasis on expenditure-tracking conditionality to measure impacts.

Part 6. Concluding Remarks

Many lessons have been learned in the use of conditionality in policy-based lending and budget support over the past decades. The initial approach was often driven by a belief that the donor community could leverage reforms with aid money. At the same time, development economists tried to implement economic liberalization policies with the aim of freeing countries from restrictive barriers to growth. However, experience has taught that a single blueprint cannot be applied universally.

Country specificity and country ownership have been increasingly recognized as key ingredients for successful policy-based programs. There is a broad consensus that domestic ownership of a reform agenda is vital to its success; the legitimate way forward is for donors to be actively involved in the policy dialogue within the country.

Critics have suggested that some of the advice disseminated by the international financial institutions has proved imperfect, indicating that donors should shoulder some of the blame as borrowing countries face a disproportionately higher cost of policy failure. Nonetheless, there also seems to be broad agreement that donors have a useful role in imparting lessons learned in development experiences elsewhere, as well as sharing expertise gained through focused country-specific analytic work in forming appropriate conditionality in the context of policy dialogue with the respective country.

With the recommendation that the donor community should be increasingly involved in the internal policy dialogue of a borrowing country, there is also a recognized need to adapt to country decision-making systems. By becoming more involved at the domestic level, process conditionality is seen as potentially contributing to successful reforms. Others caution against process conditionality, arguing that it implies political involvement in the reforming country, possibly reducing the likelihood of successful program implementation. Yet, adapting to country circumstances was viewed by all forum participants to be highly desirable.

Doubters have expressed concern that the international financial institutions are not providing the correct incentives for change. Specifically, as policy dialogue with the country is espoused, questions are being raised as to how much the negotiation process over loans has changed. In addition, although there is general agreement that streamlining conditionality is highly desirable, it is being questioned whether task managers are being provided with enticements to craft fewer and more comprehensive conditions. Cultural change within the international financial institutions is sometimes seen as critical for success.

Converging with the need to think about conditionality as part of a cycle that includes dialogue and capacity building, there is a need to take into account current capacity constraints. Country systems and capacity are not uniform, and adequate attention should be paid to improve them with the intention of becoming a more equal partner in the future.

To depoliticize the process of aid, it has been suggested to base its allocation on meeting some minimum international codes and standards. However, many err on the side of caution when advocating this approach, as it may exclude many high-risk, high-return countries with new and fragile reform-minded governments worthy of support. An additional concern is that a resurgent one-size-fits-all approach would be counter productive.

With regard to possible ways to improve the use of policy-based loans, aid to low-income countries is at issue. Concern was raised that too much attention is often being paid to narrow procedural conditions during the negotiation process. More pressingly, there is a call for more coherence on how to deal with Low-Income Countries Under Stress, where over half a billion people reside, and which may have difficulties reaching the Millennium Development Goals.

In sum, although there is an emerging consensus on various aspects of conditionality, the discussion shows that many questions of best practice still remain open. There may be scope for a greater agreement on a mutual accountability framework among donors, recipient countries, and the international financial institutions on the basis of the Monterrey consensus, which would have the potential of replacing the traditional approach to conditionality. The European Union prefers outcomes-based lending with multiyear targets and indicators, while others express doubt. Everyone, however, agrees that in the future the various international financial institutions should proceed with more humility in development policy dialogue, taking into account focused, country-specific analytic work and paying more attention to country circumstances.

Keynote Address

EMMANUEL TUMUSIIME-MUTEBILE
Bank of Uganda

A Brief History: African Economic Policies

Following independence from colonial rule, African countries looked to the state as the principal driving force for industrialization and economic transformation. Governments all over Africa embraced central planning and import substitution behind high tariffs as a means of accelerating capital accumulation. State intervention in the economy was so preoccupied with expanding productive capacity that the efficiency of resource allocation and the productivity of investments were almost universally ignored.

As a result of its state interventionist policies, by the 1980s in Africa there were overbloated state-owned enterprises, closed trade regimes, inefficient use of productive capacity, neglect of incentives for agriculture, industrial protectionist policies, and gross macroeconomic imbalances, which resulted in shrinking or at least not helping stagnating economies and increasing poverty.

As the 1990s approached, a consensus was emerging, at least among the donor community, that government policy needed a radical paradigm shift. The new paradigm sought to reduce state intervention in the economy and privatize state-owned enterprises, restore macroeconomic stability, reform the tax regime, deregulate the economy and allow markets to freely determine prices and resource allocation, open economies to international trade, and reduce damaging protectionist policies. The donors sought to convince governments to spend more on reduction of poverty, on health, on education, and on infrastructure. In addition, donors sought to improve the protection of private property rights and create a conducive environment for private sector development.

Conditionality in Africa

The new aforementioned paradigm became the basis for conditionality. Conditionality refers to specific policy prescriptions imposed by the International Monetary Fund (IMF) and the World Bank and other donors that are designed to ensure that the borrowers, or recipients of aid, take steps to implement economic reforms to achieve the objectives of programs supported by foreign loans and grants, and to turn away from the bad old days that led to crisis.

At first there was no attempt to specifically target the conditions attached to the demands of the new paradigm. At least as far as the IMF was concerned, its conditionality targeted stabilization programs that were designed to deal with the balance of payments disequilibrium through fiscal austerity, tight monetary policy, and the devaluation of domestic tariffs. Gradually the scope for conditionality was extended to more areas of macroeconomic policy and structural policies as it became increasingly clear that short-run macrostabilization would not deliver economic growth and financial stability while entrenched distortions were hindering the operation of markets and the efficient allocation of resources in the economy. Therefore, the number and specificity of policy conditions imposed by the IMF and the World Bank increased.

Streamlining Conditionality in Africa: Has It Worked?

There has recently been an attempt to streamline conditionality to avoid an "overload" of conditionality and to focus conditionality on policy areas that are regarded as critical for achieving the objectives of the program. The jury is still out on the effectiveness of these efforts, except in the area of poverty reduction.

Questioning Conditionality

There is ample room for a discussion on the scope, nature, timing, sequencing, and appropriateness of conditionality. There is much disagreement on the impact of conditionality, as well as on the delivery of the objectives on which these conditions were set. There is further disagreement of the impact of conditionality on the nature of the dialogue, as well as the partnership between donors and recipients, and the impact of conditionality on the ownership of the programs.

Why Is Conditionality Needed?

Without conditionality, once a borrowing government obtains a loan it may not have adequate incentives to abandon the policies that initially caused the imbalances. By imposing conditionality the IMF and the World Bank are acting as external agents of restraint on the policy action of governments that borrow from them.

We know from political-economic theory that politicians face incentives to adopt short-run policies that lead to suboptimal outcomes in the longer term. Policies that are optimal in the long run are often inconsistent with short-term goals and hence will not be implemented. If policy makers have complete discretion, there will always be a risk of political pressure to increase public spending over and above levels that are prudent, or to cut taxes, particularly in the time leading to general elections, or to incur imprudent loans and as such imprudent levels of public debt. So the need to curb time inconsistency is also a rationale for conditionality.

Encouraging Private Sector Development:
How Does Conditionality Help?

When the private sector is trying to form expectations of the future behavior of policy makers, it is not enough for the authorities to state what they intend to do. For the government to encourage private investment, the authorities need more than just the correct current policies that are conducive to private sector investment; the authorities also need to establish credibility that they will actually follow correct policies in the future. What is needed is a credible, binding precommitment by the political authorities to particular policies that effectively prevent ex post violations of the commitments that they have made. An external agent of restraint, such as the IMF or the World Bank, provides that commitment assurance.

Of course an agent of restraint cannot substitute for a government that is committed to, and capable of, implementing sound economic policies, but it can complement the action of such a government and thereby enhance the prospects that these policies will be successful in generating economic growth and policy reform.

Criticism of IMF Conditionality in Africa

IMF conditionality is mainly set in the form of contingent targets for fiscal and monetary aggregates that are used as performance criteria in the program. While encouraging contingent economic targets in programs plays an important role by sending a clear signal of the government's commitment and the intent of the private sector, structural performance criteria that have been incorporated in Poverty Reduction and Growth Facility (PRGF) programs seem not to be as useful, and may even be counterproductive.

The failings of the aforementioned approach are not due to the fact that the supported structural reforms are not necessary, but rather because structural performance criteria suffer from several defects. First, the targets are conservative by nature and are not easily monitorable or verifiable. There is often scope for dispute about whether a particular target has been met. Second, implementation is often much more difficult politically and institutionally than quantitative targets, and these difficulties are often overlooked in negotiations between the IMF staff and the country authorities. Third, whereas the IMF clearly has expertise in the area of macroeconomics, it is not evident that it has the experience to design the structure of policy reforms in areas that are outside its normal area of competence.

Consequently, structural performance criteria are often missed, either because they are poorly designed or because insufficient consideration was taken of the political and decisional difficulties of implementing these targets. The incorporation of structural performance criteria in PRGF programs has consequences for the integrity of these programs. If PRGF programs include a plethora of structural targets, some of which are almost certain to be missed, and some of which cannot be monitored easily by outsiders, the value of the program as an agent of restraint is weakened.

Furthermore, the more structural performance criteria are included in a given PRGF program, the more likely it is that some of the targets will not be met, but a program with many targets cannot be suspended if only one or a few of the targets is not met. This means that each individual target becomes less important for the success of the program, and this inevitably weakens the incentives facing the authorities for complying with any single target. What is more, rational and well-informed private agents would also know this, which would not enhance their confidence in the country's economic management.

A Welcome Change from the World Bank: The Comprehensive Development Framework (CDF)

The introduction of the CDF by World Bank President James Wolfensohn has led to changes in the conception and use of conditionality. The CDF puts emphasis on four broad principles. First, development strategies should be owned by the developing country. Second, development strategies should be comprehensive, reflecting the dimensional nature of poverty, and they should be shaped by a long-term vision of how macroeconomic structure and human development policies will address all the core dimensions of it. Third, development outcomes depend on effective partnership of poverty reduction at all levels, involving local government, civil society, the private sector, as well as donors. Fourth, the effectiveness of development efforts should be judged on the basis of results—where the traditional emphasis was on how resources are allocated and used, the CDF now calls for a focus on development outputs and outcomes.

Many of the aforementioned principles were not new; however, what is novel is bringing them together in a unified framework of development policy and applying them systematically to all government actors.

Continuation of the CDF: The Poverty Reduction Strategy Paper (PRSP)

The PRSPs have provided an operational means of implementing the focus of the CDF. These PRSPs are prepared by the developing governments with wide consultation of stakeholders at all levels of development, including the private sector as well as donors. Once the PRSP has been agreed upon, the specific policies contained in the PRSP are then used by the IMF and the World Bank to design supporting loans. A major difference is that now the countries are imposing the conditions themselves, and the IMF and the World Bank are simply "crafting" conditionalities to those policies.

Uganda's Experience with the PRSP

Uganda was a pioneer of the PRSP process before the term was even coined. We published our Poverty Reduction Action Plan in 1997 after a period of preparation spanning two years, consulting with all stakeholders, virtually starting with zero draft. The aforementioned government strategy for guiding medium-term policy was revised in 2000, and the existing summary of this revision actually became the PRSP.

Improving Policies Using the Consultation Process of the PRSP

It is necessary to emphasize that there were extensive consultations with the advent of the PRSP, and these consultations have now become institutionalized at the core of the process. The aim of these consultations is to ensure that the policies that underlie the PRSP are fully owned by all the stakeholders. The consultation process is also important as a platform for those in the country who are pushing for reforms to put across the arguments for reform before the politicians and the public. This opportunity should not be spurned, because some of the policies that are critical for the long-term success of poverty eradication do not always have widespread support.

A good example of a policy without much support is open trade policy, which is both propoor and progrowth, but unfortunately these benefits are not clearly understood in developing countries, and for that matter even in developed countries, and McCarthyist views are still widespread among politicians. With or without the IMF and the World Bank, an open trade regime and rapid export growth are essential for sustained economic growth, development, and poverty eradication. These messages should be sent out as strongly as possible in consultations so that one can widen the understanding of the public and hopefully widen the constituency for reform.

Widespread consultation would also help to build the constituency for reform by explaining the role of public finance, the limits to fiscal policy, and the need for prudent monetary policy to control inflation. Reform of public finances, and especially the reforms of the management of government budgets, should be at the center of the PRSP process.

Part II
Conditionality Revisited: What Has Changed?

1

Country Ownership: A Term Whose Time Has Gone

WILLEM H. BUITER
European Bank for Reconstruction and Development

Words matter. They can enlighten or obscure. Jargon is an example of the destructive use of words. It creates artificial barriers to understanding and participation and, ultimately, obscurity rents that insiders can appropriate. Scientific disciplines, professions, and institutions all have their own jargon. So do the international financial institutions (IFIs) and multilateral development banks. The terms "country ownership" and the associated adjective "country owned" have become particularly pernicious examples of politically correct IFI-speak. They may have been useful at some point; however, they have been used and abused to gloss over realities deemed uncomfortable and to create a pleasant buzz to distract the uninformed and unwary, so they now need to be put out of their misery.

Country ownership refers to programs, plans, or strategies involving both a domestic party (generally a national state) and a foreign party, and particularly to the conditionality attached to these programs. The foreign parties are the IFIs, including the International Monetary Fund (IMF), the World Bank, regional development banks, and other multilateral institutions. Most of these comments, however, apply equally to bilateral relations between a developing country and a developed donor country and to the relationship between the European Union and developing countries and emerging markets. The programs in question include the Poverty Reduction Strategy Papers (PRSPs) and interim PRSPs and the consultative processes associated with it, comanaged by the World Bank and the IMF; the IMF's Poverty Reduction and Growth Facility (PRGF); the World Bank and IMF's Heavily Indebted Poor Country (HIPC) Initiative; the World Bank's Country Assistance Strategies; the World Bank's Low Income Countries Under Stress Initiative; IMF Stand-By Arrangements and Structural Adjustment Facilities; World Bank Structural Adjustment Loans and Sector Adjustment Loans; and a range of similar stabilization, structural adjustment, and reform programs.

Country ownership can refer to a number of dimensions of the multidimensional relationship of the domestic party to the program and its conditionality. Specifically, it can mean one or more of the following:

- The country has designed and drafted the program, or the country has had a significant involvement in the drafting and design of the program, or the authorities of the country were informed of the program after it had been drawn up by other parties, typically the World Bank and the IMF.

- The country agrees with the objectives of the program.

- The country believes that the implementation of the program as envisaged will achieve the program's objectives.

- The country implements the program, or the country plays a significant role in the implementation of the program, or the authorities of the country are kept informed of how and when the program has been implemented.

Up to now, the word "country" has sloppily referred to a single, purposefully acting agent. This anthropomorphic approach obscures reality and confuses the argument. Who or what is or are the country(ies) that owns the program, in any of the four senses just referred to?

A country comprises populations ranging from tens of thousands to a billion plus. All countries, even the smallest and most homogeneous—racially, ethnically, culturally, religiously—contain individuals and groups with diverse, often divergent and conflicting views, interests, policy objectives, and programs. Under what circumstances and how can the concept of country ownership be relevant to a country with myriad heterogeneous and often conflicting views and interests?

Representativeness

If the country has institutions for political and economic governance that are representative and legitimate, a limited number of national representative voices may claim with some validity to "speak for the country" or to "represent the interests of the country." The range of views and interests may be so wide, however, that not even the representatives of the legitimate government and of the worlds of work and business can claim to speak for the country whose ownership is being sought for a program. In the case of the PRSPs, recognition of this reality has led to the development of ad-hoc consultative processes of ever-increasing complexity and duration. Not only are representatives of the government (central, state, and municipal) and parliament now involved, but also representatives of many other groups, associations, agencies, institutions, and organizations. Increasingly, the PRSP process tries to involve a wide range of special interests and lobby groups, including political, environmental, cultural, and religious nongovernmental organizations and other representatives of civil society.

How the views and voices of such a range of sectional and special interests are aggregated into an operative concept of country ownership remains a mystery. Also, despite the large number of nongovernmental organizations and civil society groups, organizations, and factions involved in some of the PRSP consultative processes, the representativeness of the consultations remains an open issue. For instance, the spectacular underrepresentation of the enterprise sector, and especially the private enterprise sector in most PRSP consultative processes, represents a serious dent in its claim to be representative of all the parties whose efforts are essential to a successful attack on poverty or who are affected by it.

Moreover, in only a limited number of cases is there is a realistic prospect for putting together a consultative process (let alone a program drafting and conditionality designing process) that can claim to be representative of the interests, wishes, and views of the majority of the country's population. Unrepresentative and often repressive governments frequently preclude representative PRSP processes. This should come as no surprise.

Why do countries become candidates for stabilization, structural adjustment, or reform programs? Why do countries take part in the HIPC Initiative or the PRSP process? Because they need and seek three kinds of external assistance:

- They need external financial resources and cannot access these through the markets because they are not creditworthy.

- They need external expertise and do not have the resources to pay for this on market terms.

- They need an external commitment device because of weak domestic political institutions.

Countries that need one or more of these external desiderata—finance, expertise, commitment—are countries that are in trouble, countries that cannot help themselves, and countries that are in a mess.

It is possible for a country with good institutions, good political leadership, and good policies to be in a mess nevertheless. The cause(s) could be exogenous bad luck: bad neighbors that prevent trade and transit and restrict the country's ability to participate effectively in the regional and global economy; armed conflict inflicted on a peaceful nation; natural disasters and public health disasters such as the acquired immunodeficiency syndrome pandemic; bad initial conditions, such as those encountered by many of the new countries in the Commonwealth of Independent States following the collapse of the Soviet Union.

Most of the time, however, bad luck does not explain why a country is confronted with the programs and conditionality associated with external assistance. The most frequent explanations are bad institutions, bad political leadership, and bad policies. Countries subject to IFI programs and the associated conditionality tend to have political systems that are unrepresentative and repressive, ranging from mildly authoritarian to brutally totalitarian. The political leadership and the elites supporting them are often corrupt and economically illiterate. Rent seeking and cronyism offer higher returns to effort than socially productive labor and entrepreneurship. Public administration is weak, corrupt, and has limited implementation capacity. Moreover, the countries with the most unrepresentative and repressive governments do not permit a representative cross-section of civil society to participate. Indeed, civil society tends to be weakest precisely in those countries where it is needed most.

What would country ownership mean in Zimbabwe, in the Democratic Republic of Congo (an HIPC Initiative country), and in Sudan? These are extreme examples, and neither Zimbabwe nor Sudan currently has a World Bank or IMF program, but there are many others. What does country ownership mean in Algeria, in the Arab Republic of Egypt, or in China? In Iraq after the fall of Saddam Hussein, and in Afghanistan? Closer to home are the seven poor countries in the Commonwealth of Independent States: Armenia, Azerbaijan, Georgia, the Kyrgyz Republic, Moldova, Tajikistan, and Uzbekistan. All but Uzbekistan have produced PRSPs. In Uzbekistan the World Bank Group has a modest program of lending, technical assistance, and analytical and policy advice. There is no IMF program, although an Article 4 Consultation was completed in June 2004. What would country ownership mean in Uzbekistan? That the agreement of President Karimov has been obtained?

The term "country ownership" is used to describe both positive and normative features of IFI programs. These alternative uses are exemplified by the following two statements, both of which are commonly heard. First, "Unless an IMF program and the conditionality it embodies is country owned, it will fail." Second, "Unless an IMF program and the conditionality it embodies is country owned, it deserves to fail." The first statement presumably means that for an IMF program to be successful certain actions are required by local agents. Unless these agents are willing and able to implement these actions, the program will fail. This statement is true, but not enlightening. A program and the plan of action it involves have to be incentive compatible to be credible and to succeed.

Incentive Compatibility

The local agents whose actions are necessary for the program to succeed are, however, those who speak for the country in the meetings or consultative processes where these programs are drafted and the conditionality is designed. Those on whom the success of the program depends, however, may not include all those affected by it. Some of those affected by it may have had no voice in the design of the conditionality, and the program may not serve their interests, regardless of whether their efforts are essential to its success and regardless of whether they can be cajoled or induced to implement it and make it successful. If this is the reality in a country that is a candidate for a program, it tends to be beyond the ability of the IMF, World Bank, and other IFIs to remedy the situation. The choice for the IFIs is then between not having a program and having a program that is not country owned in the sense of not in the interest of and supported by the majority of the population. There can be little doubt that at times programs have been designed and implemented that served the interests of an unrepresentative few at the expense of the unrepresented many. Such illegitimate programs do not deserve to be implemented. In many other cases, however, the case is less clear-cut.

Even legitimate programs (that is, programs that are widely viewed as fair and desirable) are constrained by the requirement that their implementation must be incentive compatible. If they depend for their success on the adoption of rules or on actions that are not incentive compatible, the programs are not credible. Conditionality (sticks or carrots conditional on outcomes, processes, performance, or actions) is a means of enhancing the incentive compatibility and thus the credibility of programs. In practice, ensuring postimplementation irreversibility of reforms, policies, and actions is the hardest part of program design. Most incentives (for example, the disbursement of a tranche of a loan or grant) have a natural expiration date. Good conditionality creates effective and lasting or irreversible incentives to take certain actions.

Process Conditionality

Conditionality can apply to actions, outcomes, or processes. Ideally, incentives should be designed to increase the likelihood of actions that contribute to desirable outcomes. In practice, key outcomes may lag far behind actions, and the contribution of the action to the eventual outcome may be hard to identify, measure, and verify. The effect of privatization on economic performance is an obvious example. Process conditionality does not directly target specific actions, policies, or outcomes. Instead it focuses on promoting good governance, in the hope that more accountable, transparent, responsive, representative, and democratic government institutions will produce better actions, policies, and outcomes. Process conditionality focuses on capacity building broadly defined and requires that a process (such as the consultative PRSP process) be implemented, or that certain institutions be in place to enhance the transparency and representativeness of governance at different levels. Making aid available to countries whose governments and institutions for political and economic governance are most effective (or at least meet certain minimum thresholds, defined, say, by international standards and codes) is an example of process or institutional conditionality. The U.S. Millennium Challenge Account embodies this process approach to conditionality.

If process conditionality and country ownership are to be taken seriously, we need international standards and codes to benchmark acceptable practice. Failure to meet these benchmarks would prevent the country from access to the external funds, expertise, and credibility brought by an IFI-mediated program. Sources of benchmarks could be initiatives or agencies such as the Extractive Industries Transparency Initiative, the Publish What You Pay, Publish What You Receive Initiative, the Financial Action Task Force for anti-money-laundering benchmarks, the Corruption Perceptions Index of Transparency International, and, in the regions of the European Bank for Reconstruction and Development (EBRD), the reports of the Organization for Security and Co-operation in Europe and of the Council of Europe on electoral and political performance. Standards for other key aspects of the accountability of the government to the domestic population could be set by defining benchmarks or minimum standards for freedom of the media, independence of the courts, freedom to organize and register independent political parties and labor unions, the right of peaceful assembly and protest, and the right to strike.

Process conditionality *is* political or governance conditionality. The EBRD has long practiced this form of conditionality because of the political nature of its mandate, which in that regard is unlike that of the other IFIs.[1] The requirement that we operate only in "...countries committed to and applying the principles of multiparty democracy, pluralism and market economics" has meant that the EBRD no longer engages in new public sector projects in Turkmenistan and Belarus, and that similar constraints have been imposed on the bank's ability to work with the sovereign in Uzbekistan.

Although process conditionality and political benchmarks may give one a warm glow inside, an unavoidable implication of their adoption is that a number of potential countries of operation will fail to qualify. The EBRD still operates, albeit at a low level of activity, in Turkmenistan, Belarus, and Uzbekistan, because the primary mandate of the bank is in the private sector. The World Bank and IMF would be out of business altogether in a country if they could no longer operate in the public sector. More generally, if the IFIs were to get serious about country ownership, there would be many fewer programs.

In conclusion, the concept of country ownership has been used and abused in so many ways that it now is at best unhelpful and at worst misleading and obfuscating. When the statement "this program is country owned" means no more than "this program is supported by the people who own the country," it is time to purge it from our vocabulary.

Endnotes

1. The preamble to the Agreement Establishing the EBRD states that "The contracting parties, Committed to the fundamental principles of multiparty democracy, the rule of law, respect for human rights and market economics; Recalling the Final Act of the Helsinki Conference on Security and Co-operation in Europe, and in particular its Declaration on Principles; Welcoming the intent of central and eastern European countries to further the practical implementation of multiparty democracy, strengthening democratic institutions, the rule of law and respect for human rights and their willingness to implement reforms in order to evolve towards market-oriented economies; ..."

   Article 1 of the Agreement states: Purpose "In contributing to economic progress and reconstruction, the purpose of the Bank shall be to foster the transition towards open market-oriented economies and to promote private and entrepreneurial initiative in the central and eastern European countries committed to and applying the principles of multiparty democracy, pluralism and market economics."

2

International Monetary Fund Conditionality: A Provisional Update

IMF STAFF PAPER

The International Monetary Fund's (IMF) financial assistance supports the adoption and implementation of appropriate policies. These policies need to be adequate to cope with the country's balance-of-payments problem in a manner that is consistent with the purposes of the IMF (in particular, in the language of the Articles of Agreement, avoiding "measures destructive of national or international prosperity") and that will enable the country to repay the IMF within the designated maturity term (the Articles state that the IMF's resources are made "temporarily available . . . under adequate safeguards").

Significant unease with the IMF's recent practice of conditionality came to the fore in the late 1990s. Conditionality was, in principle, still ruled by conditionality guidelines adopted in 1979, but in some areas—in particular, as regards structural conditionality—practice had diverged significantly from these guidelines. Although structural measures were rarely an element in IMF-supported programs until the 1980s, by the 1990s almost all programs included some element of structural conditionality. The expansion of structural conditionality was reflected in increasing performance criteria, structural benchmarks, and prior actions. These changes were the result of several forces. First, the IMF had, over time, placed increasing emphasis on economic growth as a policy objective, recognizing that demand management may be able to solve an external problem, but does so at high cost and often in an unsustainable way. Second, the IMF became increasingly involved with different groups of countries in which structural reforms were viewed as a central part of the overall policy package (low-income and transition countries). In particular, the design of the Enhanced Structural Adjustment Facility explicitly mandated at least some structural conditionality. Over time, however, the IMF was seen, in some cases, as overstepping its mandate and core areas of expertise, using its financial leverage to promote an extensive policy agenda, and thus short-circuiting national decision-making processes and overtaxing countries' implementation capacity.

A process of reflection on these issues began in 2000 and culminated in the adoption of new Guidelines on Conditionality in September 2002 (IMF 2002a). In parallel, the new facility for low-income countries, the Poverty Reduction and Growth Facility (PRGF), established in 1999, shared some of the objectives of the new guidelines.[1]

The IMF is conducting its first review of the new guidelines, a process that is expected to be completed later in 2004. It is too early to tell whether the programs' record of achieving their ultimate objectives has improved, especially to the extent that these objectives encompass not only immediate outcomes but also issues of medium-term sustainability and growth. However, it should be possible to draw some preliminary conclusions as to whether the practice of conditionality has indeed changed, and, if it has, whether these changes have been accompanied, as had been hoped, by improvements in program implementation. Pending this first review of the guidelines, the evidence available on their implementation and impact is limited.

The New Guidelines

The new guidelines emphasize five interrelated principles as key to program effectiveness and implementation, which, in turn, are key to safeguarding IMF resources: national *ownership* of programs, *parsimony* in the application of conditionality, *tailoring* of programs to countries' circumstances, effective *coordination* with other multilateral institutions, and *clarity* in the specification of conditions. These principles interact in numerous ways. Tailoring programs and coordinating with other institutions both contribute to more appropriate program design. Emphasis on national ownership—the member's primary responsibility for designing and implementing policies—should lead to both better tailoring, through greater use of local knowledge, and stronger implementation. Parsimony supports ownership and implementation by creating explicit room for the member to formulate and adapt policies; together with clarity, it also helps the authorities focus on agreed priorities during program implementation. Parsimony and coordination also ensure that the IMF does not exceed its mandate. Finally, clarity of conditions gives the member confidence in the availability of drawings—a crucial condition if the country is to avoid adjustment measures destructive of prosperity, and thus a basic principle of IMF arrangements.

To achieve these objectives, the guidelines emphasize the need to *define program goals clearly*, to ensure the *appropriate breadth of coverage* of conditionality, to apply conditionality at the *right level of detail* and to make judicious use of the different tools of conditionality, and—an overarching goal—to make sure that *the member is ultimately responsible* for the selection, design, and implementation of its economic and financial policies.

Ownership

Ownership is an essential ingredient for effective policy change. Many of the stipulations in the new guidelines regarding the way conditionality is to be applied are intended to ensure that conditionality supports ownership. In addition, the guidelines provide guidance as to how the IMF should relate to members in the process of designing programs. The implicit model is one in which, beyond the standard that members' policies must meet in order to qualify for IMF support, there is a "policy space" in which members' choices would not affect the IMF's willingness to support the program.

Of course, it is difficult to determine whether the IMF is succeeding in giving members appropriate policy space. However, the results of a survey conducted recently in the framework of a review of IMF–World Bank collaboration are fairly encouraging (IMF 2004). Three-quarters of countries considered that they "largely" or "fully" owned the program supported by the IMF, with a third of countries reporting "full" ownership; two-thirds of countries reported that the IMF was "rather" or "very" flexible in taking the authorities' views into account during program design: and none considered the IMF "very inflexible."

Program Goals

In terms of goals, the new guidelines—much like the old ones—specify that "Fund-supported programs should be directed primarily toward (a) solving the member's balance of payments problem without recourse to measures destructive of national or international prosperity; and (b) achieving medium-term external viability while fostering sustainable economic growth." These are also among the goals of the PRGF, although they are supplemented by "fostering durable growth, leading to higher living standards and a reduction in poverty."

With the new guidelines' emphasis on ownership and parsimony, clear specification of program goals has become more important than it was previously. A necessary corollary of encouraging country ownership is selectivity in determining which programs meet the criteria for IMF financial support, and clear specification of program goals is crucial in this regard. Clear and circumscribed goals are also essential if measures critical to achieving the program's objectives are to be identified with confidence. The upcoming review of the guidelines will consider whether IMF-supported programs are, indeed, sufficiently clear in their identification of goals.

Breadth of Coverage of Conditionality

Parsimony in the breadth of coverage of conditionality is a clear requirement of the new guidelines. Conditions must be either of critical importance for achieving the goals of the member's program or necessary for the implementation of specific provisions of the IMF's Articles of Agreement. Reflecting the need to safeguard IMF resources, all measures that meet this test are expected to be subject to conditionality; otherwise, it would be possible for the program to veer seriously off track without an interruption of drawings. The criticality test pertains regardless of whether a measure is within or outside the IMF's core areas of responsibility. However, because critical measures for the IMF-supported program are likely to be within the IMF's core areas, conditions will typically be within the IMF's core areas of responsibility. Conditions outside these areas may need more detailed explanation of their critical importance.

Consistent with these expectations, there is some evidence that conditions in programs supported by arrangements in the General Resources Account (GRA) have become more heavily focused on fiscal and financial policies (IMF 2002b).[2] This is especially true for countries that have experienced serious financial crises, with most of the conditions set to reduce vulnerabilities in the financial sector. Although financial conditions generally account for about one-quarter of all conditions in stand-by programs, this ratio exceeds 50 percent for emerging-market economies in crisis. Measures range from implementing new accounting systems in line with international accounting standards to privatizing state banks.

In contrast to conditions in GRA-supported programs, conditions in PRGF-supported programs are more heavily weighted toward the fiscal sector, with a number of conditions emphasizing the need for improved allocation of expenditures to address poverty concerns. This is consistent not only with the objectives of the PRGF but also with the requirement for Heavily Indebted Poor Countries (HIPCs) reaching their decision and completion points to monitor the spending of additional resources flowing from debt relief on poverty-related needs.

Determining which actions are critical to the success of a program remains a key challenge. Some would argue that the IMF remains too heavily engaged in areas that are not macrocritical. In certain areas, macrocriticality is relatively easy to establish—for instance, where the fiscal position is significantly affected (utility price adjustments, pension reform, and new systems for taxing petroleum products) or where there is a direct and significant impact on the growth potential of the economy (efficiency gains in public companies, privatization, and trade policy changes). At the same time, it is also still possible to point to conditions that appear to be far removed from macrocriticality.

Conversely, in some individual cases, streamlining of the areas covered by conditionality may have gone too far. IMF executive directors have sometimes argued that areas critical to the success of the program were not subject to conditionality (for example, structural fiscal measures in revenue administration or public procurement). Ex post assessments have also sometimes pointed to areas that were identified only in hindsight as critical to program goals.[3]

Level of Detail of Conditionality and Conditionality Toolkit

The new guidelines also encourage fewer and less detailed individual conditions: within a given area, conditions are to be applied parsimoniously, and all conditions must be of critical importance to the program's objectives. At the same time, conditions must be clear, so as to permit the country to know in advance what it must do to qualify for IMF financial support and to encourage a focus on the critical actions. There is inevitably some tension between these objectives. Parsimony and ownership argue for allowing for different measures to achieve the same objectives, while the need for clarity suggests that measures should be specified precisely.

Different tools are available to specify conditionality in a given area, and the guidelines specify how each of these is to be used, in an attempt to achieve the right balance. The tools consist of performance criteria (PCs), structural benchmarks, program reviews, and prior actions.[4]

The guidelines specify that in addition to being objectively monitorable, PCs must be by themselves "so critical [. . .] that purchases or disbursements under the arrangement should be interrupted in cases of nonobservance." Structural benchmarks, too, must be of critical importance. They are appropriate when monitoring the implementation of a measure requires judgment or when the measure's "non-implementation would not, by itself, warrant an interruption of purchases or disbursements under the arrangement." The latter is consistent with the requirement of critical importance because, as explained in the operational guidance on the guidelines, benchmarks may be used for "key components of a broader reform measure that is judged to be critical (e.g., steps in a tax reform or privatization program)," even if the individual measure subject to a benchmark represents but a relatively small step. Program reviews can be used to monitor overall progress in a given area, and thereby give the country more flexibility in how it achieves this progress, but at the cost of a loss of clarity as to what the IMF will or will not consider to be an adequate basis for drawings.

Although there are clear pitfalls in merely comparing numbers of conditions, it is interesting to consider whether streamlining has been reflected at this most basic level. Preliminary indications from the first phase of the "streamlining" initiative (2000–1) were that the number of structural conditions had not declined among GRA recipients, although focused structural benchmarks were replacing individual performance criteria, thereby providing the authorities more leeway in achieving a specific objective, in line with the new guidelines (IMF 2002b). In PRGF countries, preliminary evidence suggested that the number of conditions had declined. For both GRA and PRGF, information on the total number of conditions and its distribution between PCs, benchmarks, and prior actions will be updated for the forthcoming review.

The guidelines also encourage use of outcomes-based conditionality and floating tranches, either of which would allow the authorities greater choice in the exact specification and sequencing of reforms, taking account of potential implementation difficulties. Although floating tranches are used in the HIPC Initiative, there has been little experimentation with these instruments in IMF arrangements. The forthcoming review will examine why, including whether the use of floating-completion-point triggers under the HIPC Initiative holds lessons for floating tranches more generally.

The guidelines also specify that prior actions are to be used sparingly, specifically "when it is critical for the successful implementation of the program that such actions be taken to underpin the upfront implementation of important measures." The operational guidance makes clear that "prior actions are to be applied parsimoniously" and states that "staff should be guided by the experience that implementing prior actions has not been shown to increase the likelihood that other subsequent measures under the program will be successfully implemented."

It is not clear at this stage whether the use of prior actions has, indeed, diminished. Some have argued that prior actions remain useful in allowing countries with weak track records to demonstrate ownership, or in screening out programs with weak ownership. The forthcoming review will examine evidence in support of this argument.

Progress has been made in specifying more clearly the areas on which program reviews will focus. The impression of mushrooming conditionality during the 1990s was driven, in part, by the inclusion of wide-ranging and detailed policy agendas in letters of intent, often with no indication of the more limited set of measures to which IMF financial support was tied. The new guidelines specify that letters of intent should clearly distinguish between the conditions on which IMF support depends and other elements of the authorities' policy program, and that detailed policy matrices covering the broader agenda should be avoided unless the authorities consider them necessary to express their policy intentions.

Conclusion

The IMF's review of conditionality over the past few years has recognized that there are several interrelated principles for successful design and implementation of IMF-supported programs. These include national ownership of reforms, parsimony and tailoring in the choice and application of conditions, and effective coordination with other multilateral institutions. Early streamlining efforts suggest that some things have changed, but there likely remains room for improvement in the implementation of the new guidelines. It is also possible that the forthcoming review of the initial experience will reveal areas of fundamental tension, where the initial expectations of what could be achieved through streamlining may have been overoptimistic. Only time will tell whether macroeconomic benefits have also been achieved.

Endnotes

1. See, in particular, IMF 2000.
2. This analysis was based on arrangements approved between September 2000 (when "streamlining" efforts began as part of the process that would lead to the adoption of the new guidelines) and November 2001.
3. Ex post assessments are conducted for countries that have had a longer-term program engagement with the IMF and were initiated in response to the findings of the IMF's Independent Evaluation Office that, in some cases, prolonged use of IMF resources reflects failures in the design and implementation of programs or hinders the development of domestic institutions. Ex post assessments have been done for about 15 countries so far.
4. Indicative targets are another tool of conditionality but are used mainly in the area of quantitative macroeconomic conditionality.

Bibliography

IMF (International Monetary Fund). 2000. "Key Features of IMF Poverty Reduction and Growth Facility (PRGF) Supported Programs." http://www.imf.org/external/np/prgf/2000/eng/key.htm.

———. 2002a. "Guidelines of Conditionality." http://www.imf.org/External/np/pdr/cond/2002/eng/guid/092302.htm.

———. 2002b. "Lessons from the Real-Time Assessments of Structural Conditionality." http://www.imf.org/external/np/pdr/cond/2002/eng/assess/032002.htm.

———. 2004. "Strengthening IMF–World Bank Collaboration on Country Programs and Conditionality—Progress Report." http://www.imf.org/external/np/pdr/cond/2004/eng/022404.htm.

3

International Monetary Fund Conditionality and Ownership

MARK ALLEN
International Monetary Fund

The International Monetary Fund (IMF) engaged in a major review of conditionality during 2000–2, the result of which was to produce new Guidelines of Conditionality, revising the guidelines of 1979. The review concentrated on the role of structural conditionality and issues of ownership in programs. These issues have come to the fore particularly since the Asian crisis, the establishment of the Poverty Reduction and Growth Facility, and the launching of the Poverty Reduction Strategy Paper process.

Current Review of IMF Conditionality

The IMF is now performing the first biennial review of these conditionality guidelines and has split this review into two parts. The Policy Development and Review Department is doing a series of papers on program design issues, which will be followed by a review of the guidelines themselves. The papers on program design are scheduled to be discussed by the Board and made public shortly before or after the Annual Meetings, and the conditionality guidelines will be reviewed at about the end of the year.

The revised guidelines were based on five principles: programs should be clearly owned by the authorities; conditions should be parsimonious; conditions should be tailored to the country's circumstances; conditions should be set in coordination with other actors, particularly the World Bank, but also the rest of the donor community; and conditions themselves should be clear. The current review will consider how conditionality has developed over the past two years, whether conditions have been implemented according to the guidelines, and whether the guidelines themselves are having the desired effect.

Objectives of IMF Programs

Before one can be clear on what conditions should be applied, one needs to be clear on the program goals that form the basis of IMF support. The IMF's task is to strengthen the balance of payments position and foster reserve accumulation, and is therefore not primarily involved in development aid, although IMF financing may be complementary to development aid in some lower-income countries.

The aforementioned review is looking quite carefully at whether program goals are clearly defined, noting that IMF-supported programs can be divided into several different groups, depending on the precise program objective: some are traditional programs aimed at strengthening the current account; some are designed to support the restoration of confidence in the markets after a capital account crisis; some are designed primarily as monitoring arrangements to give assistance either to the creditor community or to the authorities themselves, as well as ensuring that programs are on track; and others back major structural reform operations.

One of the expected results of this conditionality review is the need to be clear on program objectives. In justifying IMF assistance, IMF economists tend to highlight the perceived perverse consequences had they not gone ahead with support for a particular set of policies, rather than highlight the precise objectives of the program. In other words, the minister of finance was under pressure to take highly undesirable measures, and the IMF's support of the program succeeded in making things not quite as bad as they would have been otherwise. This type of justification does not provide an adequate basis for IMF assistance.

Breadth of Policy Conditions Supported by the IMF

The breadth of policy conditions is also an essential element of conditionality, and this clearly varies with the goals of the program. In programs that are dealing with financial crises, the vast majority of conditions are indeed financial, whereas in programs that are in the Poverty Reduction Growth Facility category (for the lower-income countries), the bulk of conditionality tends to be focused on fiscal issues and expenditure orientation.

Whether the breadth has been appropriately tailored to the country's circumstances remains to be seen. The Independent Evaluation Office's report on fiscal adjustment was rather positive on this issue, but the Policy Development and Review Department is in the early stages of its own review. Streamlining conditionality continues to be a priority, but the number of conditions in programs now seems to be fairly constant, with about 15 conditions a year per country.

Conditionality and Ownership: The Future

The basic framework for the IMF's support of countries should involve setting a minimum standard beyond which the authorities should be given space to conduct economic policies precisely as they wish, provided of course this doesn't cut into the minimal area. This implies both a retreat from extraneous conditions and more selectivity in IMF assistance. In other words, the institution needs more care in accepting the member's word that it will meet the minimum standards.

A recent survey to see how World Bank–IMF collaboration was viewed in member countries was quite encouraging in that it indicated quite a large majority of the countries found conditionality not to be particularly intrusive and that policies were clearly owned by the country.

The current debate on conditionality and ownership is centered on whether conditionality should be used as leverage, or whether it is designed primarily to protect the lending agencies, so that they can give assurance to their shareholders that the money is being lent properly. The evidence is overwhelming that conditionality as leverage is not particularly effective. Moreover, it is not legitimate for an institution such as the IMF to use conditionality to persuade a country to do things that it would not otherwise have done.

Rather, the purpose of IMF resources is to encourage the authorities to adopt appropriate measures on the basis of an active policy dialogue that incorporates program design issues, even before conditionality is actually set. In practice, however, there is a temptation to use leverage when the country is in a difficult situation, and this temptation needs to be resisted. It can be difficult to enforce selectivity when the country itself is faced with a desperate situation, or when the donor community wishes the IMF to give support on the grounds that without it, the situation would be unmonitored and could deteriorate further, thus rendering its own bilateral aid less effective.

4

Experience with World Bank Conditionality

STEFAN KOEBERLE AND THADDEUS MALESA
World Bank

This chapter summarizes key trends in the application of conditionality in World Bank policy-based lending since fiscal 1980. Many of the findings indicate that over time the World Bank has adopted a number of lessons learned and incorporated them into business practices. The analysis concluded that (a) the volume of adjustment lending has stabilized at about 30 percent of World Bank lending in the past decade; (b) the average number of conditions has decreased; (c) loans with fewer conditions are generally of higher quality; (d) single-tranche adjustment operations are usually of higher quality; (e) World Bank adjustment lending is selective, favoring better-performing countries; (f) the average number of conditions is lower in better-performing countries; and (g) the focus of conditionality has changed from short-term reforms to longer-term and more complex issues. This chapter also attempts to answer the question: Given the experience with conditionality, should the World Bank continue to use it in its present form? It concludes with a discussion of programmatic lending as a fairly robust approach to reconcile numerous tensions and concerns.

Adjustment Lending Has Stabilized

Adjustment operations have accounted for 10–20 percent of all Bank lending operations (see figure 4.1) in recent years, with a far smaller share in the early 1980s. There has been a greater fluctuation in the share of lending volumes, with adjustment lending commitments representing about one-third of the World Bank portfolio on average (see figure 4.2). The number of adjustment operations approved to date has been almost evenly split between the International Bank for Reconstruction and Development (IBRD) and the International Development Association (IDA; see figure 4.3), but the share of commitments to middle-income countries by the IBRD has been far larger (see figure 4.4). This is also reflected in regional lending comparisons: the Africa Region accounts for 34 percent of adjustment operations but only 16 percent of commitments (see figures 4.5 and 4.6).

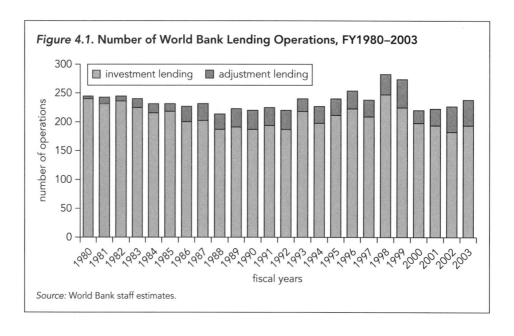

Figure 4.1. Number of World Bank Lending Operations, FY1980–2003

Source: World Bank staff estimates.

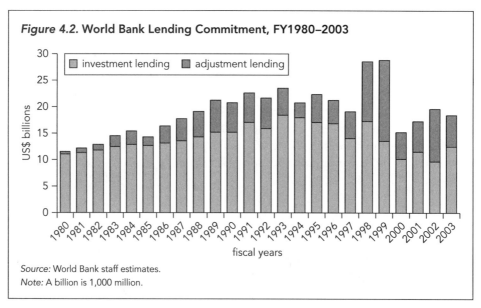

Figure 4.2. World Bank Lending Commitment, FY1980–2003

Source: World Bank staff estimates.
Note: A billion is 1,000 million.

The Average Number of Conditions Has Decreased

The average number of conditions[1] fell from above 35 in the late 1980s to below 18 in fiscal 2003 (see figure 4.7), with the exception of fiscal 1992–3 when the average number of conditions exceeded 40. If nonbinding conditions or desired actions are

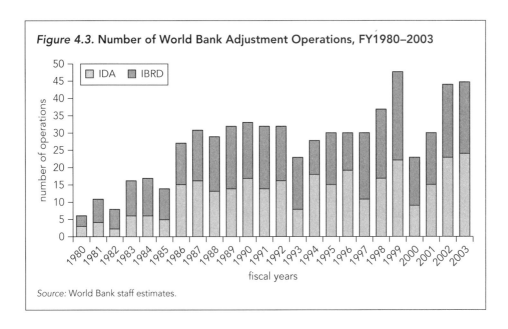

Figure 4.3. Number of World Bank Adjustment Operations, FY1980–2003

Source: World Bank staff estimates.

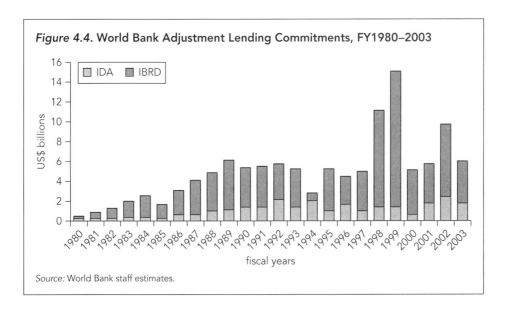

Figure 4.4. World Bank Adjustment Lending Commitments, FY1980–2003

Source: World Bank staff estimates.

included,[2] the total number has fallen from about 60 to 42 during the same period—somewhat above previous years' averages (34 in fiscal 2001 and 27 in fiscal 2002). Furthermore, the average number of conditions has been decreasing across all types of adjustment lending[3] used by the World Bank in recent years (see figure 4.8). While the average number of conditions has decreased across all Bank adjustment

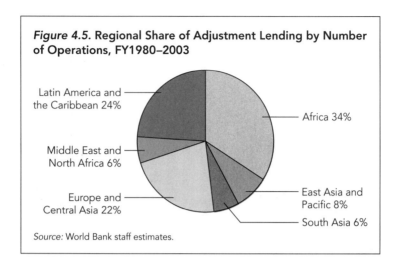

Figure 4.5. Regional Share of Adjustment Lending by Number of Operations, FY1980–2003

Latin America and the Caribbean 24%

Middle East and North Africa 6%

Europe and Central Asia 22%

Africa 34%

East Asia and Pacific 8%

South Asia 6%

Source: World Bank staff estimates.

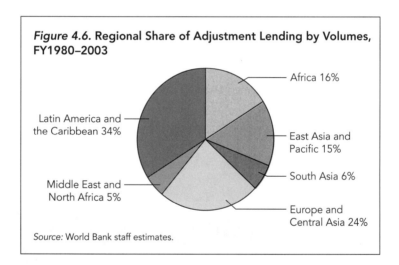

Figure 4.6. Regional Share of Adjustment Lending by Volumes, FY1980–2003

Latin America and the Caribbean 34%

Middle East and North Africa 5%

Africa 16%

East Asia and Pacific 15%

South Asia 6%

Europe and Central Asia 24%

Source: World Bank staff estimates.

loans, the number of conditions in IBRD and IDA countries has been converging (see figure 4.9).

Loans with Fewer Conditions Are Generally Higher Quality

In general, quality of adjustment operations, as judged by the independent Operations Evaluation Department, has improved markedly in the past decade. Quality-at-exit ratings increased from 69 percent of operations with satisfactory ratings in fiscal 1992 to 81 percent of operations with satisfactory ratings in fiscal 2003 (see figure 4.10). A lower number of legally binding conditions is generally associated with higher quality (see figure 4.11).

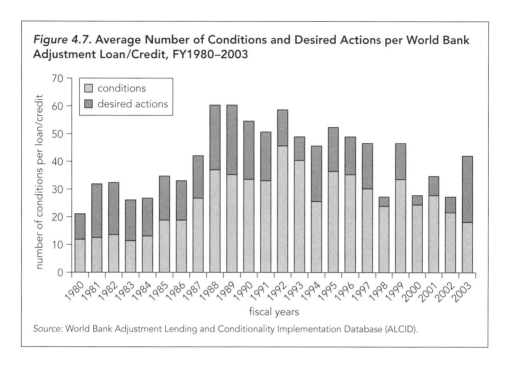

Figure 4.7. Average Number of Conditions and Desired Actions per World Bank Adjustment Loan/Credit, FY1980–2003

Source: World Bank Adjustment Lending and Conditionality Implementation Database (ALCID).

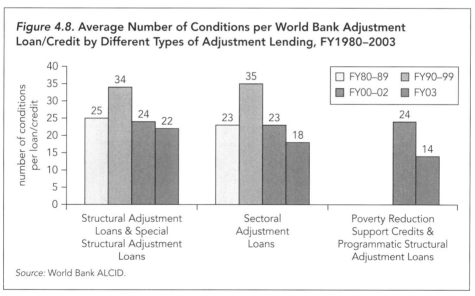

Figure 4.8. Average Number of Conditions per World Bank Adjustment Loan/Credit by Different Types of Adjustment Lending, FY1980–2003

Source: World Bank ALCID.

Single-Tranche Adjustment Operations Are Usually Higher Quality

As shown in figure 4.12, single-tranche adjustment operations tend to be more satisfactory than multiple-tranche adjustment operations. This result has not been not affected, however, by a significant increase in the share of single-tranche adjustment operations in the overall portfolio (see figure 4.13).

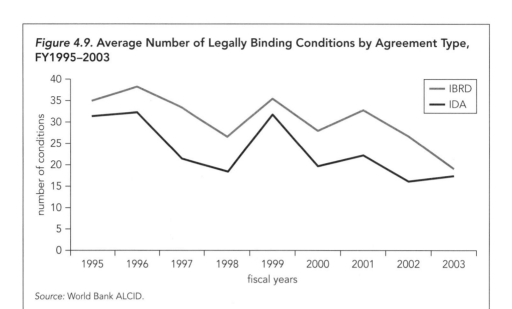

Figure 4.9. Average Number of Legally Binding Conditions by Agreement Type, FY1995–2003

Source: World Bank ALCID.

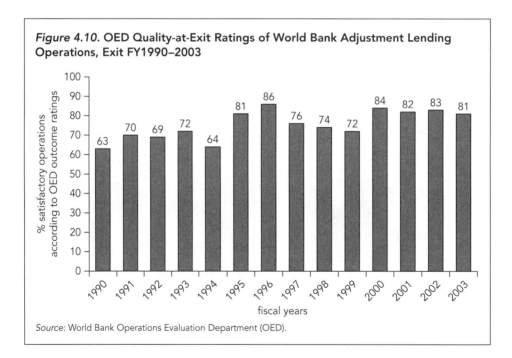

Figure 4.10. OED Quality-at-Exit Ratings of World Bank Adjustment Lending Operations, Exit FY1990–2003

Source: World Bank Operations Evaluation Department (OED).

Selective Lending Favors Better-Performing Countries

The majority of adjustment lending commitments go to high- and good-performing country groups,[4] according to the countries' Country Policy and Institutional Assessment (CPIA) rating (see figure 4.14).

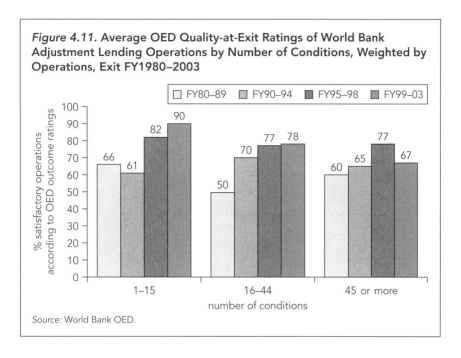

Figure 4.11. Average OED Quality-at-Exit Ratings of World Bank Adjustment Lending Operations by Number of Conditions, Weighted by Operations, Exit FY1980–2003

Source: World Bank OED.

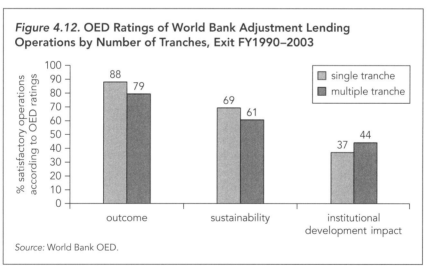

Figure 4.12. OED Ratings of World Bank Adjustment Lending Operations by Number of Tranches, Exit FY1990–2003

Source: World Bank OED.

Average Number of Conditions Is Lower in Better-Performing Countries

On average for fiscal 1998–2003, adjustment loans in very-high-performing countries (CPIA 4.5 or more) contain an average of 23 legally binding conditions, whereas for very-low-performing countries (CPIA 2.49 or less) the average number of conditions is 47. Operations in countries with higher overall CPIA ratings have higher average outcome ratings.

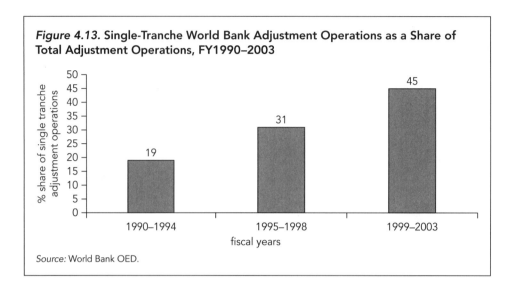

Figure 4.13. Single-Tranche World Bank Adjustment Operations as a Share of Total Adjustment Operations, FY1990–2003

Source: World Bank OED.

BOX 4.1 The CPIA Rating

The CPIA rating is carried out once a year. Its main purpose is to assess the quality of a country's current policy and institutional framework on the basis of observable policies, not on the amount of improvement since the previous yearly exercise, nor on intentions for future change, unless the latter are virtually in place. "Quality" means how conducive that framework is to fostering poverty reduction and sustaining growth and the effective use of development assistance. Bank staff follow specific guidelines to rate countries based on these guidelines and to benchmark countries in each region. Bank staff assess and rate 20 policy and institutional performance areas every year, which are then grouped and averaged into four clusters: (a) economic management, (b) social inclusion and equity, (c) public sector management and institutions, and (d) structural reform policies. The CPIA rating (a numerical value between 1 and 6) is then discussed and agreed to by World Bank Regional management. Some aspects of the CPIA ratings are disclosed. CPIA ratings for 1995 existed only for IDA countries, while IBRD ratings for 1995 were staff estimates. CPIA ratings for 1995–97 were rescaled from a 1–5 scale to a 1–6 scale.

Focus of Conditionality Has Changed to Longer-Term, More Complex Issues

The focus of overall conditionality has changed: from an initial focus on short-term macroeconomic and trade-related reforms to longer-term and more complex social sector and public sector management issues (see figures 4.15 and 4.16). The change in concentration of policy-based lending is also reflected in the sharp decline of supported public enterprise restructuring and privatization reforms in recent years (see figure 4.17).

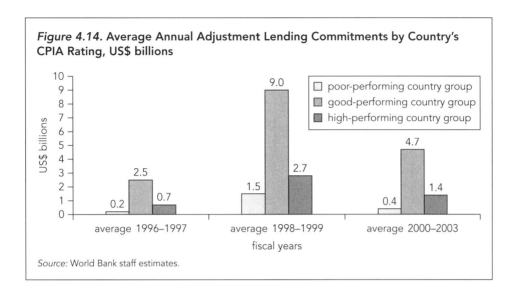

Figure 4.14. Average Annual Adjustment Lending Commitments by Country's CPIA Rating, US$ billions

Source: World Bank staff estimates.

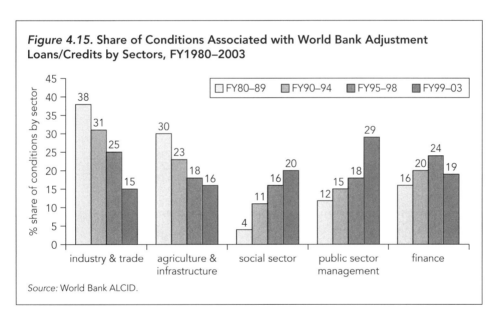

Figure 4.15. Share of Conditions Associated with World Bank Adjustment Loans/Credits by Sectors, FY1980–2003

Source: World Bank ALCID.

Should the World Bank Continue to Use Conditionality?

Although ex ante conditionality has often been criticized as corrosive and ineffective, leading to volatility of resource flows, straining the donor-recipient relationship, and undermining the respective country's sovereignty, it is still a necessity. If for no other reason, donors have a fiduciary responsibility to exercise due diligence while spending their taxpayers' money. However, alternative approaches such as ex post

---

BOX 4.2 Sectors

Sectors are high-level, mutually exclusive groupings of economic activities based on the types of goods or services produced. Sectors are used to indicate which part of the economy is supported by the World Bank intervention. For our analysis we classified the sectors into five categories:

Industry & Trade: Industry & Trade Sector Group

Agriculture & Infrastructure: Agriculture, Fishing and Forestry Sector Group, Information and Communications Sector Group, Energy and Mining Sector Group, Transportation Sector Group, and Water, Sanitation and Flood Protection Sector Group

Social Sector: Education Sector Group, Health and Other Social Services Sector Group, Compulsory Pension and Unemployment Insurance Sector, and Health Insurance Sector

Public Sector Management: Central Government Administration Sector, Law and Justice Sector, Subnational Government Administration Sector, and General Public Administration Sector

Finance: Banking Sector, Capital Markets Sector, Housing Finance and Real Estate Markets Sector, Noncompulsory Pensions, Insurance and Contractual Savings Sector, Payment Systems, Securities Clearance and Settlement Sector, General Finance Sector, and Micro- and Small and Medium Enterprise Finance Sector

---

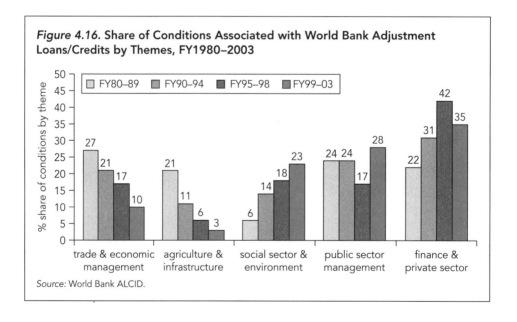

Figure 4.16. Share of Conditions Associated with World Bank Adjustment Loans/Credits by Themes, FY1980–2003

Source: World Bank ALCID.

---

conditionality and outcome-based conditionality have been under consideration as possible ways forward. Yet such approaches are thought to be fraught with practical difficulties, including the identification of meaningful intermediate indicators on which to base disbursements and the considerable time lag resulting from the collection and measurement of results indicators in often challenging circumstances.

BOX 4.3 Themes

Themes are goals or objectives of World Bank activities and are used to capture World Bank support for the Millennium Development Goals. For our analysis we classified the themes into five categories:

Trade & Economic Management: Trade and Integration Theme Group and Economic Management Theme Group

Agriculture & Infrastructure: Infrastructure Services for Private Sector Development Theme, Access to Urban Services for the Poor Theme, Other Urban Development Theme, Rural Nonfarm Income Generation Theme, Rural Policies and Institutions Theme, Rural Services and Infrastructure Theme, and Other Rural Development Theme

Social Sector & Environment: Social Protection and Risk Management Theme Group, Social Development, Gender and Inclusion Theme Group, Human Development Theme Group, and Environment and Natural Resources Management Theme Group

Public Sector Management: Public Sector Governance Theme Group, Rule of Law Theme Group, and Municipal Governance and Institutional Building

Finance & Private Sector: Corporate Governance Theme, Regulation and Competition Policy Theme, Small and Medium Enterprise Support Theme, Standards and Financial Reporting Theme, State Enterprise/Bank Restructuring and Privatization Theme, Other Financial and Private Sector Development Theme, Rural Markets Theme, and Municipal Finance Theme.

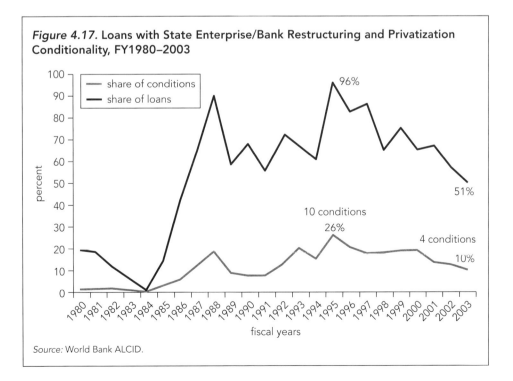

Figure 4.17. Loans with State Enterprise/Bank Restructuring and Privatization Conditionality, FY1980–2003

Source: World Bank ALCID.

Programmatic Lending Emerges as an Approach to Reconcile Numerous Tensions and Concerns

Many concerns remain with outcome-based adjustment lending, such as the diminishing predictability of available aid resources for the client, as well as having a country's aid program tied to indicators that are not necessarily under its control. Meanwhile, programmatic lending is emerging as a promising way to reconcile focus on performance with resource predictability by having support be reflected by a country's track record while supporting sustained engagement for a prudent mix of medium-term institutional and policy reforms. Not only is the lending product able to assist the implementation of complex reforms, but it also serves as a vehicle for policy dialogue that also typically involves transfer of advice and knowledge.

Endnotes

1. Legally binding conditions are prior actions preceding Board presentation, effectiveness conditions, and conditions for tranche release set out in the legal agreements signed by the borrowing government and the World Bank.

2. Nonbinding conditions are other desired actions included in the loan documentation but not included in the legal agreement. Client government compliance with these actions is not tied to the release of funds.

3. The different types of adjustment lending include Structural Adjustment Loans and Special Structural Adjustment Loans, Sectoral Adjustment Loans, and Poverty Reduction Support Credits and Programmatic Structural Adjustment Loans.

4. The unofficial groupings of high, good, and poor performers were made using CPIA ratings during the period between fiscal 1996 and 2003. A country with a CPIA rating of 4.00 and above is assigned to the high-performing group, those countries with a rating between 3.00 and 3.99 are assigned to the good-performing group, and the countries with an overall CPIA rating 2.99 and below are included in the poor-performing group. These groupings were made exclusively for this exercise, and are not in line with any official World Bank classifications.

5
Conditionality: Under What Conditions?

STEFAN KOEBERLE
World Bank

Policy-based lending has inspired much debate, with much of the controversy revolving around the use of conditionality—the conditions attached to funds disbursed by international finance institutions. With research on aid effectiveness highlighting the importance of good policy and institutional environments and country ownership, the shortcomings of traditional conditionality have become increasingly apparent. Selectivity, partnerships, and outcome orientation have been suggested to address these shortcomings.

Under what conditions is conditionality still useful? With donors focused on achieving the Millennium Development Goals, what type of conditionality remains useful and relevant? This chapter reviews experiences with conditionality in the World Bank's policy-based lending in light of the ongoing debate between the traditional approach to conditionality based on ex ante commitments to reforms and recent calls for a results-oriented approach stemming from the literature on aid effectiveness.[1]

The chapter concludes that approaches to policy-based lending and conditionality have evolved considerably over the past decade and that conditionality has a central role to play when tailored to country circumstances. Country-specific conditionality requires a careful mix of traditional ex ante elements and new approaches. But this type of programmatic adjustment lending offers a promising way to reconcile tensions between country ownership and commitment to donors, and between a medium-term strategy and flexibility.

Adjustment lending was originally conceived as a way of financing short-term balance of payments support—and to improve the policy environment for traditional project lending. Although the World Bank's Articles of Agreement envisage the provision of project financing as the Bank's primary activity, adjustment lending was introduced in 1980 under "special circumstances" allowed in article IV (though, in fact, the Bank's first loans were program—that is, nonproject—loans). But in response to changing borrower needs and broader reform agendas, new approaches to adjustment lending have evolved over the past two decades.

As a result adjustment lending has become an important tool for supporting social, structural, and sector reforms and is increasingly focused on long-run structural, social, and institutional issues. The narrow focus in the 1980s on achieving short-term stabilization and addressing distortions gave way in the 1990s to a more developmental perspective, with growing attention to reducing poverty, building institutions, and implementing complex social and structural reforms. This included an explicit focus on good governance, with strong support for public sector management reforms.

The Bank's adjustment lending now provides quick-disbursing policy-based financing based on actual or anticipated external financing gaps in the balance of payments or fiscal accounts (World Bank 1996). Policy-based lending is used to provide a cushion against economic shocks, deliver external financing that generates local counterpart funds in support of government development programs, and promote policy reforms.

These three goals are often pursued concurrently. But there has been an evolution in the mix, with a shift away from short-term balance of payments support toward increased emphasis on medium-term external financing of government spending and support for social and structural reforms.

Over the years World Bank policy-based lending has stirred substantial controversy. It has been the subject of extensive research and numerous internal Bank reviews (World Bank 1986, 1990, 1992b, 1994; Thomas and others 1991). The Bank has been considering its experience with adjustment lending and conditionality as part of its periodic reviews of operational policies and lending instruments in support of country strategies and programs (World Bank 2001c, 2002c). The mixed performance of adjustment lending has been well documented (Mosley, Harrigan, and Toye 1991). A more recent evaluation of developments in adjustment lending examined its appropriate use and the design of conditionality within the Bank's menu of lending instruments (World Bank 2001b). Based on several country studies, the Structural Adjustment Participatory Review Initiative drew broader conclusions on specific areas of policy reform, including privatization, agriculture, and the public sector (Structural Adjustment Participatory Review Initiative 2002; World Bank 2001a).

This chapter first discusses critiques of traditional conditionality, along with evidence on the validity of such criticisms. It then assesses new approaches to conditionality in the context of World Bank experiences. The next section discusses how suggestions for greater emphasis on country ownership and selectivity play out in real lending decisions. It then reviews the implications of new approaches to conditionality, followed by an examination of a partnership approach to conditionality. The final section provides a summary of lessons on the use of conditionality.

Critiques of Traditional Conditionality

Conditionality is central to policy-based lending, linking financial support from donors to policy reforms considered critical for a country's economic and social development. The Bank memorandum introducing adjustment lending defines it as an agreement with a borrower to implement structural changes over a three- to five-year period, with financial support and technical assistance provided throughout (World Bank 1980).

Adjustment lending starts with the Bank and the borrowing government agreeing on needed policy reforms. The Bank then provides financing conditional on the implementation of specific reforms. This approach provides assurances to both parties—to the Bank that the reforms will be implemented and to the country that compliance will make financing available. Thus conditionality also involves monitoring whether country programs achieve their goals.

Conditionality has generated many contentious debates in the development community. The two biggest questions are: Does conditionality influence policy choices? And have the policies associated with adjustment lending led to better outcomes?

When assessing the effects of conditionality and adjustment lending, it is difficult (if not impossible) to devise appropriate counterfactuals and attribute outcomes to specific operations, especially because Bank adjustment lending often accounts for a small portion of government resources. To interpret results correctly, the effects of adjustment programs must be separated from the dire economic conditions that prompted them. It is also useful to distinguish World Bank adjustment lending from adjustment efforts supported by the International Monetary Fund (IMF), multilateral development banks, and other institutions. But methodological problems are compounded by the complexity of distinguishing the effects of different adjustment measures on different groups. For example, a currency devaluation may benefit poor rural farmers producing cash crops, but its inflationary effect may hurt poor urban workers.

Notwithstanding these empirical difficulties, assessments of conditionality have been mixed and inconsistent. Critiques generally fall into the following areas:

- *Efficacy and enforcement.* Traditional ex ante conditionality has been described as a failed instrument for promoting reform and growth—one that is useless and potentially damaging (Collier 1997; Easterly 2001). Its usefulness is undermined by difficulties in monitoring compliance and by incentives for donors to continue disbursing funds despite lax reform efforts. Because borrowers do not see the withholding of funds as a credible threat, they may not follow through on program commitments. The usefulness of conditionality is further diminished when donors engage in defensive lending—that is, grant new loans to help countries pay off old ones—regardless of whether the countries have implemented reforms.

- *Sustainability.* Another critique of conditionality questions the sustainability of externally induced reforms. Many analysts argue that once financing for a donor-supported adjustment program ends, reforms are often reversed or abandoned.

- *Process.* Conditionality is often seen as infringing on the sovereignty of borrowing countries. Some critics also question the legitimacy of the World Bank and the IMF, describing them as unelected and unrepresentative bodies that force countries to adopt policies that are not in their best interests. In addition, there are concerns that agreements on conditionality are reached in nontransparent discussions between small groups of government officials and World Bank (and IMF) representatives without due consideration and participation by stakeholders, including civil society.

- *Content.* Some critics suggest that the main problem is the content of conditions, not conditionality itself. In this view conditions are often based on best practices and theoretical fixes, with no objective investigation of their actual economic effectiveness and no consideration of political, social, cultural, and environmental features and limitations (Wood and Lockwood 1999). Policy-based lending is thus seen as the handmaiden of the supposedly malignant "Washington consensus." For example, Milanovic (2003) asks why—despite numerous adjustment loans and IMF programs—Africa's per capita income is the same as it was 20 years ago.

- *Proliferation of conditions.* Critics also charge that that recipient countries have been micromanaged by conditions that are too numerous, too detailed, and too intrusive. Wood and Lockwood (1999) argue that more conditions have been placed on more areas of government policy, yet the central focus of reform programs has not changed. There is also concern that the number of conditions has increased as more bilateral donors have moved from project lending to policy-based lending in areas where they have an interest, including efforts to promote human rights, combat corruption, and build social capital.

Efficacy, Enforcement, Sustainability, and Process

Criticisms of conditionality in World Bank policy-based lending suggest an inconsistent perception of its influence on country policies. On the one hand there is widespread concern about its intrusiveness. On the other hand attention is drawn to the limited effectiveness of traditional Bank adjustment lending.

Yet several country studies have found that conditionality has been useful, with reformers welcoming it and using the associated external commitment to push through reforms—especially when conditionality focuses on a few important measures to which governments were already committed. For instance, government officials in Ghana and Uganda welcomed conditionality that helped them identify, implement, and cement reforms (Devarajan, Dollar, and Holmgren 2001). Kenya, Tanzania, and Zambia offer less effective examples of the positive role of adjustment lending in supporting reforms (Burnside and Dollar 1997). But in other countries commitments to reform have been delayed, not carried out, or were implemented but subsequently reversed.

Disappointing economic performance and uneven progress in policy reforms have been variously interpreted as failures of adjustment or as failures to adjust (World Bank 1994, 2001a). A clear verdict is thwarted by the serious identification problems inherent to evaluations of conditionality. Still, it is instructive to consider the regular evaluations of adjustment operations conducted by the World Bank's independent Operations Evaluation Department (OED). These evaluations assess projects' outcomes, likely sustainability, and institutional development impact (figure 5.1). Projects are considered to have satisfactory outcomes if they achieve or exceed their main

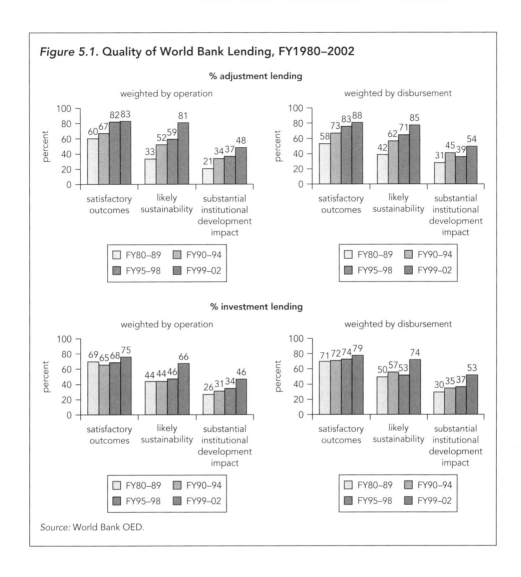

Figure 5.1. Quality of World Bank Lending, FY1980–2002

% adjustment lending

weighted by operation

weighted by disbursement

FY80–89   FY90–94
FY95–98   FY99–02

% investment lending

weighted by operation

weighted by disbursement

FY80–89   FY90–94
FY95–98   FY99–02

Source: World Bank OED.

goals; in the case of adjustment operations this includes the relevance of and compliance with conditionality (World Bank 1999a).

These ratings may be subject to methodological biases because of the problem of attributing outcomes to projects and given that evaluations are undertaken shortly after the funds are fully disbursed, before long-term results can be observed. Nevertheless, the evaluations indicate that most World Bank adjustment operations seem to meet their development objectives, are likely to be sustainable, and have significant impacts on institutional development—with significant improvements in the 1990s. OED outcome scores for adjustment lending increased from 60 percent satisfactory in the 1980s to 67 percent in fiscal 1990–94, then rose to 83 percent in fiscal 1999–2002.

The likely sustainability of adjustment operations also increased considerably, from 33 percent in the 1980s to 81 percent in fiscal 1999–2002, as did their institutional development impact, which rose from 21 percent to 48 percent. For all three indicators the findings for adjustment lending exceed those for investment lending. And as discussed further below, most ex ante conditions in World Bank adjustment loans have been met.

While most examples of involving civil society in the preparation or implementation of conditionality have emerged on an informal basis, recent adjustment programs based on the participatory processes involved in preparing Poverty Reduction Strategy Papers (PRSPs) have increasingly recognized the importance of building consensus among stakeholders (World Bank 2001b). Thus, in contrast to the failures in efficacy, enforcement, sustainability, and process claimed by many critics, a systematic evaluation suggests that policy-based lending has on balance yielded measurable benefits for recipient countries.

Content

Criticisms of conditionality often claim that a standard blueprint—presumably based on the Washington consensus—is used in all borrowing countries regardless of their circumstances (Wood and Lockwood 1999). Although the Bank's current operational policy contains prescriptive passages, this interpretation ignores the profound changes in World Bank policy-based lending over the past two decades (World Bank 2001b). The Bank's update of its operational policy on adjustment lending suggests refraining from using any blueprint for country-specific policy reforms (World Bank 2002b). Moreover, the validity of adhering to the Washington consensus has been called into question, including by the Bank's former chief economist (Stiglitz 1998).

The nature of conditionality in adjustment lending has evolved in line with the content of policy-based lending, reflecting the changing reform agenda in borrowing countries. Since being introduced in 1980 to help developing countries adjust their balance of payments after the 1979 oil shock, the Bank's policy-based lending has shifted from an early focus on supporting fiscal adjustment in response to external shocks to removing obstacles to growth and helping countries grow out of debt (figure 5.2). In the early 1990s policy-based lending began focusing on adjusting relative prices that had been distorted by decades of import-substituting industrialization policies.

Today policy-based lending more often supports institutional reforms in public sector management and in the financial and social sectors. Many borrowing countries have moved beyond first-generation reforms involving the removal of economic distortions and are predominantly engaged in more complex reforms—building capacity and developing institutional infrastructure. As a result the share of policy conditions applied to agriculture and infrastructure reforms fell from 27 percent in fiscal 1980–8 to 4 percent in fiscal 2001–02. During the same period the share of conditions for public sector reforms increased from 19 percent to 33 percent, and for financial and private sector reforms from 20 percent to 32 percent. Across all sectors, the reforms supported by adjustment lending are increasingly long term, institutional, and microeconomic.

The content of conditionality used in World Bank policy-based lending does not follow a standard blueprint, but differs by type of country. Conditionality in the

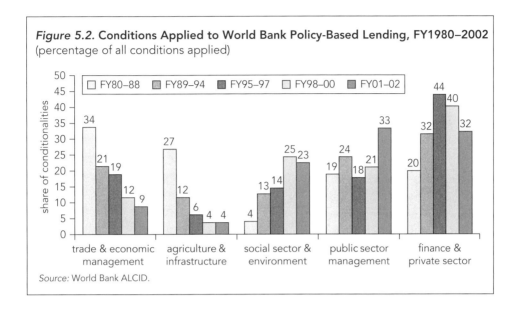

Figure 5.2. Conditions Applied to World Bank Policy-Based Lending, FY1980–2002 (percentage of all conditions applied)

Source: World Bank ALCID.

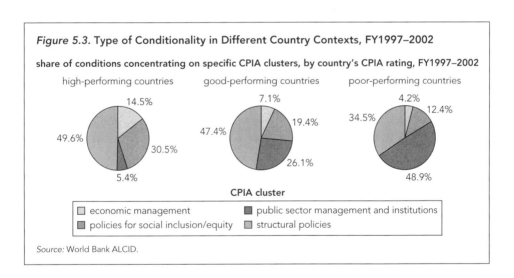

Figure 5.3. Type of Conditionality in Different Country Contexts, FY1997–2002

share of conditions concentrating on specific CPIA clusters, by country's CPIA rating, FY1997–2002

Source: World Bank ALCID.

better-performing countries[2] (those with a CPIA rating of 4.0 and above) focuses largely on structural polices (such as financial stability, financial sector depth, competitive environment for the private sector, trade and environmental sustainability). By contrast, conditionality in the poor-performing countries (those with a CPIA below 3.0) has a stronger focus on public sector management and institution building, including property rights, quality of budgetary and financial management, efficiency of revenue mobilization, quality of public administration, and transparency, accountability and corruption in the public sector (figure 5.3).

Proliferation of Conditions

Disillusionment with traditional conditionality tends to focus on the number of conditions imposed, often calling them excessive (Wood and Lockwood 1999). There is no "right" number of conditions: according to the World Bank's operational policy, a priori limits on the number of conditions are undesirable because they restrict the number of reforms that can be supported.

Moreover, determining actual conditions in adjustment loans is often not straightforward. Not only do policy agendas often contain a multitude of conditions, they also tend to mix reform measures, desired actions, and detailed processing steps. The average number of conditions in adjustment operations has fallen significantly—from above 36 in the late 1980s to below 18 in fiscal 2003 (figure 5.4a). If nonbinding conditions or desired actions are included,[3] the total number has fallen from about

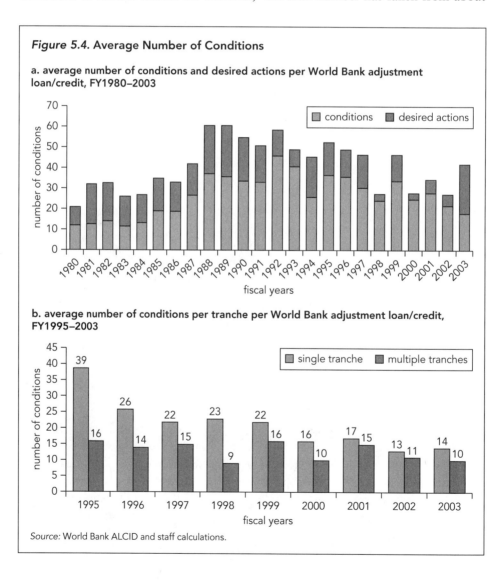

Figure 5.4. Average Number of Conditions

a. average number of conditions and desired actions per World Bank adjustment loan/credit, FY1980–2003

b. average number of conditions per tranche per World Bank adjustment loan/credit, FY1995–2003

Source: World Bank ALCID and staff calculations.

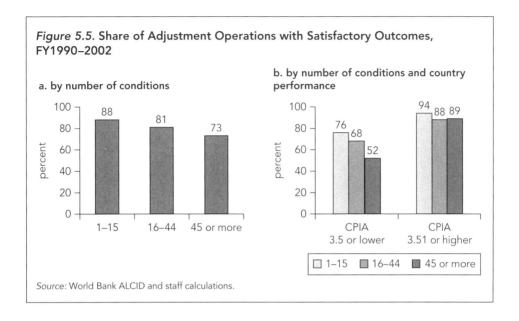

Figure 5.5. Share of Adjustment Operations with Satisfactory Outcomes, FY1990–2002

a. by number of conditions

b. by number of conditions and country performance

Source: World Bank ALCID and staff calculations.

60 to 42—somewhat above previous years' averages (34 in fiscal 2001 and 27 in fiscal 2002). However, because the overall number is of course higher the more tranches an operation has, it is more relevant to look at the number of conditions per tranche. The average number of conditions tied to a single-tranche operation (which accounted for 45 percent in fiscal 1999–2003) has declined from 39 in fiscal 1995 to an average of 14 conditions in fiscal 2003 (figure 4b).

Fewer conditions tend to be positively correlated with higher quality, as measured in the percentage of satisfactory outcome ratings for adjustment loans (figure 5.5a). Efforts to address performance deficiencies and capacity limitations through a larger number of conditions are generally ineffective.

This holds especially in countries with weak policies and institutions, as measured by the World Bank's annual CPIA. Adjustment operations were less successful in countries with weak policy performance subject to more conditions, while countries with stronger performance did well regardless of the number of conditions (figure 5.5b). This suggests that a country's policies and institutions are typically more important than specific design features—such as the number of conditions—in determining the success of a program.

At the same time, reflecting the growing focus on the long-run structural and institutional aspects of country reforms, conditionality has grown more complex (from 73 percent of adjustment operations in fiscal 1990–4 to 86 percent in fiscal 1999–2000, as rated by OED), demanding (from 82 percent of adjustment operations in fiscal 1990–4 to 93 percent in fiscal 1999–2000), and risky (from 72 percent in fiscal 1990–4 to 81 percent in fiscal 1999–2000) (World Bank 2001b).[4] Adjustment operations considered complex also tended to have more waivers and lower ratings for outcomes and sustainability.

These results can be largely explained by the fact that the number of conditions tends to be higher and complexity a greater challenge in countries with weak policy

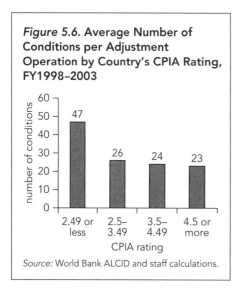

Figure 5.6. Average Number of Conditions per Adjustment Operation by Country's CPIA Rating, FY1998–2003

Source: World Bank ALCID and staff calculations.

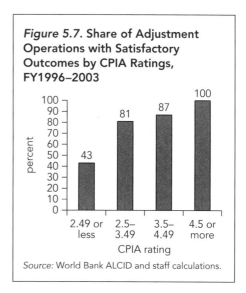

Figure 5.7. Share of Adjustment Operations with Satisfactory Outcomes by CPIA Ratings, FY1996–2003

Source: World Bank ALCID and staff calculations.

performance and institutional capacity, where adjustment lending is less successful. For example, in fiscal 1998–2003 adjustment operations in countries with low policy performance (CPIA ratings of 2.0–2.5) had an average of 47 binding conditions, compared with 23 in countries with high policy performance ratings (CPIA rating of 4.5 or higher) (figure 5.6). In sum, country conditions are decisive for the likelihood of success, as underlined by the general observation that the share of satisfactory outcome ratings tended be higher in countries with a better policy environment (figure 5.7).

Suggested New Approaches to Conditionality

Because traditional conditionality has not been entirely successful, many critics have wondered whether it should be dropped altogether. Various new approaches have been suggested to address the inherent tensions in conditionality:

- *Increasing country ownership and selectivity.* One issue involves the potential conflict between country ownership and a lender's due diligence and enforcement of loan conditions. The importance of strong policies and institutions for successful reform, as highlighted by the literature on aid effectiveness, has also given rise to calls for selectivity in favor of better-performing countries.

- *Improving the design of conditionality.* Because the traditional approach to policy-based lending—using ex ante conditionality based on promised actions—has been perceived as useless (at best) and even corrosive, an approach based on reputation and results has often been advocated.

- *Strengthening partnerships on conditionality.* A renewed focus on partnerships and coordination—between recipients and donors, and among donors—has gained currency in response to traditional conditionality perceived as overly intrusive.

Increasing Country Ownership and Selectivity

Many debates on conditionality have focused on the importance of country ownership—that is, commitment to aid-supported reforms by country authorities and a majority of domestic stakeholders. Country ownership has always been a central concept in development aid, on the assumption that it makes the policy and institutional changes associated with lending operations more likely to be implemented even in the face of political opposition. But in recent years the literature on aid effectiveness has increased the emphasis on ownership, driven by the proposition that donors can only advise and support but cannot buy or induce economic reforms (World Bank 1998a). Thus government willingness to reform—ideally supported by a broad consensus among members of civil society—is considered essential to successful adjustment programs.

The World Bank has long recognized the importance of country ownership and readiness to reform as critical factors for effective policy reforms and sustained development (Johnson and Wasty 1993). In light of the past two decades of policy-based lending, the Bank now shares the view that conditionality can reinforce country ownership—but cannot substitute for it (World Bank 2001b).

More recently, the Bank has made concerted efforts to form results-oriented partnerships for development to reflect three main lessons highlighted at the 2002 United Nations Conference on Financing for Development (held in Monterrey, Mexico). First, good development outcomes require appropriate policies and institutions. Second, sustained development progress requires that policies and institutions be country owned and country specific. And third, when these conditions are in place, development assistance can be highly effective (World Bank 2002a).

Country ownership and reform readiness are difficult to assess. Several conceptual frameworks have been developed to assess the level and quality of country ownership (box 5.1). Each of these approaches has merits and limitations (Morrow 1999). The

---

BOX 5.1 Conceptual Frameworks for Assessing Country Ownership

Leadership analysis assesses senior policy makers in terms of their initiative in formulating and implementing reforms, their level of intellectual conviction, their expression of political will, and their efforts to build consensus among various constituencies (Johnson and Wasty 1993). Leadership is important for successful reform, but senior policy makers may underestimate difficulties in securing support from other political actors and sustaining institutional efforts.

Stakeholder analysis focuses on understanding the power relationships, influences, and interests of stakeholders affected by policy reforms, including those in government (Heaver and Israel 1986). This analysis also captures the extent to which stakeholders can make their voices heard, participate in decision making, reach consensus, and accept short-term costs in exchange for long-term gains and uncertainties in the distribution of benefits.

Reform readiness analysis captures the commitment and performance of key policy makers and interest groups and so requires detailed knowledge of a country's political situation (Haggarty and Matuda 1999). Based on findings that successful reforms must be politically desirable, feasible, and sustainable, this approach examines institutional arrangements for policy making and analyzes the political rationale for particular policy decisions.

challenge is identifying robust indicators for judging whether policy-based lending is appropriate in a specific country situation. These might include the authorities' willingness to prepare an action plan outlining the government's reform intentions and the extent of consultations with and participation of civil society in designing and implementing reforms.

A country's track record of policy performance is among the most robust predictors of whether reforms will be implemented. But some countries with weak track records have managed to turn themselves around fairly quickly. Such cases require a judgment that the risks of failure are outweighed by the potential rewards of continued engagement.

Decisions on policy-based lending cannot overlook the tensions between limited country ownership and the use of conditionality to ensure that reform objectives are achieved. If a country's commitment or implementation capacity is weak, conditionality is unlikely to be effective. By itself conditionality cannot lead to the adoption of better policies if there is no consensus for reform. When there is commitment and capacity to reform, adjustment lending can accelerate, broaden, and deepen it, enhancing its impact and hopefully contributing to growth and development. But in the absence of such commitment, adjustment lending may fail to support improvements in policies and institutions—and indeed, may contribute to delays in reform and leave the country burdened with debt.

One way to bolster country ownership is to forgo ex ante conditionality in favor of ex post allocations of policy-based loans based on the policies a country adopts. Although successful adjustment can deliver significant long-term benefits, research on aid effectiveness suggests that these benefits can be realized only if a country's policy environment is favorable (World Bank 1998a). This suggests that policy-based lending should focus on countries where it is most likely to be effective—those with good policies and high poverty.

Empirical studies emphasize that policy changes are driven primarily by domestic political economy, not by foreign assistance or policy-based lending (Devarajan, Dollar, and Holmgren 2001). Alesina and Dollar (1998) find that there is no tendency for surges in finance to lead to policy reforms. In fact, policy is generally quite persistent, and sharp policy changes are the exception, not the rule.

Greater selectivity in World Bank lending, based on country performance, is among the main suggestions for increasing aid effectiveness (World Bank 1998a). Taking that argument further, the International Financial Institutions Advisory Commission, chaired by Allan Meltzer, advocated limiting policy-based lending to countries with good policies (Meltzer and others 2000). Despite several obvious shortcomings, these proposals have been influential.

First, although many advocates see it as a way of avoiding traditional ex ante conditionality, selectivity based on judgments of country performance may implicitly result in similar bargaining between the Bank and borrowing countries. Unless selectivity is based on a few measurable, objective indicators (such as spending allocations), assessing a country's performance is inherently subjective—particularly if it involves judging the relevance and effectiveness of a country's policy choices.

Second, selectivity would not eliminate the tensions between country ownership and donor intrusiveness. Instead the bargaining process would shift from conditionality to policy assessments.

Finally, there is no reasonable basis to objectively distinguish countries with good policies (where policy-based lending would make sense) from countries with bad policies (where it would not). Most of the Bank's borrowing countries fall between these two extremes, with mixed performance resulting in rather subjective judgments and lending decisions. Moreover, the countries in this heterogeneous middle ground are home to most of the world's poor people. If selectivity meant that adjustment loans went only to the small handful of countries with unquestionably good policy performance, these poor people would not benefit from any policy-based lending, however ineffective.

Aid allocations based on country performance are not a novel idea for the Bank. It already uses CPIA ratings in determining the relative country financing shares from the International Development Association (IDA). In addition, its Country Assistance Strategies include different lending scenarios based on triggers typically driven by country performance. Moreover, in recent years considerable selectivity has emerged in decisions on adjustment lending.

The World Bank's policy-based lending has been selective, favoring better-performing countries. Since the mid-1990s most—though not all—adjustment lending has gone to countries with above-average policy performance, for sectors with good track records and for issues with adequate supporting analytical work. In fiscal 1995–2003 borrowers with above-average CPIA ratings received 76 percent of adjustment loans by volume (amount) and 65 percent by number (figure 5.8).

When adjustment lending has gone to countries with poor track records, assessments of potential risks and rewards have typically argued that such loans were needed to exploit brief windows of opportunity for long-overdue reforms. But some less successful examples—such as adjustment lending to the Russian Federation shortly before it defaulted on its foreign debt in 1998—show that, despite the best intentions, it is extremely difficult to assess such situations.

Improving the Design of Conditionality

Recognizing the importance of country ownership, the country's policy and institutional environment, and the changing nature of policy programs, what are the implications for the design of conditionality? Some analysts have called for a results-oriented approach to conditionality based solely on outcomes and for the use of different loan disbursement procedures to align conditionality with country performance rather than promises.

Should Conditionality Be Outcome-Based?

Disillusionment with ex ante conditionality has led to suggestions that loan disbursements be linked to outcomes rather than policies. It is argued that specifying the

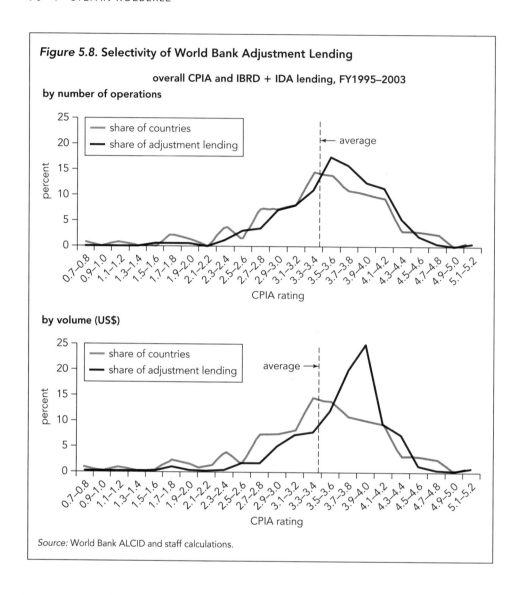

Figure 5.8. Selectivity of World Bank Adjustment Lending

overall CPIA and IBRD + IDA lending, FY1995–2003

by number of operations

by volume (US$)

Source: World Bank ALCID and staff calculations.

desired results of reforms rather than policies on how to achieve them would signal that donors are concerned with the destination rather than the journey. Giving country authorities more discretion in achieving agreed outcomes is an attractive proposition that could eliminate intrusive donor micromanagement of policy and institutional reforms. Freed from the principal-agent problem of bargaining with donors, countries would have greater scope to define their policies and so have greater ownership.

But linking disbursements to outcomes creates several problems (Gunning 2000): First, outcomes result from many factors other than policy choices. Moreover, the link between government actions and outcomes is often not clear—as exemplified by the complex relationship between social spending and social outcomes (Filmer, Hammer, and Pritchett 2000; Thomas and others 2000). Thus countries might suffer if disbursements are withheld on the basis of inadequate outcomes beyond the government's control. Collier, Guillaumont, and Guillaumont (1997) suggest correcting for this bias by identifying important determinants of outcomes beyond the government's control (such as landlockedness and ethnolinguistic fractionalization). But this approach is limited to a few indicators and presupposes a good understanding of determinants and available data.

Second, it is harder to monitor outcomes than policies, and data on outcomes are often not available or are fraught with methodological problems. Finally, even if there is a clear link between government actions and outcomes and data on outcomes are available, outcomes typically change slowly and can be monitored only over the medium term—implying that current governments would be held responsible for the actions of their predecessors. Linking disbursements to outcomes would also be impractical for policy-based lending, which usually involves disbursements over periods of less than three years.

Outcome-based conditionality has been tested in a few countries. Under the leadership of the European Commission, the Special Programme of Assistance for Africa—sponsored by a group of multilateral and bilateral donors—experimented with a pilot approach in Burkina Faso that linked the release of funds to program outcomes rather than policy reforms. This effort involved joint evaluations by all donors of overall results rather than individual conditions (Emblad and Gilles 2000). Preliminary evaluations suggest that this approach increased country ownership and donor coordination (Special Programme of Assistance for Africa Task Team on Contractual Relationships and Selectivity 2000), with implementation issues revolving around the choice of outcome indicators, realistic targets given time lags, and the quality of data (European Commission 2001).

In World Bank policy-based lending, conditionality based on outputs and outcomes has been used increasingly in recent years. Such conditionality does provide more flexibility to countries and makes conditionality more effective—provided outcome-related benchmarks are quantifiable, narrowly defined, and complemented by action-based conditions where appropriate. Benchmarks should also be clearly linked to measures over which policy makers have discretion, to reduce borrower uncertainty about the release of financing. These indicators should be agreed upon at the outset of lending programs, with a clear understanding of which ones (primarily those related to policy actions) are within government control.

Options for Phasing and Tranching

Debates on the best approach to conditionality also involve the timing and phasing of performance benchmarks supported by policy-based lending. When adjustment loans provide fast-disbursing financial support in response to economic distress, they tend to focus on problems amenable to short-term solutions—such as stroke-of-the-pen reforms of tariffs and regulations.

But when policy-based lending supports complex structural reforms in areas such as public sector management, privatization, and the financial sector, there is a tension between the rapid provision of financing and the often slower pace of intensive reforms. To reflect these timing considerations, adjustment loans are disbursed in tranches—that is, portions of funding are withheld until certain conditions are met. Tranches have typically been designed on the basis of ex ante conditionality, though in principle they could be used for ex post approaches. Among 452 World Bank adjustment loans approved in fiscal 1990–2002, 85 percent fully disbursed all tranches as planned (World Bank ALCID). Thus the majority of operations did not experience waivers, restructuring, or cancellations, suggesting that a common criticism of traditional conditionality—that it leads to frequent noncompliance with policy conditions—has limited validity.

Still, appropriate phasing of policy-based lending to support countries' growing focus on complex medium-term structural and institutional reforms involves difficult choices among various options:

- *Multiple tranches.* The World Bank's traditional approach using ex ante conditionality has typically been based on multiple tranches to support reform commitments as they are achieved in a single operation. Multiyear and multitranche operations have been used to demonstrate country commitment and to lock in reforms through conditionality covering future actions. It is largely this type of ex ante conditionality that has given rise to charges of noncompliance, corrosion of sovereignty, and low efficacy. But in several countries this approach has been welcomed by reformers, strengthening their hand against vested interests, or served as a signaling device (Devarajan, Dollar, and Holmgren 2001). In principle, multiple tranches can also clarify future commitments when a country's track record is weak. But in practice, multiyear and multitranche operations account for the bulk of implementation difficulties that occasionally hamper adjustment programs. For example, during fiscal 1990–9, 39 percent of all approved two-tranche operations and 63 percent of three-tranche operations involved waivers or cancellations (World Bank ALCID). Such problems are especially pronounced in multiyear operations owing to the challenge of setting out during negotiations a detailed policy plan covering actions to be taken a few years later.

- *Floating tranches.* The Bank has increasingly used floating tranches—that is, tranches disbursed when specific conditions are fulfilled rather than according to a set schedule. This approach can be appropriate for clearly defined discrete reform actions with uncertain timing, such as privatization of public enterprises. Preliminary evidence suggests that floating tranches for different parts of a reform program can increase the credibility of loan conditionality. Floating tranches generate complementarities and synergies among reform measures and avoid delays in specific reforms holding up progress in the overall program. In addition, OED evaluations of the Higher Impact Adjustment Lending Initiative in Sub-Saharan Africa have found that floating tranches provided considerable flexibility in timing and increased country ownership—especially when combined with fewer but well-focused conditions (World Bank 1998b, 1999b).

- *Single tranches.* Single-tranche operations have become more common. During fiscal 1998–2000 the Bank approved 36 single-tranche adjustment operations worth

$12.8 billion, and by fiscal 2000 single-tranche loans accounted for nearly 40 percent of the number and volume of adjustment operations. Experiences with single-tranche operations have been encouraging, with OED evaluations for fiscal 1990–2002 showing higher ratings than for multitranche operations in terms of satisfactory outcomes (88 percent compared with 78 percent) and likely sustainability (72 percent and 63 percent). The higher ratings may partially reflect the wider use of single-tranche operations in countries with better policies and less need for conditionality. Although single-tranche operations received slightly lower ratings in terms of their impact on institutional development, this may reflect their shorter disbursement periods. Indeed, concern about the sustainability of single-tranche operations is the main reason for the Bank's operational policy provision that such operations may be appropriate in environments of high uncertainty—provided there is adequate ex ante conditionality and a satisfactory medium-term program in which the operations can be evaluated (World Bank 1996). Again, country conditions matter for effective conditionality design. In countries with below-average policy and institutional performance, single-tranche operations are associated with better outcomes and fewer waivers, while higher-performing countries achieve good outcomes regardless of the number of tranches.

- *Programmatic adjustment lending.* Over the past few years the Bank has increasingly used a programmatic approach for its policy-based lending. This approach involves a series of single-tranche operations that are subsequently presented to the Bank's Board of Executive Directors, with a medium-term framework specified at the outset—including completed prior actions, monitorable progress indicators, and expected prior actions for subsequent operations. To the extent possible, programmatic approaches align disbursements with the borrowing country's annual budget cycle. By building on completed actions specified and agreed to in advance (instead of future promises), a programmatic approach combines country ownership with systematic reform implementation. Programmatic lending is usually used to support complex medium-term institutional reforms. Poverty Reduction Support Credits are emerging as a vehicle that incorporates these principles, basing social and structural reforms in IDA countries on the poverty reduction strategies articulated in these countries' PRSPs (World Bank 2001b).

Country experiences suggest that an exclusive focus on conditionality on the basis of ex ante commitments or ex post results may not be practical or useful for World Bank policy lending. The tranching and phasing options described above are not appropriate in every country or sector. Traditional multiyear, multitranche designs may still be useful, especially for supporting in-depth sector reforms. Floating tranches can help with discrete reforms with uncertain timing, without holding up the rest of the program. For strong performers with good track records—such as Brazil, Latvia, Mexico, and Uganda—the programmatic approach has been used to provide sustained, flexible, and predictable support to credible medium-term reform programs. The programmatic approach has also been useful in countries with sound reform programs but weaker capacity or track records or in countries emerging from crisis or instability—such as Jamaica, Peru, Turkey, and Ukraine. Early experience suggests

that the programmatic approach is well suited for its goals of fostering country ownership, providing reliable financial support for successful medium-term programs,
and accommodating the uncertainties inherent in medium-term reforms (World Bank
2004).

Monitoring Results

Debates on conditionality implicitly emphasize the importance of monitoring its
development impact, using specific indicators to judge its effect on the borrowing
country's compliance (in the case of ex ante conditionality) or performance (in the
case of a results-based approach). Borrower implementation and Bank supervision of
lending operations have been key issues for the World Bank—especially since the
Wapenhans Report stressed their importance (World Bank 1992a). Past efforts to
strengthen monitoring and evaluation of the Bank's loan portfolio focused on investment lending (World Bank 2000).

For policy-based lending, monitoring has typically focused more on compliance
with ex ante conditionality than on progress, outcomes, and poverty impacts. All programs supported by policy-based lending, whether based on an ex ante or an ex post
approach, involve implicit assumptions about the expected effects of certain actions
on economic performance and incentives, social conditions, poverty reduction, and
the environment. But it is difficult to define and apply performance indicators that
compare actual and expected outcomes and allow for program corrections. Linking
policy measures supported by conditionality and their associated financing to specific
economic and social outcomes entails several problems: (a) reform programs have
complex economywide repercussions, (b) poverty reduction and economic performance are influenced by many other factors, (c) reliable and timely data are often not
available, and (d) changes in countrywide economic, social, and environmental trends
may be realized only with a considerable lag. Evaluations of policy-based lending are
further complicated by the difficulty of specifying counterfactuals—that is, what
would have happened without the operations.

The Millennium Development Goals—the product of the UN Millennium Declaration adopted by the international community in 2000—pose a new challenge for
increasing the focus on results (IMF and others 2000). Tying adjustment lending to
development outcomes is a critical part of the Bank's commitment to align country
and sector strategies with the eight development goals (World Bank 2001d). These
goals provide an ambitious yardstick against which to measure the contribution of
conditionality to alleviating poverty, increasing school enrollments, reducing child
and maternal mortality, expanding access to reproductive health services, eliminating
gender disparities, and improving environmental management.

Aligning conditionality with the Millennium Development Goals requires realistic
time frames, intermediate goals, and measures differentiated by countries and regions.
Country programs for policy and institutional reforms should monitor clear performance targets over the medium term while maintaining scope for adapting reform

efforts to changing country circumstances. Programmatic adjustment lending offers a promising way to do both.

Still, it has been challenging to develop a road map for policy-based operations that allows meaningful assessment of reform progress and goes beyond mere compliance with policy conditions, whether ex ante or ex post. Policy-reform plans must spell out a practical framework that links strategies to results using monitorable progress indicators. (For programmatic operations, such indicators should complement the actions selected as expected prior actions—or "triggers"—for subsequent operations.) It is no trivial task to define performance indicators precise enough to guide implementation and enable unambiguous monitoring of results, but pragmatic and flexible enough to allow for the inherent unpredictability of institutional reforms over the medium term (see World Bank 2001b for a discussion of performance benchmarks).

Regardless of whether an ex ante or ex post approach is chosen, conditionality will yield results only if its design reflects a country's institutional capacity. Clear monitoring arrangements are integral to effective implementation, including by local governments and civil society where appropriate. In addition, governments must build domestic capacity for monitoring economic, social, poverty, and environmental outcomes.[5]

Strengthening Partnerships on Conditionality

Increased partnerships and collaboration between donors and borrowers and among donors have been part of the response to the claim that traditional ex ante conditionality is overly intrusive. It is hoped that transparent partnerships between donors and countries will encourage true country ownership of reforms. The most sweeping proposal in this area is to channel all development assistance through a common pool instead of financing individual programs and projects—augmenting the general budgets of poor countries less obtrusively (Kanbur and Sandler 1999).

The World Bank supports coordination and harmonization efforts, which attempt to combine partnerships with a focus on results—most recently in the Rome Declaration on Harmonization (World Bank 2003). The Bank's Comprehensive Development Framework advocates a long-term holistic approach, with borrowing countries owning and directing their development strategies and stronger partnerships among governments, donors, civil society, the private sector, and other development stakeholders in implementing the strategies. The goal is to make aid more effective through coordinated support for country programs and to benefit from synergies and avoid duplication among different development partners, including the IMF, other multilateral development banks, and bilateral donors.

Applying these principles to conditionality requires aligning the design and implementation of policy-based lending supported by the Bank, the IMF, and other multilateral development banks, which have traditionally provided the bulk of policy-based lending. Efforts to coordinate policy-based lending aim to strengthen government ownership by reducing the scope and number of conditions, making policy-based lending more effective in supporting poverty reduction efforts, reducing burdens on country capacity, and enhancing the predictability of aid flows. In addition, as bilateral donors shift away from projects toward direct budget assistance supporting poverty reduction strategies their support needs to be coordinated with country processes and other donors.

One risk of these partnership approaches to conditionality is that they tend to ignore tensions between stakeholders with different incentives. It is in the choice of conditionality where potential conflicts between ownership and intrusiveness are played out, when the agenda of donors diverges from that of reluctant reformers. And because few countries are monolithic, policy choices reflect the various influences that domestic stakeholders and competing vested interests have on policy makers. The political economy of borrowers might also create incentives for policy reversals after an adjustment program has been concluded.

Moreover, because the effectiveness of donors such as the World Bank is measured as much by lending volumes as by program outcomes, such donors tend to overestimate the likelihood of successful reforms in borrowing countries. In addition, different donors may have different agendas, potentially leading to conflicting incentives. If these complexities are not addressed, the partnership approach to conditionality risks generating disenchantment similar to that with traditional conditionality.

Coordination of Conditionality with the IMF

Efforts to coordinate conditionality among multilateral development institutions have focused on the World Bank and the IMF—the largest providers of policy-based lending. The Bank and the IMF have distinct but complementary responsibilities and expertise for supporting member countries' adjustment programs. Both institutions have long had a framework for collaboration to help ensure that their advice is consistent and fully exploits each institution's expertise and financial resources—as reflected in the so-called joint guidelines (World Bank and IMF 1998).

PRSPs and the Heavily Indebted Poor Countries Initiative have contributed to more systematic arrangements for Bank and IMF collaboration in many low-income countries, with each institution's conditionality focused on its areas of primary responsibility. Extending similar principles to other countries, the Bank and the IMF have been strengthening their collaboration in supporting country development efforts through more coherent, streamlined conditionality (World Bank and IMF 2001). Based on the premise that increased collaboration on conditionality would strengthen program designs, a "lead agency" concept was introduced to deal with specific policy issues, along with systematic information sharing and monitoring. Enhanced collaboration is being operationalized through increased interaction between the staff of the two institutions and through transparent reporting in Board documents of each institution's views on borrowing countries' reform priorities, program conditionality, and progress in program implementation (World Bank and IMF 2002, 2004).

Among the forces driving increased Bank and IMF collaboration are ongoing efforts by the IMF to streamline its conditionality and increase country ownership of the programs it supports. In the past the extended use of structural benchmarks in IMF-supported programs contributed to significant overlap in the structural conditions of IMF and World Bank–supported programs (World Bank 2001b, IMF 2001a). By contrast, conditionality in the Bank's policy-based lending has tended to focus on structural reforms in areas within its mandate, with a general provision that countries receiving adjustment loans maintain an adequate macroeconomic framework. The main aim of the IMF's review of its conditionality was to focus it on measures critical to monitoring and achieving the macroeconomic objectives of IMF-supported programs, and to apply it sparingly outside the IMF's core areas of responsibility (IMF 2001a, 2001b, 2002).

The Boards of the IMF and the Bank stressed that the streamlining of IMF conditionality should result in an overall reduction in the conditions imposed on borrowing countries—and not just shift them from one institution to the other. In addition, enhanced reporting on conditionality to the Boards of both institutions is designed to ensure that areas no longer covered by IMF conditionality will be adequately addressed by the Bank or other institutions.

Success in both institutions' efforts to streamline and focus conditionality hinges on effective collaboration. The staffs of both institutions must develop a shared vision of their support for each borrowing country, with a clear division of labor based on each institution's areas of expertise and frequent dialogue and information sharing.

Donor Harmonization on Conditionality

The problems of donor-driven project proliferation are well known, including the stress it imposes on country capacity, the potential substitution of donor-driven agendas for country ownership, and the fragmentation of country budget processes. In response, donors (especially bilateral donors) have sought to enhance the effectiveness of their aid programs by replacing or supplementing traditional project financing with direct budget support, particularly in low-income countries developing PRSPs. Recent recipients of such support include Ghana, Tanzania, and Uganda.

Whether intended or not, this type of aid resembles the policy-based lending provided by the World Bank, the IMF, and other multilateral development institutions. Although the objective is typically to provide predictable and less-intrusive financing and greater country ownership, by its nature budget support implies that conditionality explicitly or implicitly guides donor decisions.

The shift from project to nonproject financing may raise a host of new issues, including concerns about PRSPs that are not specific on programs, action plans, and output indicators, with weak or no links to the budget cycle or medium-term spending framework; discrepancies between poverty reduction strategies and donor programs; and contradictions or overlap between the budget support provided by different donors.

Moreover, instead of facilitating the alignment of donor support with the borrowing country's budget cycle, there is a risk that discordant donor priorities or processes may excessively strain country capacity. Even the goal of predictable resource flows could be undermined if donor decisions on disbursements are based on different performance criteria.

These issues call for much closer coordination of policy-based lending, with explicit recognition of the need for a systematic approach to conditionality. Such efforts may involve coordinating the timing, content, and process of donor negotiations with governments, assigning clearer divisions of labor or even lead agencies for specific areas, and focusing conditionality on a small set of country priorities and plans developed by the borrowing country. Such approaches would make it possible to better integrate sector programs and capacity building with countries' regular budget processes. Although donors would maintain distinct accountability for their decisions, they would aim to increase the predictability of resource flows through coordinated assessments of borrowing countries' performance against agreed benchmarks.

Conclusions

Development financing in support of country policies has become more important as donors increasingly recognize the need for strong country policies and institutions and shift away from narrow project financing. Yet conditionality remains controversial and is often considered intrusive, ineffective, or even harmful. Disillusionment with traditional ex ante conditionality has led to proposals for more results-oriented approaches focused on ownership, selectivity, and partnerships.

These approaches have merits and drawbacks in the reality of World Bank lending decisions. Moreover, many of their elements have already been incorporated into the Bank's policy-based lending—and the improving quality of adjustment lending suggests that Bank conditionality reflects some of the lessons from the past two decades of experience. In the future these approaches should be made more systematic and transparent by spelling out how the policies and institutional reforms they support will contribute to the achievement of country objectives. In addition, monitoring of the poverty outcomes of policy-based lending should include indicators linking conditionality to progress toward the Millennium Development Goals wherever possible. Developing such indicators will require concerted diagnostic and analytical work.

Overall, policy-based lending remains a useful tool for supporting government reforms. Conditionality is integral to policy-based lending, whether explicitly included ex ante or implicitly recognized ex post. But while conditionality can be a useful commitment device, it cannot substitute for country ownership. Conditionality should be used with judicious selectivity and tailored to country circumstances. Moreover, its limitations and opportunities must be recognized in designing a new generation of conditionality.

Because economic policies are driven primarily by domestic political processes, conditionality is appropriate only if there is commitment and capacity to reform. Research on aid effectiveness emphasizes the importance of focusing adjustment support on countries with good policies and institutions. Building capacity and providing advice on the basis of analytical work are better ways of nurturing reforms in their early stages. Moreover, although country ownership of reforms is critical, it is difficult to assess. A country's track record is among the most robust indicators of its readiness and capacity to reform. But though there are exceptions, the history of policy-based lending is littered with inaccurately assessed windows of opportunity for reform.

Enhancing the development effectiveness of policy-based lending also requires making judicious use of the various design options that allow conditionality to be customized to country circumstances, including in terms of the number and nature of conditions and the phasing and tranching. Most attempts to address performance deficiencies and capacity limitations through a larger number of more complex conditions have been ineffective. Thus conditionality should focus on priorities grounded in country ownership and capacity and be limited to policy and institutional actions under the control of the executive branch.

Although research on aid effectiveness encourages phasing and tranching based on performance rather than promises, a pure outcome focus is fraught with practical difficulties: expected results may evolve over time; results are often subject to exogenous factors; information on results measurement/indicators often comes with a considerable time lag; and identification of meaningful intermediate indicators (on which to base disbursements) is often difficult. An outcome focus cannot be a substitute for conditionality, for which policy actions over which the government has meaningful control remain relevant. Good practice also suggests the need for a clear medium-term framework for policy-based lending linking policy actions, progress indicators, and expected outcomes. In addition, conditionality customized to country circumstances implies strengthening countries' capacity to monitor and evaluate progress toward development objectives.

These principles are embedded in the programmatic approach to policy-based lending, which recognizes the importance of country ownership through increased flexibility, reflects countries' track records, and supports sustained engagement for complex medium-term institutional and policy reforms. This approach to conditionality does not just involve providing financing, it also serves as a vehicle for policy dialogues that typically involve transfers of advice and knowledge. Programmatic policy-based lending calls for a prudent mix of government policies, intermediate benchmarks, and ultimate outcomes embedded in a medium-term policy framework and involving a series of operations linked by specific but flexible triggers. Thus it has emerged as a promising way to reconcile the debate between the traditional ex ante approach and the aspirations of the results-based approach to conditionality.

Endnotes

1. Conditionality is defined here as conditions attached to policy-based lending, although conditions are sometimes involved indirectly in other lending activities such as investment lending or triggers defined in Country Assistance Strategies or programs for Heavily Indebted Poor Countries. "Policy-based lending" is used as a generic term for the World Bank's adjustment lending, which is proposed to be renamed "development policy lending" in fiscal 2005.

2. The unofficial groupings of high, good, and poor performers were made using Country Policy and Institutional Assessment (CPIA) ratings during the period between fiscal years

1996 and 2003 (see worldbank.org/IDA/Resources/CPIA2003.pdf). A country with a CPIA rating of 4.00 and above is assigned to the high-performing group, those countries given a rating between 3.00 and 3.99 are assigned to the good-performing group, and the countries with an overall CPIA rating 2.99 and below are included in the poor-performing group. These groupings were made exclusively for this exercise, and are not in line with any official World Bank classifications.

3. Nonbinding conditions are other desired actions included in the loan documentation but not included in the legal agreement. Client government compliance with these actions is not tied to the release of funds.

4. OED defines *demandingness* as the extent to which the project could be expected to strain the economic, institutional, and human resources of the government or implementing agency. *Complexity* refers to such factors as the range of policy and institutional improvements contemplated, the number of institutions involved, the number of project components and their geographic dispersion, and the number of cofinanciers. *Riskiness* refers to the likelihood that the project, as designed, would be expected to fail to meet relevant project objectives efficiently.

5. An important factor that allows borrowers to take on responsibility for monitoring reform implementation is to assign performance indicators to specific government agencies— ideally the same agencies responsible for implementing the program or its components. The importance of adequate monitoring is reflected in the proposed update of the Bank's operational policy on policy-based lending (World Bank 2002b).

Bibliography

Alesina, Alberto, and David Dollar. 1998. "Who Gives Foreign Aid to Whom and Why?" NBER Working Paper 6612, National Bureau for Economic Research, Cambridge, MA.

Baird, Mark, Michael Lav, and Deborah Wetzel. 1995. "Performance Indicators for Adjustment Programs: A First Edition Note." Development Economics Vice Presidency, World Bank, Washington, DC.

Burnside, Craig, and David Dollar. 1997. "Aid, Policies, and Growth." Policy Research Working Paper 1777, World Bank, Washington, DC.

Collier, Paul. 1997. "The Failure of Conditionality." In *Perspectives on Aid and Development*, ed. Catherine Gwin and Joan Nelson. Washington, DC: Overseas Development Council.

Collier, Paul, Patrick Guillaumont, and Sylviane Guillaumont. 1997. "Redesigning Conditionality." *World Development* 25 (9): 1399–1407.

Devarajan, Shantayanan, David Dollar, and Torgny Holmgren. 2001. *Aid and Reform in Africa*. Washington, DC: World Bank. www.worldbank.org/research/aid/africa/intro.htm.

Dollar, David, and Svensson, Jacob. 2000. "What Explains the Success or Failure of Structural Adjustment Programmes?" *Economic Journal* 110 (October): 894–917.

Easterly, William. 2001. *The Elusive Quest for Growth*. Cambridge, MA: MIT Press.

Emblad, Stefan, and Hervio Gilles. 2000. "Conditionality Revisited: A New Approach in Burkina Faso." PREMnote 35, World Bank, Washington, DC. www1.worldbank.org/prem/PREMNotes/premnote35.pdf.

European Commission. 2001. "Conditionality Reform: Some Results of the Burkina Faso Pilot Case." Paper presented at the Organisation for Economic Co-operation and Development Seminar on Aid Effectiveness, Selectivity and Poor Performers, Paris, January 17. www.oecd.org/pdf/M00021000/M00021252.pdf.

Filmer, Deon, Jeffrey S. Hammer, and Lant Pritchett. 2000. "Weak Links in the Chain: A Diagnosis of Health Policy in Poor Countries." *The World Bank Research Observer* 15: 199–224.

Gunning, Jan Willem. 2000. "The Reform of Aid." Centre for the Study of African Economies, Oxford University.

Haggarty, Luke, and Yasuhiko Matuda. 1999. "Assessing Clients' Commitment to Sectoral Reforms: A Reform Readiness Analysis." Development Economics Vice Presidency, World Bank, Washington, DC.

Heaver, Richard, and Arturo Israel. 1986. "Country Commitment to Development Projects." World Bank Discussion Paper 4, Washington, DC.

IMF (International Monetary Fund), OECD (Organisation for Economic Co-operation and Development), United Nations, and World Bank Group. 2000. *A Better World for All: Progress towards the International Development Goals.* Washington, DC. www.paris21.org.

IMF. 2001a. "Structural Conditionality in Fund-Supported Programs." Washington, DC. http://www.imf.org/external/np/pdr/cond/2001/eng/struct/index.htm.

———. 2001b. "Streamlining Structural Conditionality: Review of Initial Experience." Washington, DC. www.imf.org/external/np/pdr/cond/2001/eng/collab/071001.pdf.

———. 2002. "Guidelines on Conditionality." SM/02/276, Revision I, Washington, DC. www.imf.org/External/np/pdr/cond/2002/eng/guid/092302.htm.

Johnson, John H., and Sulaiman S. Wasty. 1993. "Borrower Ownership of Adjustment Programs and the Political Economy of Reform." World Bank Discussion Paper 199, Washington, DC.

Kanbur, Ravi, and Todd Sandler. 1999. *The Future of Development Assistance: Common Pools and International Public Goods.* Policy Essay 25. Washington, DC: Overseas Development Council.

Killick, Tony, with Ramani Gunatilaka and Ana Marr. 1998. *Aid and the Political Economy of Policy Change.* London: Routledge.

Meltzer, Allan, C. Fred Bergsten, Charles W. Calomiris, Tom Campbell, Edwin J. Feulner, W. Lee Hoskins, Richard L. Huber, Manuel H. Johnson, Jerome I. Levinson, Jeffrey D. Sachs, and Esteban Edward Torres. 2000. *Results and Recommendations of the International Financial Institution Advisory Commission.* Final report to the U.S. Congress and Department of Treasury. Washington, DC. www.bicusa.org/usgovtoversight/meltzer.htm.

Milanovic, Branko. 2003. "The Two Faces of Globalization: Against Globalization as We Know It." *World Development* 31 (4): 667–83.

Morrow, Daniel. 1999. "Assessing Borrower Ownership Using Reform Readiness Analysis." PREMnote 25, World Bank, Washington, DC.

Mosley, Paul, Jane Harrigan, and John Toye. 1991. *Aid and Power: The World Bank and Policy-Based Lending, Volume 1—Analysis and Policy Proposals.* New York: Routledge.

Stiglitz, Joseph. 1998. "Towards a New Paradigm for Development: Strategies, Policies, and Processes." Prebisch Lecture presented at the United Nations Conference on Trade and Development, Geneva, October 19.

Special Programme of Assistance for Africa Task Team on Contractual Relationships and Selectivity. 2000. "Conditionality Reform: The Burkina Faso Pilot Case." Brussels. www.oecd.org/pdf/M00021000/M00021255.pdf.

Structural Adjustment Participatory Review Initiative. 2002. "The Policy Roots of Economic Crisis and Poverty." Washington, DC. www.saprin.org/SAPRIN_Findings.pdf.

Thomas, Vinod, Ajay Chhibber, Mansoor Dailami, and Jaime de Melo, eds. 1991. *Restructuring Economies in Distress: Policy Reform and the World Bank.* New York: Oxford University Press.

Thomas, Vinod, Mansoor Dailami, Ashok Dhareshwar, Daniel Kaufmann, Nalin Kishor, Ramón López, and Yan Wang. 2000. *The Quality of Growth.* New York: Oxford University Press.

Wood, Angela, and Matthew Lockwood. 1999. "The 'Perestroika of Aid'? New Perspectives on Conditionality." Bretton Woods Project, Washington, DC. www.brettonwoodsproject. org/topic/governance/poa2.pdf.

World Bank. 1980. "Structural Adjustment Lending." R80-122, IDA/R80-83, Washington, DC.

———. 1986. "Structural Adjustment Lending: A First Review of Experience." Operations Evaluation Report 6409, Washington, DC.

———. 1990. "Report on Adjustment Lending: Policies for the Recovery of Growth." R90-57 IDA/R90-49, Washington, DC.

———. 1992a. "Effective Implementation: Key to Development Impact—Report of the World Bank's Portfolio Management Task Force (Wapenhans Report)." Washington, DC.

———. 1992b. "Third Report on Adjustment Lending: Private and Public Resources for Growth." R92-47, IDA/R92-29, Washington, DC.

———. 1994. *Adjustment in Africa: Reforms, Results, and the Road Ahead.* A World Bank Policy Research Report. New York: Oxford University Press.

———. 1996. "Issues in Adjustment Lending." SecM96-18, Washington, DC.

———. 1998a. *Assessing Aid: What Works, What Doesn't and Why.* A World Bank Policy Research Report. New York: Oxford University Press.

———. 1998b. "Higher Impact Adjustment Lending (HIAL) in Sub-Saharan Africa: An Update." Chief Economist's Office, Africa Region, Washington, DC.

———. 1999a. "Annual Review of Development Effectiveness: Toward a Comprehensive Development Strategy." Operations Evaluation Department, Washington, DC.

———. 1999b. "Higher Impact Adjustment Lending (HIAL)—Initial Evaluation." Operations Evaluation Report 19797, Washington, DC.

———. 2000. "Report of the Working Group on Improving Quality of Monitoring and Evaluation in Bank Financial Operations." CODE2000-72, Washington, DC.

———. 2001a. "Adjustment from Within: Lessons from the Structural Adjustment Participatory Review Initiative." Washington, DC. www.worldbank.org/research/sapri/ WB_SAPRI_Report.pdf.

———. 2001b. "Adjustment Lending Retrospective." Operations Policy and Country Services, Washington, DC.

———. 2001c. "Supporting Country Development: Strengthening the World Bank Group's Support for Middle-Income Countries." DC2001-0005, Washington, DC. www.worldbank.org/ html/extdr/pb/pbmiddleincome.htm.

———. 2001d. "World Bank Group Strategic Framework." Washington, DC.

———. 2002a. "Better Measuring, Monitoring and Managing for Development Results." DC2002-0019. Development Committee, Washington, DC.

———. 2002b. "From Adjustment Lending to Development Policy Support Lending." Washington, DC.

———. 2002c. "Supporting Country Development: World Bank Role and Instruments in Low- and Middle-Income Countries." DC/2000-19, Washington, DC. http://wbln0018. worldbank.org/DCS/DevCom.nsf/(documentsattachmentsweb)/ September2000EnglishDC200019/$FILE/DC-2000-19-SCD.pdf.

————. 2003. "Rome Declaration on Harmonization: High Level Forum on Harmonization." Rome. http://siteresources.worldbank.org/NEWS/Resources/Harm-RomeDeclaration2_25.pdf.

————. 2004. "Programmatic Adjustment Lending Retrospective." Operations Policy and Country Services, Washington, D.C.

World Bank Adjustment Lending and Conditionality Implementation Database (ALCID). Washington, DC.

World Bank and IMF (International Monetary Fund). 1998. "Report of the Managing Director and the President on Bank-Fund Collaboration." SecM98-733, Washington, DC.

————. 2001. "Strengthening IMF-World Bank Collaboration on Country Programs and Conditionality." Washington, DC.

————. 2002. "Strengthening IMF-World Bank Collaboration on Country Programs and Conditionality—Progress Report." Washington, DC.

————. 2004. "Strengthening IMF-World Bank Collaboration on Country Programs and Conditionality—Second Progress Report." Washington, DC.

6

Streamlining Conditionality in World Bank– and International Monetary Fund–Supported Programs

ZHANAR ABDILDINA AND JAIME JARAMILLO-VALLEJO
World Bank

A recent paper produced jointly by the staffs of the World Bank and the IMF and discussed by the Executive Boards of both institutions has led to a number of comments on how the effort to streamline conditionality has had a tangible effect in IMF programs, but not so in Bank loans (IMF and World Bank 2004). These comments are based on a chart that showed how conditionality in programs with low-income countries had evolved from the period 1998–2000 to the period 2001–2 (figure 6.1). Although a broad definition of Bank conditionality may give support to that conclusion, *a narrower definition actually shows that the streamlining effort is producing noticeable results in low-income countries in all areas except for that of fiscal management.* A slight increase in conditionality in this area has followed the greater emphasis on improving development effectiveness in all public expenditures, and the move toward a more aggressive stance on debt with the Heavily Indebted Poor Countries Initiative and the development of Poverty Reduction Strategy Papers. Moreover, *when middle-income countries are brought into the picture, overall conditionality has declined in recent years, including in the area of fiscal management.*

The Streamlining Effort

In the late 1990s, the Bank and the IMF decided to streamline conditionality, following the perceived surge at the time of the debt crisis as well as a growing discomfort with the effectiveness of the support provided by both institutions. The streamlining effort entailed reducing the number of conditions in programs while sharpening their focus. For the Bank and the IMF, that meant being flexible and responsive in discussing alternatives with the client countries, so that the smaller conditionality set could produce better development outcomes. The expectation was that streamlined conditionality would lead to greater ownership of the reform programs, which would in turn lead to less policy reversals and a more sustained implementation. The move also addressed the need for a better-tailored approach in the design and follow-up of second-generation reforms, and in bringing about lasting institutional development.

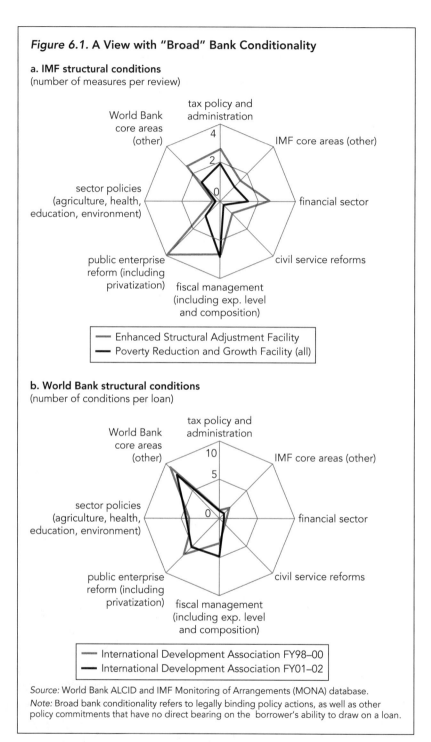

Figure 6.1. A View with "Broad" Bank Conditionality

a. IMF structural conditions
(number of measures per review)

— Enhanced Structural Adjustment Facility
— Poverty Reduction and Growth Facility (all)

b. World Bank structural conditions
(number of conditions per loan)

— International Development Association FY98–00
— International Development Association FY01–02

Source: World Bank ALCID and IMF Monitoring of Arrangements (MONA) database.
Note: Broad bank conditionality refers to legally binding policy actions, as well as other policy commitments that have no direct bearing on the borrower's ability to draw on a loan.

The Executive Boards and management of both institutions provided clear signals in this regard, by stressing ownership in each case, while following closely the number and content of conditions. Thus, the concept of conditionality gradually shifted, moving the due diligence of the institutions to ensure the effectiveness of their support toward greater emphasis on the quality and appropriateness of policy actions, and away from the sheer number of those actions. Within this framework, both the Bank and the IMF sought to focus more intensely in their respective areas of expertise, reducing conditionality overlap (see IMF and World Bank 1998, 2000, 2001, 2004). The idea was to adopt a coherent approach based on an efficient division of labor, with each institution focusing its conditionality on measures critical to its respective programs' success.

From Broad to Narrow Conditionality in Low-Income Countries

Focusing on low-income countries and with a broad concept of Bank conditionality, figure 6.1a shows how the streamlining effort in the IMF led to a sharp decrease in the average number of structural policy conditions under Poverty Reduction Growth Facility arrangements, with a heavier load remaining in the institution's core areas of responsibility—economic management, tax policy, exchange rate policy, monetary policy, and capital account. In parallel, figure 6.1b shows that the Bank expanded structural conditionality in its core areas—poverty reduction strategies and governance and regulatory reforms—while remaining strong in other social and economic sectors such as agriculture, infrastructure, and so forth. In the two areas where both institutions share a strong mandate—financial sector and fiscal management—both institutions reduced their emphasis on the former, while increasing the average number of conditions on fiscal management issues.

The picture on the Bank side changes significantly when only binding conditions are taken into account. While the broad concept includes policy actions that borrowing countries intend to implement, the stricter concept of binding conditions only includes those policy actions that need to be taken in order to allow the borrower to draw on the loan. With the advent of the Poverty Reduction Strategy Papers and the ensuing Poverty Reduction Support Credits (PRSC), the policy matrix associated with these credits and grants included actions that were central to the overall strategy, but that were not elevated to the level of program conditions. The attribute of being a binding condition is typically reserved for those policy actions that are judged as necessary for the success of the overall strategy.

As figure 6.2 shows, streamlining has also had a significant impact on the average number of binding conditions in Bank programs with low-income countries. Conditions have declined in all areas, except in fiscal management. The decline has been more noticeable in the core areas of the IMF, including tax policy and administration, economic management, exchange rate policy and monetary policy, as well as on public enterprise reform. The Bank remains focused on poverty reduction and other social policies, as well as on sectoral policies.

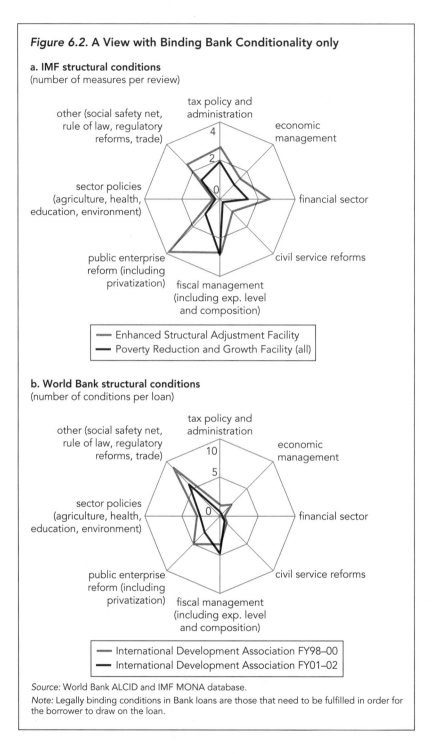

Figure 6.2. A View with Binding Bank Conditionality only

a. IMF structural conditions
(number of measures per review)

Legend:
— Enhanced Structural Adjustment Facility
— Poverty Reduction and Growth Facility (all)

b. World Bank structural conditions
(number of conditions per loan)

Legend:
— International Development Association FY98–00
— International Development Association FY01–02

Source: World Bank ALCID and IMF MONA database.
Note: Legally binding conditions in Bank loans are those that need to be fulfilled in order for the borrower to draw on the loan.

The Shared Emphasis on Fiscal Management

Fiscal management is the only area where the streamlining effort resulted in an increase in the average number of conditions for low-income countries when comparing 1998–2000 with 2001–2. Nevertheless, and *in line with the overall trend, when middle-income countries are brought into the picture, the average number of conditions has begun to taper off* (figure 6.3).

The emphasis on fiscal management reflects the decision to improve the effectiveness of all development expenditures, and not just those financed with the support from the IMF and the Bank. This improvement is the element that brings comfort regarding a judicious resource use, thus facilitating the streamlining of conditionality. Fiscal management covers four basic topics: fiduciary issues (financial management, procurement, and transparency), public expenditure management (structure, efficiency, and medium-term framework), debt management (debt and debt service

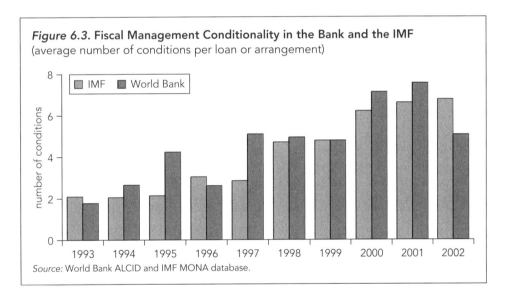

Figure 6.3. Fiscal Management Conditionality in the Bank and the IMF
(average number of conditions per loan or arrangement)

Source: World Bank ALCID and IMF MONA database.

BOX 6.1 Analytical Work and Fiduciary Conditionality

The emphasis on fiduciary conditionality has gained structure from the Country Financial and Accountability Assessments and from the Country Procurement Assessment Review. Using these two pieces of analytical work prepared jointly with the country and with other external partners, the Bank and the IMF are now approaching the necessary institutional strengthening in these areas in a more systematic and coordinated way. A major actor in bringing together this kind of analytical work has been the Public Expenditure and Financial Accountability (PEFA) partners. The PEFA program is a partnership of the World Bank, European Commission, IMF, U.K. Department for International Development, Swiss State Secretariat for Economic Affairs, French Ministry of Foreign Affairs, Norwegian Ministry of Foreign Affairs, and Strategic Partnership with Africa. The PEFA program is managed by a Steering Committee consisting of headquarters representatives of the member agencies.

workouts and development and management of domestic debt markets), and decentralization and local governments (transfers of revenue and expenditure, administrative independence, local delivery of services).

The Bank's interventions in support of fiscal management programs in low- and middle-income countries gained momentum in the second half of the 1990s, with the heightened interest in fiduciary issues and the change in the paradigm for debt management (figure 6.4). These leaps topped the increasing awareness of the relevance of

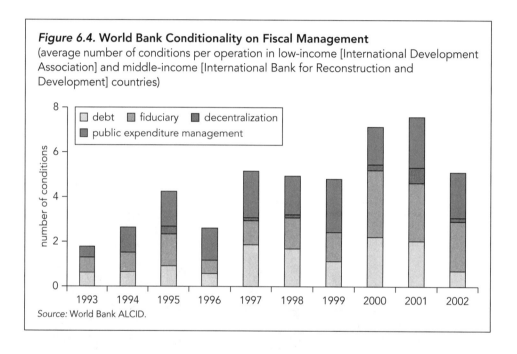

Figure 6.4. World Bank Conditionality on Fiscal Management
(average number of conditions per operation in low-income [International Development Association] and middle-income [International Bank for Reconstruction and Development] countries)

Source: World Bank ALCID.

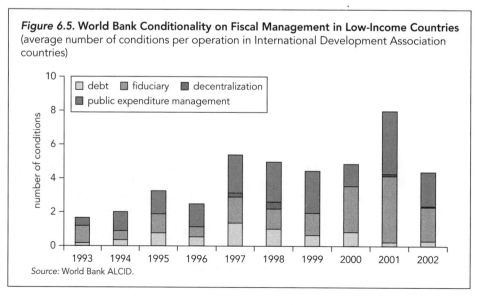

Figure 6.5. World Bank Conditionality on Fiscal Management in Low-Income Countries
(average number of conditions per operation in International Development Association countries)

Source: World Bank ALCID.

public expenditure management that had already started to pick up in the early 1990s.[1] Beginning in 1997, more attention was provided to increasing transparency in public resource management initially, and improving financial management and procurement later. At the same time, the approach for solving the problems faced by debt-ridden countries began to change significantly with the introduction of the Heavily Indebted Poor Countries Initiative in the fall of 1996.

A long view of how conditionality on fiscal management has evolved suggests that the average number of conditions stepped up to a new level in 1997, but has remained rather constant since (figures 6.4 and 6.5). Indeed, the peaks observed for the universe of countries in 2000 and 2001 (figure 6.4) correspond to specific programs intended primarily to boost fiscal management, which happened to bunch in those two years. While in 2000 fiscal management conditionality increased mostly because of programs in middle-income and blend countries, in 2001 the increase was due to low-income countries (figure 6.5).[2]

Endnotes

1. The observed blip in 1995 corresponds to two operations: Argentina's Provincial Reform Structural Adjustment Loan and Ecuador's Structural Adjustment Loan.

2. The 2000 programs that account for the increase in the bar were Brazil's Administrative and Fiscal Reform Structural Adjustment Loan, India's Uttar Pradesh Fiscal Reform and Public Sector Restructuring Credit, and Papua New Guinea's Governance Promotion Adjustment Loan. The 2001 programs that contributed most to the blip were Benin's Public Expenditure Adjustment Credit, Kenya's Economic and Public Sector Reform Adjustment Credit, and Uganda and Vietnam's Poverty Reduction Support Credits.

Bibliography

IMF (International Monetary Fund) and World Bank. 1998. "Report of the Managing Director and the President on Bank-Fund Collaboration." IMF document SM/98/226 and World Bank document SecM98-733.

———. 2000. "The IMF and the World Bank Group: An Enhanced Partnership for Sustainable Growth and Poverty Reduction." Joint Statement by Horst Köhler, Managing Director, and James Wolfensohn, President. SecM2000-536.

———. 2001. "Strengthening IMF-World Bank Collaboration on Country Programs and Conditionality." IMF document SM/01/219 and World Bank document SecM2001-0461/1.

———. 2002. "Strengthening IMF-World Bank Collaboration on Country Programs and Conditionality—Progress Report." IMF document SM/02/271 and World Bank document SecM2002-443.

———. 2004. "Strengthening IMF-World Bank Collaboration in Programs and Country Programs and Conditionality—Progress Report." IMF document SM/04/57 and World Bank document SecM2004-0070.

7

Did Conditionality Streamlining Succeed?

TONY KILLICK
Overseas Development Institute

What Do We Mean by Conditionality?

There are two opposing points of view. One, which I would describe as the view of the international financial institutions (IFIs), sees conditionality as "an instrument of mutual accountability." An alternative view says that in essence that conditionality is controversial because it is an exercise of financial leverage, requiring governments to do things they wouldn't otherwise do, or to do things more quickly than they would choose to do. This is significant because the mutual accountability view is consistent with the idea of domestic ownership; the second is much more difficult to reconcile with it. This distinction is important because research in this area indicates that where there is a perceived conflict of interest between the lender and the borrowing government, domestic politics usually comes out on top.

What Has Changed?

This chapter briefly discusses changes within the policy environment, debt relief, critiques of conditionality, streamlining measures, and attitudinal changes.

The Policy Environment

If we examine differences over a period of, say, two decades, one major change is that the overall policy environment has improved. This is extremely important. Governments everywhere around the world view policy differently from how they did 20 years ago. Essentially, the view long promoted by the IFIs has prevailed. This is relevant because it ought to reduce the need for conditionality, or at least the required rigor of conditionality. The significance of these changes in attitude is particularly large for the International Monetary Fund (IMF), because the change is most evident in macroeconomic management. The improvements in the policy environment ought to have improved compliance with conditionality by bringing policy preferences closer together. But has it actually had these effects?

Other questions include: To what extent did conditionality contribute to this turn-around in the way governments look at policy, as distinct from other influences, such as the research and persuasion of the IFIs and other donors, and changes in the intellectual climate coming from universities and think tanks? To what extent did conditionality contribute to this or did the sometimes confrontational nature of conditionality-based negotiations actually get in the way?

Multilaterals Have Been Brought into Debt Relief

The fact that since the advent of the Heavily Indebted Poor Countries (HIPC) schemes the credits to low-income countries of multilateral lenders have been brought within the purview of debt relief is relevant because it should reduce the incentive for the IFIs to undertake defensive lending: new lending in order to make sure the past loans are serviced according to schedule. There is quite extensive evidence showing the importance of defensive lending in the past, because of all the complications that arise when countries go into default. Conditionality exerts little leverage in such situations. Getting the IFIs' credits into debt relief ought to have taken away much of the incentive for defensive lending, at least for low-income countries, and that should be favorable to more effective conditionality. But does the reality conform to these expectations?

There Has Been Some Acceptance of the Critiques of Conditionality

There has been acceptance within the IFIs of some of the critiques of conditionality, and of the adverse evidence that has been accumulated by researchers on the subject. World Bank and IMF officials have acknowledged as much and have contributed to the evidential base. Some bilateral donors and major shareholders on the Boards of the IFIs remain unconvinced, however, which creates problems within these institutions in deciding how to move forward. This dilemma may be particularly acute for the IMF, to the still limited extent that there is a desire to move away from its traditional conditionality-based approach.

The IFIs *have* responded to the accumulating evidence and have sought to adapt in varying degrees (for example, see Stefan Koeberle's [2004] paper). The concern that remains, however, is whether the extent of IFI adaptation has been proportional to the severity of the limitations of conditionality. Most likely, the IFIs still remain far too reliant on a modality of questionable effectiveness. It should be stressed that over-reliance on conditionality can result in a large waste of aid resources. One must reflect on all the money that went into structural adjustment from the IMF and the World Bank in the 1980s and early 1990s to governments with no serious commitment to policy reform. There was formerly a tendency to use conditionality as a substitute for government commitment; today it is universally recognized that to do so is a recipe for unsuccessful programs—which is not to say that it no longer happens!

Streamlining Has Occurred

A streamlining of conditionality has been under way in the IFIs, particularly in the IMF, which has formally adopted such a policy. There also has been evidence of streamlining at the World Bank, in the sense that the number of conditions has been coming down. However, questions remain about how much staff buy-in there is to the streamlining agenda. Judging from personal observations made 18 months ago, there appeared to be variable acceptance of this policy among IMF staff, which was rather surprising and indicated that management was having difficulty implementing the policy.

But while the IFIs have been streamlining, HIPC countries have had a whole new dimension of conditionality added, that is, that associated with Poverty Reduction Strategy Papers and with HIPC itself. This new layer of conditionality has included the introduction of so-called process conditionality, in other words, stipulations that the government will do things in certain ways (for example, adopting participatory approaches). This new development has the potential to take conditionality more deeply into institutional and political structures.

At the same time there has been a move on the part of some bilateral donors toward direct budget support, which probably has increased economywide conditionality. Because no organization is charged with maintaining oversight of the totality of conditionality that a government faces at a given time, or its internal consistency, there is no way to assess the net effect these developments have had on borrowers. However, there is a suspicion that low-income countries have experienced no net reduction, despite streamlining.

Attitudes on Aid Relationships and Modalities Have Shifted

Attitudes on aid relationships and aid modalities have changed in favor of ownership, partnership, and program lending. This is a positive and important change, but the buy-in across donors has been uneven and some remain skeptical. A major subject of concern with the shift to program aid is its potential for adding substantially to conditionality. It could be that the relationships that have developed on a partnership basis are evolving as a substitute for conditionality, but it could easily result in more old-style policy stipulations. It could go either way.

Conclusion

Overall, there is not enough up-to-date information on how the situation has developed in the most recent years and what the results have been. Better information would probably show that the changes in approach have been indecisive thus far. Reliance on a flawed instrument remains high, especially in operations in low-income countries, and with it the potential for low-productivity assistance.

Bibliography

Koeberle, Stefan. 2004. "Conditionality, Under What Conditions." World Bank, Washington, DC.

8
Part 2 Discussion Summary

The discussions following the presentations on conditionality from the perspective of the International Monetary Fund (IMF), the World Bank, and the Overseas Development Institute focused primarily on four key issues relating to conditionality: the number of conditions and their complexity, the predictability of aid flows, the extent to which conditionality actually supports the reform process, and the actual role of conditionality in IMF budget support.

The Number of Conditions and Their Complexity

One of the consistent themes in the debates on conditionality is the number of conditions attached to a particular lending program and, related to this, the cumulative effect when the overall aid picture is looked at. The speaker from the World Bank stated that it is important to distinguish between legally binding conditionality and those conditions that are included in the matrix but don't have disbursement implications. Referring back to the Poverty Reduction Strategy Papers (PRSPs), he commented that these are essentially government wish lists for help, and that the donors then pick and choose among these items the ones they are going to support.

While acknowledging that the matrices attached to lending programs can be excessively complicated and may make reference to the bulk of the country reform program as outlined in the PRSP, an analysis of recent trends points to the fact that the number of legally binding conditions has come down. The focus should be on what the conditionality is trying to achieve, and not merely on the pure number of conditions. Nonetheless, efforts should be made to contain lending program matrices to a reasonable size so that the focus on the required actions is not confused in the process. Another consideration is that while the PRSP lays out the reforms that a country ultimately wants to achieve, it does not necessarily spell out the steps required to get there, and this is where conditionality plays a role. At times, having multiple donors simultaneously engaged in budget support may not be conducive to clear and specific results; there needs to be emphasis on coordination between donors to alleviate this problem.

Predictability of Aid Flows

One of the key issues for recipient countries is the predictability of aid flows from all donors and the impact that it will have on their budgets. It was agreed that aid flows risk being interrupted for a number of reasons. A government can fail to meet the conditionality requirements of a loan for a number of reasons, including exogenous factors such as natural disasters, instability in surrounding countries, as well as domestic political issues. For example, a country may decide to adjust the share of defense spending in its budget in response to a crisis in a neighboring country, and thereby fail to meet a condition requiring specific expenditure allocations as a share of the overall budget. It was pointed out that when conditionality is not met, it can be difficult to pinpoint the precise reason. Participants voiced a further concern that even if conditionality is met, the client country may not receive the expected amount of aid because a given donor is unable to provide the expected volume of aid.

As lending programs move from a primarily sector-based approach to one that is more programmatic, governments will need to assess the capacity of their federal budgets to absorb not only the debt, but also all of the fiscal costs associated with the loans as the responsibility for repayment of the loans and the cost of borrowing shift from the line ministries to the central government. A number of lenders, such as the European Union, Asian Development Bank, and the European Bank for Reconstruction and Development, still continue to focus primarily on the individual sectors; however, with the gradual shift to programmatic lending by the World Bank and the inevitable piggybacking by bilateral donors, the impact at the federal level in the recipient countries will not be negligible. One issue facing the donors whose aid is targeted at the sector level is the level of commitment they are actually getting from the line ministries, and what exactly their incentive is to follow through. In many cases the primary commitment is coming from the central agencies, and the actual funding for the sectoral programs is coming in via the central budget. Another concern is that as lending becomes more programmatic, donors expect to have a greater say in the design of the policy, which can infringe on the government's ownership of the program. In addition, as the transaction cost is shifted from the line ministries to the central ministries, the level of trust within the government can be affected.

The speaker from the Overseas Development Institute voiced concern over the prospect of substantially larger aid flows, which he sees as coming primarily from the bilateral side. The bilateral lenders have traditionally piggybacked on the conditionality outlined in the lending programs of international financial institutions. This will put increasing pressure on the international financial institutions to reach agreement with the borrowing country and keep those agreements on track so that aid is not held up by failure to satisfy conditions.

The Extent to Which Conditionality Supports the Reform Process

Several participants raised questions regarding the role of conditionality with respect to IMF programs, and the extent to which the IMF seeks to use conditionality as a leverage tool to force the pace of reforms. One perception is that IMF programs force countries to undertake reform actions more quickly than they would do on their own. This was seen as a benefit not only by the IMF representative, but also by some of the other participants because it pushes the borrowing countries to prioritize the actions that need to be taken immediately and get reforms/stabilization under way. Another question raised with respect to the IMF sought clarification on the basic level of engagement for the IMF—whether it was about fiduciary accountability, macroeconomic stability, or having a certain policy framework in place.

The IMF representative did concede, however, that IMF programs lose their value when they begin to be used for the sake of leverage. One of the perceived problems that contributes to this is that the IMF staff is not always consistent in applying conditionality and that some departments/individuals may still use the programs to exercise leverage in country. The IMF is currently undertaking the first biennial review of the Guidelines on Conditionality; this review will focus primarily on program design issues and subsequently on the guidelines themselves—whether they have been implemented and whether the guidelines themselves are having the desired effect.

A participant from a low-income African country expressed his impression that the IMF didn't look as if it really wanted to get involved in low-income countries because their conditions are on the ambitious side and therefore not very practical. Further fueling this perception is the fact that, unlike visitors from the World Bank and other institutions who conduct extensive policy dialogues, the IMF arrives only once a year for an assessment. It is important that there is sufficient dialogue between the borrowing country and the lending institution for the latter to have a clear understanding of the current sociopolitical and economic climate in the country. This would help the donor craft more appropriate and realistic conditionality to its lending program so that the lending program and attached conditionality can be structured in an appropriate and realistic manner.

The representative from the European Commission raised the issue of the role of political conditionality, an important issue requiring further clarification in light of its increasing relevance for bilateral governors. Political conditionality can prove to be difficult because the reality of requiring parliament to pass a specific law in order to satisfy the lender may not be realistic, and in some cases may be impossible if the legislative branch does not see eye to eye with the executive branch. Such conditionality is also vulnerable to changes within the government resulting from elections or no-confidence votes. There has been some discussion as to whether the inclusion of such conditionality in lending program matrices is advantageous.

Conditionality can be effective, particularly when it is able to tip the balance between reformers and nonreformers. However, one must be careful not to put too much pressure on the government to speed up the reform process. This may reduce the government's ability for political management and room for maneuver, and thereby tip the balance in the wrong direction.

While conditionality itself remains a much-debated topic of discussion, a shift toward results-based conditionality is emerging, both at the World Bank and with other donor organizations, and there is much hope that this shift will shed a more positive light on the concept of conditionality. One should be cautious, however, in moving to an entirely outcome-based approach because some results cannot be measured on an annual basis and others are beyond the influence of the government. Holding governments accountable for such outcomes should be avoided.

Part III
Policy Approaches and Policy-Based Lending: What Have We Learned?

9

Introduction

JOHN WILLIAMSON
Institute for International Economics

Policy-Based Lending: What Have We Learned?

The international financial institutions started with project lending and evolved into policy-based lending for three main reasons. First, at the time of the second oil crisis and the ensuing debt crisis, there was a need to increase lending substantially and quickly, and policy-based lending was one way to do it. Second, growing evidence that the policy environment was critically important, even for the success of project lending, implied that lending simply on a project basis didn't make sense. Third, the growing recognition of the fact of fungibility (that is, a borrowing country can put up its best projects to be financed by donors, and then at the margin use the cash to finance other projects, so that what is enabled by the loan isn't necessarily what is put up to the donors to finance) meant that one needed to examine a borrower's total investment program.

Those three issues led to the growth of policy-based lending. Initially, an attempt was made to change the policy environment by imposing conditions on a whole array of things, including fiscal policy, trade, public sector management, privatization, social spending, and so forth. The conditions varied depending on the program and country, but there could be a wide array of conditions. Later, that attempt evolved to a greater emphasis on public sector and social reforms, but there was still a wide array of policies on which conditions could be imposed.

In due course, however, it was discovered that this approach wasn't working: unless borrowing countries wanted to do what the conditions proscribed, the policy environment would not change in the intended way. In reaction, the international financial institutions went through a change toward consensual rather than coercive conditionality, away from "leverage." There was instead a reliance on selectivity, and in particular on selectivity based on the Country Policy and Institutional Assessment, which seeks to measure how well a country is managing its affairs.

Approach to Middle-Income Countries

Might the answer to the conundrum of what sort of strategy to have regarding the middle-income countries be addressed by the proposal that was advanced several years ago by Ravi Kanbur and Todd Sandler, for what they called a "common pool approach" to the supply of aid to developing countries?

Under this system developing countries would announce the programs they intend to pursue and then convene a conference rather like a consultative group, at which donors would say how much they wanted to subscribe in support of that program. If these were middle-income countries, clearly the donors would give loans rather than grants. In any event donors would announce the amounts that they intend to make available in support of the announced program. This would become a contractual obligation, not something the donors could go back on.

There would be problems if donors don't have complete trust in a country and fear that it might deviate violently from the program that it has announced. But in general a country would have to bear in mind that it would be unlikely to get comparable support next time if it deviated from the sense of the program. Of course, if it made a change because circumstances changed, the country would be able to explain its actions, and presumably the donors would not object.

This could be an interesting and worthwhile proposal, at the very least so far as countries that have their policies in order are concerned. Perhaps there would be greater problems in extending it to all developing countries, and yet it is something that has received very little attention among the donor community.

10

Policy-Based Lending, Conditionality, and Development Effectiveness

AJAY CHHIBBER
World Bank

The Operations Evaluation Department (OED) is an independent unit within the World Bank that reports directly to the Bank's Board of Executive Directors. It provides an objective assessment of the Bank's work and its clients' performance, thereby ensuring accountability in the achievement of Bank objectives. Every year, OED draws upon recent evaluation and research findings to examine a current development effectiveness issue. The 2003 Annual Review of Development Effectiveness (ARDE 2003) examines the effectiveness of World Bank support for policy reform.

This chapter provides a context for the discussion on conditionality, although by itself it doesn't go very deeply into the issue of conditionality. The OED also has recently completed a joint review with the International Monetary Fund's independent Evaluation Office of the Poverty Reduction Strategy Paper process, and this chapter briefly discusses one or two preliminary findings on that. The chapter touches on three points. First it reviews the evidence bearing on recent trends in developing countries' policies; second, it reviews the role of the World Bank in support of developing countries' policy reforms; and, third, it comments on the effectiveness of policy-based lending and conditionality in the much broader context of policy change that is taking place in developing countries.

Recent Trends in Developing Countries' Policies

OED's assessment found that policies have improved modestly in roughly two of every three countries; that policies have improved in all regions of the world; that improvements were registered in almost all areas of policy; and that countries with good and improving policies grew more rapidly than countries with bad and deteriorating policies.

ARDE 2003 examined four different indicators of developing countries' policy over the period 1999–2003. The Bank's Country Policy and Institutional Assessment (CPIA) is the Bank's internal policy index and is used mainly to allocate International Development Association (IDA) resources.[1] Figure 10.1 illustrates improvement in average CPIA ratings between 1999 and 2003, in both low-income countries that are eligible

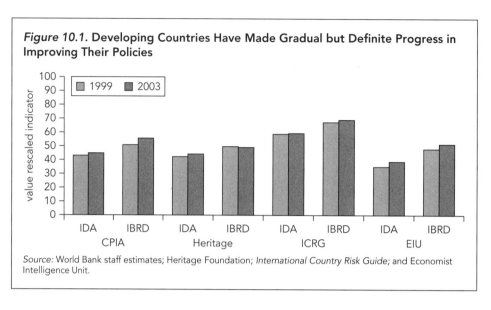

Figure 10.1. Developing Countries Have Made Gradual but Definite Progress in Improving Their Policies

Source: World Bank staff estimates; Heritage Foundation; *International Country Risk Guide;* and Economist Intelligence Unit.

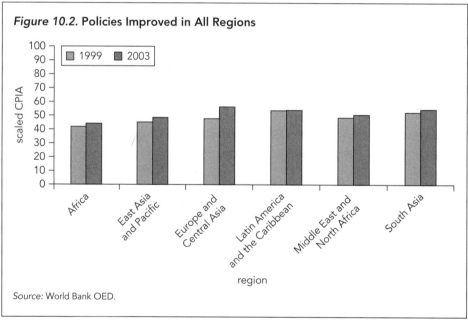

Figure 10.2. Policies Improved in All Regions

Source: World Bank OED.

to borrow from IDA and middle-income countries that are eligible to borrow from the International Bank for Reconstruction and Development (IBRD). It also demonstrates that other indicators, external to the Bank, including the Heritage Foundation/Wall Street Journal's Index of Economic Freedom, the Political Risk Services Group's International Country Risk Guide (ICRG), and the Economist Intelligence Unit's Index of Country Risk (EIU), show a broadly similar pattern. This indicates that the Bank's own internal indicator is doing a good job of evaluating country policies.

Figure 10.2 shows that the improving trend in policies has been widespread geographically, with improvements—albeit to differing degrees—in all regions of the

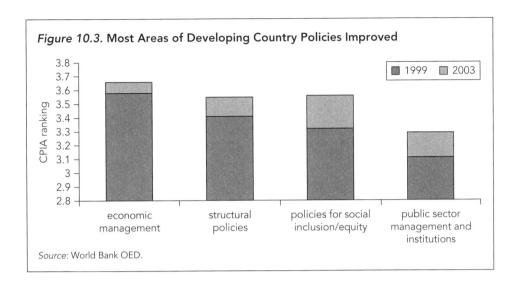

Figure 10.3. Most Areas of Developing Country Policies Improved

Source: World Bank OED.

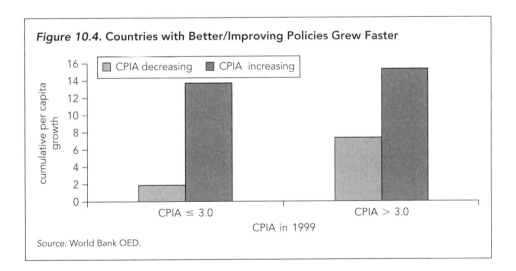

Figure 10.4. Countries with Better/Improving Policies Grew Faster

Source: World Bank OED.

world. As shown in figure 10.3, when the CPIA is classified into four broad categories (economic management, structural policies, policies related to equity, and public sector management and institutions), the improvements took place in almost all categories.

OED found that countries with better policies or improving policies grew more rapidly than did countries with weak policies or deteriorating policies (see figure 10.4). There is a close association between high CPIA rankings and improvements in CPIA rankings with growth outcomes. Cumulative per capita growth between 1998 and 2002 (the most recent period for which growth data are available that overlap with the period covered by the CPIA data) in countries whose policies were improving was more than twice that in policy-deteriorating countries.

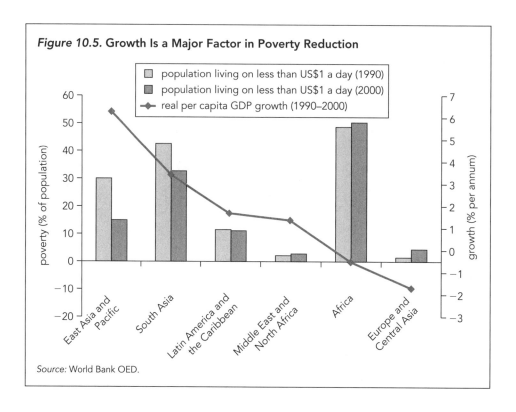

Figure 10.5. Growth Is a Major Factor in Poverty Reduction

Source: World Bank OED.

There also is a close correlation between economic growth and poverty reduction. As illustrated in figure 10.5, the regions that achieved significant reductions in poverty during the 1990s were those where real per capita growth exceeded 3 percent.

The World Bank's Role

Given this broad picture of recent trends in developing countries' policies across the world, let's examine the role of the World Bank in support of policy reforms. Of course, it is difficult to precisely attribute favorable policy outcomes to the World Bank or other donor agencies and to what has been happening in the countries themselves.

The environment confronting many developing countries in the years immediately before and during the period examined by the ARDE has been unusually favorable for reform. Most of the cases of strong reform were driven by necessity (for example, transition or crisis) or opportunity (for example, accession to the European Union). Development research suggests that these kinds of factors are frequently associated with episodes of policy reform. The environment for policy reform in the 1990s was unique in some respects. A number of developing countries were in or coming out of crises (conflict, natural disaster, financial), and 26 countries in Europe and Central Asia were in various stages of transition to a new economy. OED found

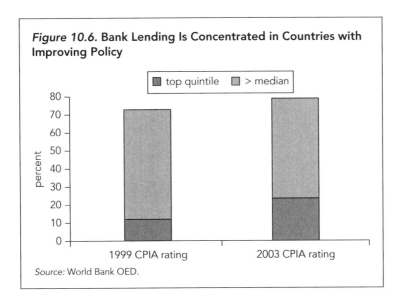

Figure 10.6. Bank Lending Is Concentrated in Countries with Improving Policy

Source: World Bank OED.

that of the 12 countries that had the greatest improvements based on two or more of the four policy indicators examined, 9 were transition countries (Azerbaijan, Brazil, Croatia, Estonia, Kazakhstan, Lithuania, Nicaragua, Republic of Yemen, Romania, Russian Federation, Slovak Republic, Ukraine). The group of countries that had the greatest deterioration based on similar criteria was more diverse (Arab Republic of Eygpt, Argentina, Dominican Republic, Lebanon, Malawi, Panama, Trinidad and Tobago, Uruguay, Zambia, Zimbabwe). Financial crisis played a role in some, while several others had long vacillated on reform.

Figure 10.6 illustrates that the Bank's lending in general was more strongly associated with good policy environment in 2003 than in 1999. About 23 percent of total lending was going into countries that were in the top quintile of the 2003 CPIA ratings relative to about 12 percent for the 1999 CPIA ratings. The same trend is evident in countries ranked above the median.

ARDE 2003 also examined the quality ratings that OED gives to bank programs in different countries. OED's rating evaluates programs in terms of how successful they have been in helping countries reach certain outcomes. In the aggregate, OED's recent country assistance evaluations have rated outcomes of Bank assistance as moderately satisfactory or better about 70 percent of the time, while about 30 percent of the programs were rated moderately unsatisfactory or worse (see figure 10.7).

Good results have been obtained with different mixes of instruments and sectoral/thematic focuses. The key is finding a mix that fits the country situation. There is no evidence that policy-based lending per se is associated with improvements in policy indicators. As figure 10.8 illustrates, the share of adjustment lending has no correlation with improvements in policy outcomes. Bank programs have contributed to reforms in a number of countries without the use of policy-based lending instruments. And the Bank has made heavy use of policy-based lending

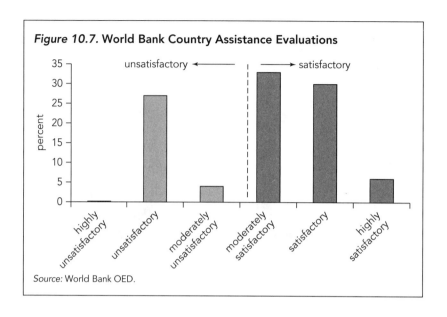

Figure 10.7. World Bank Country Assistance Evaluations

unsatisfactory ←   → satisfactory

percent

highly unsatisfactory | unsatisfactory | moderately unsatisfactory | moderately satisfactory | satisfactory | highly satisfactory

Source: World Bank OED.

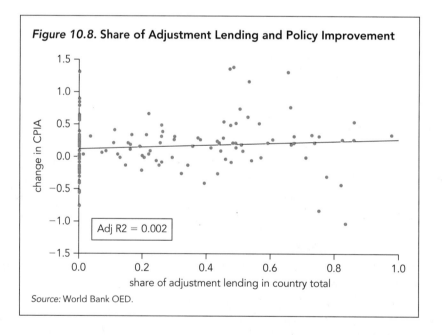

Figure 10.8. Share of Adjustment Lending and Policy Improvement

change in CPIA

Adj R2 = 0.002

share of adjustment lending in country total

Source: World Bank OED.

with little or no impact on policy as reflected in no changes or deteriorations in policy indicators. There is no single recipe for success. Program architecture has to be tailored to country policy-making styles and preferences and has to evolve over time. However, one characteristic that seems to cut across successful outcomes is a strong country and sectoral knowledge base provided by Bank economic and sector work.

In examining the 30 percent of Bank programs that had unsatisfactory outcomes, ARDE 2003 found that knowledge was again an important factor that cut across countries. Insufficient knowledge before starting to engage with countries, a poor analytical base, and lending into ignorance without track record were factors that led to failures. Country fit has been another important failure factor—programs failed when the Bank's advice was not custom fit to local conditions and programs were disconnected from country-owned strategies. For example, in Costa Rica, the World Bank's program, which was conditional on certain legislation being passed, was rated unsatisfactory by OED because it was not well suited to what the Costa Ricans were demanding. Another failure factor is overoptimism regarding the potential for policy reform in some countries, especially in turnaround countries. This has led to false starts (for example, Kenya in the past). The Bank has also been overoptimistic with regard to key determinants—particularly overall growth and export growth—of countries' macroeconomic environment leading to unsustainable debt.

Based on these analyses, OED recommends not lending in nonemergency/noncrisis situations without adequate prior economic and sector work, phasing in policy-based lending according to track record, customizing World Bank strategies and products to local conditions, and strengthening debt sustainability analysis before ramping up lending.

Effectiveness of Conditionality

The role of conditionality is to improve the development effectiveness of support for policy reform by linking aid flows to these reforms. The key effectiveness issues are the effect of conditionality on adoption of reforms, the effect of conditionality on implementation of reforms, and the effect of conditionality on outcomes.

It seems that conducive internal factors or outside pulls had a big impact on the overall improvement of policies during the period examined by the 2003 ARDE (for example, necessity [crisis] and/or opportunity [EU accession of transition countries]). The World Bank itself did not have a big impact on the adoption of reforms. It had some impact on the implementation of reforms and on the speed with which they have or have not been implemented; however, it had little impact on the outcomes themselves.

The design of conditionality and its effectiveness depend on the circumstances in which it is applied. OED has analyzed four variables that determine the effectiveness of conditionality: shared objectives or ownership, means and policies, monitorability of outcomes, and the urgency of resource needs. Table 10.1 summarizes the results for different typologies. Ownership is critical to conditionality effectiveness. If the objectives sought to be achieved by conditions are not shared, then any conditionality is harmful. However, even if the objectives are shared, differences on means or policies depending on the monitorability of certain issues and urgency of resource needs can lead to quite different implications of outcome-based and action-based conditionality.

TABLE 10.1 Working Hypotheses on the Effectiveness of Conditionality

Objectives	Means/ Policies	Monitorability	Urgency of Resource Needs	Conditionality
Not shared				Harmful
Shared	Shared	High	Low/Medium	Outcomes
Shared	Shared	Low	Low/Medium	Actions
Shared	Shared	High/Low	High	Actions
Shared	Not shared	High	Low	Outcomes
Shared	Not shared	Low	High	Actions— possibly harmful
Shared	Not shared	Low	Low	Outcomes— possibly ineffective

In conclusion, this analysis shows that there is an important role for outcome-based conditionality in certain situations, and OED recommends that the World Bank encourage piloting and experimenting with outcomes-based lending. One possibility would be to provide incentives to agreed outcomes. Another would be to introduce an outcomes element into the Bank's performance-based allocation system. The basic idea is to find ways to better align incentives with bottom-line results.

Endnote

1. A task force has recently reviewed this rating and has made some suggestions on its improvement.

11

Policy-Based Lending in LICUS

PAUL COLLIER
Oxford University

The Low-Income Countries Under Stress (LICUS) in Africa are the countries that have the weakest governance policies and institutions. This group of countries is an unsolved problem, and a large group of poor people is living in these countries. The performance of these countries is not improving—on the list in chapter 10, there were no African countries among the countries with significant improvement in their policy environment, but there were three African countries among the countries with deteriorating policies. So, these countries are starting from the worst policies and institutions, dreadful outcomes in terms of poverty, and, even from this low base, conditions are tending to deteriorate. Thus, we shouldn't lull ourselves into a pretence that things are going well.

Conditionality versus Partnership in LICUS

The language used for the issue of conditionality versus partnership is saturated with political correctness. Underpinning the issue of conditionality was the idea that there should be a bargain between donors and recipients of aid. However, bargains or deals are made in situations where objectives differ. After recognizing that objectives differ, bargains or deals are created where each side gets some of what they want in return for giving the other side some of what they want. Partnership, by contrast, presupposes shared objectives: the only problem one overcomes with partnerships is a collective action problem.

With selectivity (that is, for countries with acceptable policy and governance), it is sensible to think in terms of a partnership framework. In these countries there is indeed a reasonable basis for presuming that the objectives are common, and so what is required is to overcome the collective action problem. However, it's not helpful to pretend that we are in the world of partnership in LICUS because there are insufficient shared objectives. Conditionality fails in these countries not because its premise of different objectives is wrong, but because its premise of different objectives is actually right. Conditionality fails because deals are not enforceable. We have to face this

113

fact and not hide this in politically correct language where we pretend that we're all agreed on the objectives. In LICUS we are not.

Problems of Old-Style Conditionality

The old-style policy conditionality ran up against two massive problems. First, there is a psychological problem called "reactiveness," which is nothing distinctive to economics. It is a well-known concept in psychology, and if only we had had one psychologist at the time we were planning conditionality, we would never have gone down that route. The point of reactiveness is that if we tell a person what he's got to do, he does not like being told what to do, and to reestablish his liberty and independence and convince himself that he is free, he will try to do the opposite. So, if the condition was pretty sensible, his incentives now become to do something that is actually rather foolish. Thus, the fundamental problem with policy conditionality is that when countries are ordered to do a list of things, their governments can establish their independence only by trying to do the opposite.

The second problem is the credibility of ex ante conditionality. If the basic motivation of donors for going into policy conditionality is to disburse big money fast, then the credibility of an enforcement agency is destroyed, and the experience with conditionality over the years has just reinforced this fundamental problem.

From Policy to Institutions and Forward

Recently, the focus of donors has shifted from policy to institutions and policy rules, and there is growing evidence that policy results are basically embedded in institutions. So, attempts to change policy without changing policy rules face a fundamental credibility problem. This is the message coming from recent research such as that of Acemoglu, Johnson, and Robinson (2001, 2002).

However, even the institutions themselves may not be fundamental, since they themselves are embedded in the beliefs and attitudes of a society. For example, why did post–World War II Germany have low inflation? Ostensibly, it was because it had an independent central bank; however, the learning experience that the German population had had with hyperinflation in the 1920s underpinned the authority of the central bank.

The Importance of Learning Experiences

More attention needs to be paid to the learning experiences that cumulatively build beliefs and attitudes in societies. Aid should reinforce the effects of reform, so that it accelerates favorable learning experiences. The most powerful learning experiences in a society tend to come from crises.

Let's examine the biggest single reform experience in Africa. Unfortunately, it went drastically wrong, and it was a collective mistake on the part of international financial institutions (IFIs) that made it go wrong. In 1986, Nigeria, for the first time in its recent history, adopted a decent set of economic policy reforms. In economic terms the outcomes were remarkably encouraging—right through the second half of the 1980s. This was the fastest-growing period of recent Nigerian economic history. It is even more remarkable because it coincided with a severe depression following the crash in oil prices. So, in economic terms the reform program worked out well in the short term. As a learning experience, however, it was a total disaster.

In 1986, the world oil price dropped by about 50 percent, causing a shock to Nigeria as a large oil exporter. In addition, Nigeria moved from a strategy of irresponsible borrowing to a strategy of debt repayment. These coincident shocks (that is, the fall in oil price and the move from borrowing to repayment) halved real expenditure within a year. As a result, the population experienced a huge drop in living standards. At the same time, the IFIs introduced a reform program, so everybody in Nigeria now believes that reform causes poverty. This is the single biggest impediment for any reform program in current Nigeria, and therefore it is a disastrous example of the failure to separate stabilization from reform.

The IFIs need to learn the lesson that the stabilization should have been done quite separately from reform, and the consequences of that crash in living standards should clearly have been attributed to the failures of past policy, specifically the disastrous policies of the early 1980s. Instead, the Nigerian population looks back on the early 1980s and the policies associated with them as the golden age—and that's what they want to reestablish.

Errors versus Shocks

It is critical to determine the cause of each crisis and to distinguish between errors and shocks. The Nigerians experienced a crisis partly because of cumulative errors but also because of external shocks.

The two star reformers in Africa, Uganda and Ghana, faced external shocks caused by crashes in their export prices a few years ago. Living standards fell due to substantial deteriorations in the terms of trade, and this situation coincided with an election year. As a result, we nearly lost both of the continent's star performers. We need better strategies to cushion external shocks so they don't mislead electorates.

Selectivity and Credibility

If ex ante conditionality works as an incentive, then selectivity is bound to work as an incentive because it has all the incentive effects of ex ante plus no credibility problems. Ex ante conditionality is now so contaminated by the credibility problem that the only way we get an incentive effect is with ex post conditionality (that is, with selectivity). If one is keen to get incentive effects from aid, then ex post conditionality is the only hope.

Process Conditionality

The big gap in LICUS is in accountability. Not accountability to IFIs and the international community, but accountability to the domestic population. Conditionality can become more legitimate by insisting on accountability to the domestic population. At the moment, even where there are the formal mechanics of democracy, it is generally without genuine accountability.

There are two epicenters of domestic accountability. One is a set of checks and balances associated with media, courts, and elections. It is entirely legitimate to condition aid on those checks and balances. The second is accountability around budgets, and it is absolutely fundamental that we have transparency in budgets. Transparency is a critical input into domestic scrutiny, not an end in itself. Until budgets are transparent they can't be scrutinized domestically. And even if they are transparent, a collective action problem has to be overcome to generate domestic scrutiny.

How can we get this domestic accountability? What should we be insisting on? We should try to get more international standards and codes describing minimum acceptable practice (not necessarily best practice)—standards that are pertinent for the particular circumstances of LICUS. The Extractive Industries Transparency Initiative is a good example of creating a new standard and code in an area that is hugely important for low-income Africa (that is, through the use of natural resource rents). Similar standards should gradually be made a condition for the other significant rents of sovereignty.

Bibliography

Acemoglu, D., J. A. Robinson, and S. Johnson. 2001. "The Colonial Origins of Comparative Development: An Empirical Investigation." *American Economic Review* 91: 1369–1401.

Acemoglu, D., S. Johnson, and J. A. Robinson. 2002. "Reversal of Fortune: Geography and Institutions in the Making of the Modern World Income Distribution." *Quarterly Journal of Economics* 117: 1231–94.

12

The Experience of Brazil

JOAQUIM F. LEVY
Ministry of Finance, Brazil

This chapter will attempt to give the practitioner's perspective and will raise some issues on conditionality regarding both the International Monetary Fund (IMF) and the World Bank that are important for countries in the same stage as Brazil. It will also discuss some of the challenges to making Brazil's relationship with the World Bank consistently meaningful in the future.

In chapter 11, Paul Collier mentioned that in some countries an external shock due to, for example, falling commodity prices could ruin several years of reform efforts. In the case of countries such as Brazil, similar problems can be caused by capital flows. Brazil is strongly committed to free capital flows, but they can generate large tides and can create turbulences and disturbances that can be mixed with the direct effects of policies. As a result, the outcome may become hard to judge by both experts and voters on the street. Thus, because, when judging the performance of countries, it is always important to consider external factors in addition to domestic policies, multilateral organizations should strive to devise instruments to reduce the risks that external shocks can impose on developing countries that have otherwise adjusted their economies and policies.

One of the key issues for Brazil is how to have conditionality and facilities that could respond to the potential problems resulting from big changes in capital flows due mainly to external factors. When Brazil experienced a sharp contraction in flows in 2002, it developed an effective arrangement with the IMF, but that was an ad hoc construction. Looking forward, it is critical to design structured facilities, especially for middle-income countries, with conditionality that ensures quick and effective financial support.

IMF Program Conditionality

Brazil certainly supports the streamlining of IMF conditionality. It has had, especially in the past three years, quite a successful relationship with the IMF. This relationship has been based on IMF streamlined programs focused on the basics, that is, on safeguarding IMF resources. In addition, the IMF did not try to use structural conditionality to impose a predetermined reform agenda.

Mr. Lula's government in Brazil is strongly committed to reforms and has moved forward in many key areas. Some of the elements of reform, mainly the ones related to core areas of the IMF, gradually became part of the IMF program in Brazil. Other elements were left outside of the program because, despite their importance, they were not related to core areas, and Brazil strongly believes that it should never try to hide behind the IMF to advance its reforms. Brazil has to do what it believes is important. Although the dynamics of operating in a noncrisis situation can sometimes be different from operating in a crisis situation, the same principle can find broad application.

In the context of discussions about outcomes, Brazil has been quite adamant never to promise things that do not depend only on the executive branch. In a democratic system, to ensure the right functioning of programs, the government should not commit on behalf of other branches, even when it has a majority in congress.

Brazil has had some meaningful results in the past few years. It has had no need for waivers or other artifices to accommodate underperformance and try to make the program look better. On the contrary, Brazil has overperformed in many cases, especially in key areas. One of those key areas is fiscal, and when the new government came into power in 2003, it went to the general public, and later to the IMF, and said that, based on its calculations, the primary target should be raised somewhat. Of course that meant additional efforts, especially in a year of low economic activity in the wake of a 5 percent of gross domestic product (GDP) adjustment of the external sector. However, it paid off, and fiscal discipline with a view to reduce the debt burden is now at the core of other economic policies as well.

Looking back further, it is noteworthy that, starting back in 1999 with inflation targeting, trust on the part of the IMF has served both parties well. Dropping quantitative monetary targets and sticking to inflation targets was an important innovation in the context of a program. It paid off handsomely for Brazil, which has been able to keep inflation under control and overcome the huge external shock of 2002 without disorganizing its economy. It also proved effective for the IMF, which has undoubtedly learned from this experience and has considered applying it elsewhere. This result has also helped change the perception of the IMF by Brazilian society and opened the way to discussions—in a structured fashion—of issues such as how to protect and promote high-return investments in the face of strong budget constraints.

Looking ahead, it is important to assess whether the 2000 guidelines on streamlining conditionality have been really implemented, before evaluating if they have achieved their goal and proposing any change in course. Our substantive recommendations for IMF conditionality are: (a) program design should be adjusted to avoid the serious issue of blackout periods; (b) the use of prior actions as a modality of conditionality should be limited to a minimum; (c) there should be no conditionality in areas that diminish the odds of program implementation; (d) there should be no conditionality associated with policy initiatives or structural measures that unnecessarily corner country authorities (for example, stiff targets for variables that depend essentially on market demand); (e) under certain preconditions, financing for public investment in infrastructure should be accommodated under program fiscal targets; and (f) further discussions on the greater use of outcomes-based conditionality should be carried out before being enshrined.

World Bank Conditionality

Some of the issues and recommendations above are also relevant for the World Bank. In particular, minimizing the use of prior actions and other coercive mechanisms is fundamental to ensure the development of a trust-based relationship. Conditions and conditionality have to be adapted to the situation, and sensitivity is critical for the success of programs in any country.

Of course, there is good news. Apparently, there is growing recognition that the Bank's new policy for policy-based lending should ensure a unified policy framework, although leaving room for customization in the context of the Country Assistance Strategy (CAS). Programs' analytical underpinnings are being strengthened, as they should be. Also, Brazil's experience shows that it is important that the expected total volume for a borrower be determined in the CAS. This step is beneficial for the borrowers because it enables better planning of financial and personnel resources for the administration of programs. The central role of the CAS is quite compatible with a need to have a good policy dialogue with the government, and Brazil certainly supports the strengthening of this understanding.

The following examples from the past two or three years illustrate the possibility of success in some of the conditionality issues discussed. The first example is a programmatic loan for the electricity sector agreed upon with the previous government in Brazil. Electricity is an extremely complex sector, and the beauty of the relationship with the Bank in this area was the fact that, although there was an important contribution from World Bank staff, there was also, from the beginning, a clear understanding that these were complex issues and nobody had a complete answer. The loan conditionality emerged from rigorous analytical work, but it was geared toward providing clear support to changes already achieved in a difficult environment. The trust of the Bank on the appropriateness of the policy choices was expressed by a big disbursement in addition to technical assistance. The results included not only high performance, but also the success in avoiding a rupture by the new government. This highlights one of Brazil's best partnership experiences with the Bank, which is yielding results many years after the program was signed.

The second example is the more recent sectorwide approaches in social areas. In this case, an understanding of the hard fiscal constraints of the government and trust in the improved design-and-control mechanisms of new social programs were critical. In many cases, if the World Bank just comes with a new project involving a lot of new spending, it does not support Brazil's policy and reform agenda—given the serious budget constraints all levels of government face in Brazil. In this case, we had to develop a mechanism that would allow a meaningful participation of the World Bank, so that it could bring all the best it has, without going against the core aspects of the general policy. The new mechanism relies on national fiduciary and safeguard systems that take advantage of existing mechanisms in World Bank programs (for example, reimbursements), but conform to general policies in Brazil. It has provided a means for the Bank to participate in an innovative program of high visibility, granting the way for the Bank to contribute to the improvement of the design of government initiatives while learning the complexities of a large-scale, transfer-and-requirement program and reinforcing the macroeconomic framework of the federal government.

The third example is subnational loans. The key here is an understanding of fiscal constraints of subnational governments, which are typically cash hungry and often debt burdened. So, it is clear that programs can happen only where subnational governments can afford additional debt. Meanwhile, where the existing debt dynamics allow, programs should support investments or social reform with minimum financial requirements from the counterpart—thus providing an effective source of cash for states that have little other access to liquidity.

The fourth example is from the sensitive area of the environment. It again shows the importance of trust, and is an example of how conditionality has worked in Brazil. A recent programmatic loan has a significant disbursement based on the mutual agreement that what has been already achieved is meaningful and in the right direction, and that it is the result of a policy effort of the government. Then, of course, Brazil laid out the expected path for the future. However, this is not conditionality in the standard sense—it is a common view. The resulting policy matrix supports the achievements and priorities of the present administration—recognizing existing constraints and letting the government choose its actions according to the circumstances. In the future, Brazil and the World Bank are going to come together and assess what has happened and see if both sides are happy. If this is the case, the process may be repeated, with a new loan based on what has been achieved so far. This is mainly a process of building confidence and exchanging experiences, and, if one can call this conditionality, it certainly shows a constructive approach to conditionality.

Of course, although the experience of Brazil is more applicable to middle-income countries, some aspects may be applicable to lower-income countries as well. In particular, the boundaries between incentives and coercion may in some cases be blurred, especially if a country administration is weak (for example, on technical terms) in relation to multilateral institutions and donors in general. In this case, those imposing conditionality must take special care to avoid narrow or self-righteous views, which could do more harm than good, especially if attitudes and operational approaches fail to acknowledge the numerous factors and conflicting incentives often faced by authorities in small and poor countries. These factors, all too often, transcend domestic boundaries and reflect powerful economic forces elsewhere.

World Bank Support to Middle-Income Countries

World Bank total lending to this group of countries has undergone a significant decline (26 percent in nominal terms) from an average of $15.7 billion per year in fiscal 1990–7 to an average of $11.6 billion per year in fiscal 2000–3 (see figures 12.1–12.3).

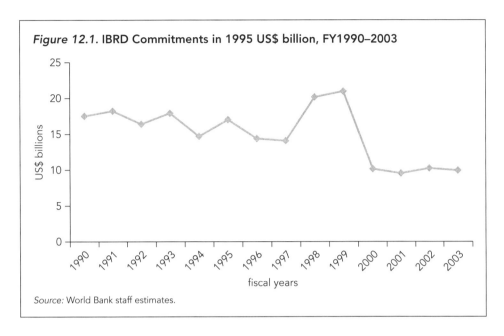

Figure 12.1. IBRD Commitments in 1995 US$ billion, FY1990–2003

Source: World Bank staff estimates.

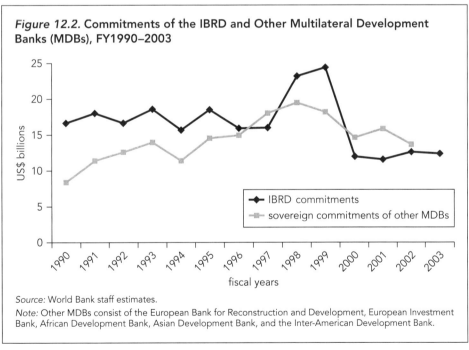

Figure 12.2. Commitments of the IBRD and Other Multilateral Development Banks (MDBs), FY1990–2003

Source: World Bank staff estimates.

Note: Other MDBs consist of the European Bank for Reconstruction and Development, European Investment Bank, African Development Bank, Asian Development Bank, and the Inter-American Development Bank.

Since the mid-1990s, investment lending declined in all regions except South Asia, with the greatest decline in East Asia. It also dropped in all sectors, except education and health, with infrastructure being the most affected (see figures 12.4–12.7).

Figure 12.8 shows the development of World Bank commitments to Brazil since fiscal 1990. Although there were more resources committed in loans in 2001–2 than

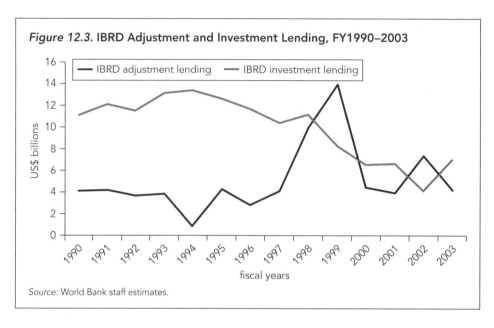

Figure 12.3. IBRD Adjustment and Investment Lending, FY1990–2003

Source: World Bank staff estimates.

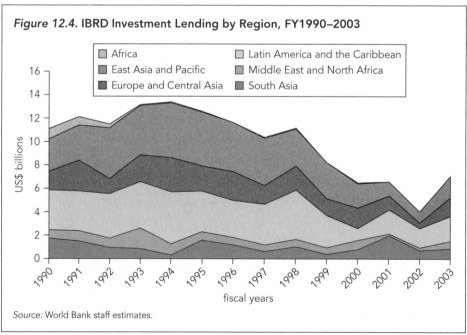

Figure 12.4. IBRD Investment Lending by Region, FY1990–2003

Source: World Bank staff estimates.

in most previous years, there was a sharp drop in 2003, which persisted in 2004. Of course, the flow of investment loans to some areas envisaged in the heyday of the second half of the 1990s proved unsustainable, while the World Bank signaled limits to the scope of adjustment loans. Thus, although Brazil has recently successfully discussed a CAS, many challenges are ahead to ensure a meaningful role of the Bank in Brazil and to avoid a continued reduction of the Bank portfolio (Brazil was a net payer to the Bank in 2003 and for part of 2004).

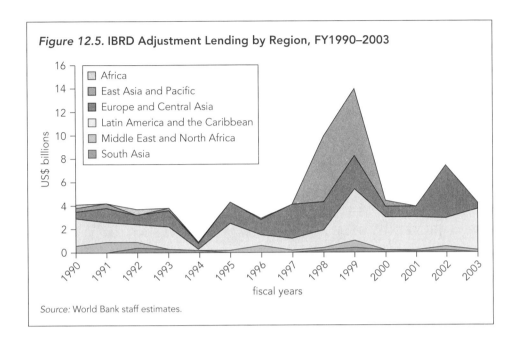

Figure 12.5. IBRD Adjustment Lending by Region, FY1990–2003

Source: World Bank staff estimates.

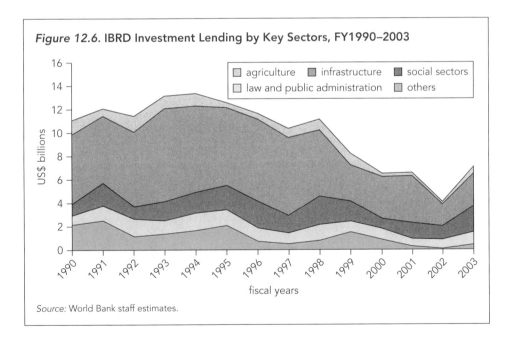

Figure 12.6. IBRD Investment Lending by Key Sectors, FY1990–2003

Source: World Bank staff estimates.

Looking ahead, some things appear quite evident. In particular, the World Bank has an approach for low-income countries on the basis of the Poverty Reduction Strategy Paper process and, similarly, for Low-Income Countries Under Stress. It is also time to develop a structured approach for middle-income countries. Efforts are already under way, but it is important to build something together, because the contribution

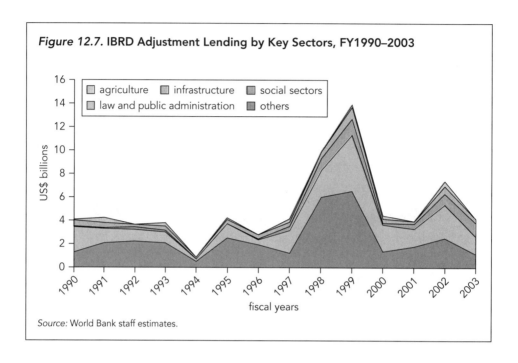

Figure 12.7. IBRD Adjustment Lending by Key Sectors, FY1990–2003

Source: World Bank staff estimates.

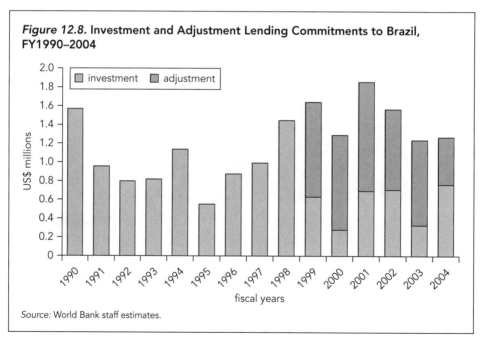

Figure 12.8. Investment and Adjustment Lending Commitments to Brazil, FY1990–2004

Source: World Bank staff estimates.

of countries in the same stage as Brazil could be extremely positive for the Bank if it is based on open dialogue.

More specifically, the World Bank should take the following actions toward middle-income countries. First, it should reassess and integrate country exposure limits, because several middle-income countries do want to increase the role of the private sector in infrastructure, and the International Finance Corporation (IFC) has been unable to handle this demand in view of limits to credit exposure. This may result in idle resources in the World Bank (because governments cannot borrow more for fiscal reasons), and shortage of room in the IFC. One possibility to improve this area—in addition to swapping risks between the two branches of the World Bank Group (the International Bank for Reconstruction and Development and IFC)—would be to take a comprehensive view of risk along sectors or even corporate borrowers in given regions.

Second, it would also be important to reduce the cost of doing business with the Bank by, for example, finding ways to issue in local currency to fund infrastructure projects that generate revenues in local currencies (this could also be achieved by issuing derivatives, given the existing restrictions on the funding policies of the World Bank). Such a policy would facilitate public-private partnerships in many middle-income countries. Another way to reduce costs is to rely more on national fiduciary and safeguard systems (for example, by employing the country systems of budgetary control, where they are developed enough). Third, in the area of conditionality, the World Bank's approach should be realistic and pragmatic in order to reduce the burden of sector policy conditions on individual projects. The Bank should also make continued efforts to simplify its procedures and harmonize its policies with other MDBs.

The Bank's new commitment to infrastructure loans is an opportunity to revitalize its relationship with middle-income countries. It is important that in its dialogue with the IMF, the Bank develop a real framework to make operational the insight that stifling investment to ensure debt service may be a suboptimal choice. Among other issues, the framework has to show how to measure the additional resources that may become available to service the public debt in the wake of a relaxation of budget constraints, and how to make these resources available. The Bank has advantages compared with simple investment banks in assessing macrosustainability of additional spending and could use them in moving this dialogue forward.

Conclusions

The meaning of conditionality has changed over time. The principle will remain important, because it will be important that facilities and programs from multilateral financial institutions continue to be backed by actual and meaningful resources. In some cases, these resources may not need to be withdrawn immediately, and they may not entail significant increases in fiscal spending by governments. But they ought to remain an integral part of programs. This is particularly important for middle-income countries. Conditionality for these countries should reflect, however, the stage of the administrative structures and the sophistication of policy making, implementation, and monitoring in these countries and should never be used to attempt to impose preestablished policies from the outside. The recent experience of Brazil with both the IMF and MDBs shows that these objectives can be approached and should be pursued further, because the building up of trust through streamlined and focused conditionality reduces the risks of moral hazard and reinforces good policies.

13

Does World Bank Effort Matter for Success of Adjustment Operations?

THADDEUS MALESA AND PETER SILARSZKY[1]
World Bank

The approach the World Bank has taken with its clients has changed significantly over time, starting with large reconstruction projects in Western Europe to what is now largely a poverty-driven agenda in mid- and low-income countries. The initial loans made by the institution in the 1940s and 1950s concentrated on infrastructure projects. In the 1970s, the International Development Association (IDA) enabled the expansion of the Bank's activities to low-income countries, and the scope of the Bank's work expanded beyond infrastructure to human capital. Subsequent years of experience indicated that such investments, without change to inadequate policies in place, were not as advantageous as they could have been in many client countries. An inadequate policy environment was recognized to be a major barrier to growth. As a result, adjustment lending emerged in 1980 with the intent of positively influencing the policy reform process in developing economies. The promotion of propoor growth policies was added to the goals of adjustment lending in the 1990s. Given the nearly 25-year history of adjustment lending within the World Bank, an examination of the factors determining its success is highly appropriate and should shape the approach toward this instrument in the future.

A large number of studies of policy-based lending have been conducted, and most take a case-study approach. Ranis (1995) concludes that policy-based lending and the embedded conditionality process work well only when countries have decided on their own to reform, and his findings seem to be confirmed by a number of other studies. A more systematic approach to the reasons for successful adjustment operations is taken by Dollar and Svensson (2000), who analyze a database covering 272 operations and conclude that the success of reforms supported by the World Bank through its adjustment operations is strongly related to political-economic factors in the borrowing country. Dollar and Svensson go further, asserting that there is no relation between any of the donor-effort variables and the success of reforms. More specifically, having treated those variables under the World Bank's control as endogenous to the probability of success of adjustment operations,[2] Dollar and Svensson find no evidence that these variables affect the probability of success of an adjustment operation. The operationally significant conclusion they draw is that the donor community should be more selective in providing this kind of assistance, concentrating it in countries with good political-economic environments.

This is a daunting conclusion—clearly, countries with meager political-economic indicators often have an equal or greater need for reforms and financial support from the donor community—and begs the question: is there any evidence that the World Bank can contribute significantly to the success of reform programs in borrowing countries with meager political-economic environments?

This study reexamines the results of previous studies using a newly compiled database that covers all 643 adjustment operations designed to support specific reform programs from the International Bank for Reconstruction and Development and the IDA since 1980 through fiscal 2003. Further evidence for the conclusion of previous studies that domestic political-economic factors have a major impact on the success of supported reforms is provided by our analysis of the newest data available. However, political-economic variables are not the sole significant factors determining the success of reform programs. Specifically, we find that some of the variables under the World Bank's control, such as preparation costs, are not endogenous (as prior papers have assumed) and are significant contributing factors to the success of adjustment operations. This finding suggests that the World Bank does have the ability to positively affect the outcome of supported reforms in client countries, including among them countries with meager political-economic environments. In short, World Bank inputs do matter.

Measuring Reform Outcomes

Case studies constitute most of the literature analyzing the outcomes of policy-based lending, probably because the lack of consistent data inhibits systematic, quantitative studies. The latter analysis requires both a measure of success of policy reform (to be used as a dependent variable) and variables capturing aspects of country-specific political-economic factors and of donor input (to be used as explanatory variables). However, a large number of development institutions and aid agencies provide support for reforms in developing countries and they report varying amounts of information in their own format.

Given the constraint of inconsistent data, this study follows in the footsteps of Dollar and Svensson (2000) and focuses on World Bank adjustment operations. The outcome ratings of the independent Operations Evaluation Department (OED) of the World Bank are used as a consistent measure of reform success (that is, as our dependent variable). OED's outcome rating measures the extent to which the World Bank project's major relevant objectives were achieved efficiently. Specifically, we use a zero-one dummy variable reflecting failure or success of each operation as determined by OED. There are two major disadvantages to this approach: this measure is subjective and it evaluates only the short-term success of the reform.

As argued by Dollar and Svensson (2000), this measure is an acceptably objective measure of success for at least two reasons. First, the OED evaluation assesses whether reform has taken place and the larger objective of reform has been met, not simply whether the loan conditionalities were met. Second, although there is clearly a subjective element to such an assessment, it remains a dispassionate subjectivity: OED's independence within the World Bank means that there is no necessary bias in the results.

Because OED's evaluation is carried out within six to eight months of the loan's disbursement and so can only be recognized as an indicator of short-term success, we considered a number of other options for our dependent variable. However, we struggled to identify a superior alternative. As the World Bank is in the privileged situation of a preferred creditor, the issue of repayment is not as relevant as it would be to a private lender. We also considered an index combining OED's outcome rating with an objective medium-term (three to five years after the operation's completion) indicator of reform success, such as change in inflation or change in budget balance. Reform measures differ across countries and operations, however, and it proved impossible to find a single quantitative measure of success. Furthermore, these objective measures are also influenced by external shocks, and it is difficult to distinguish the effects of these shocks from policy effects. Instead, the stated objectives of each project could be measured against the actual progress achieved. Again, however, the stated objectives also differ across countries and operations. There is no database where these objectives are stated and stored, and no way to efficiently compile data and measure any advancements achieved across the breadth of World Bank loans and credits.

Thus, we concluded that although OED's outcome rating is imperfect, it is preferable to alternative feasible measures of success of policy reforms. Moreover, it has the advantage that it can be linked to a wide range of internal data on World Bank operations, including the resources invested in project design and in supervision of implementation.

Data

Our dataset covers all 643 World Bank adjustment operations approved since 1980 through fiscal 2003 ending on June 30, 2003.[3] To compile our dataset we made use of multiple sources within the World Bank and selected outside sources. Specifically, we made use of OED's database, which tracks project outcome ratings for projects evaluated by OED and information covering costs associated with the preparation and supervision of operations, and the Adjustment Lending Conditionality and Implementation Database (ALCID), which is maintained by Operations Policy and Country Services—Country Economics (OPCCE) and has recently been improved. ALCID now also tracks data on economic sector involvement and development objectives by condition. Another internal source of information is the World Development Indicators (WDI) database, which provides various macroeconomic indicators by year and country. We also made use of external sources such as the *Europa Yearbook,* which provides detailed information on country governments and their political arrangements. The ethnic fractionalization indicator was drawn from Beck, Levine, and Loayza (1999), which updates the dataset originally compiled in 1964 and that is used by Easterly and Levine (1997). The political instability variable was taken from Banks (2001). Please see Annexes 13.1 and 13.2 for further clarification of the variables used in our study.

The breadth of operations included has its largest concentration in the Sub-Saharan Africa Region with 35 percent of operations, followed by the Latin America and the Caribbean Region with 23 percent, and the Europe and Central Asia Region with 22 percent. East Asia and Pacific as well as the Middle East and North Africa Regions accounted for 7 percent of operations, and South Asia 6 percent. The key descriptive statistics of the most important data series in our dataset are tabulated in table 13.1.

The average number of legally binding conditions[4] associated with the loans and credits in our dataset is 28 (ranging from 1 to 136), coupled with an average 14 desired actions,[5] amounting to an average total of 42 overall conditions per operation. Since the early 1990s there has been a trend to reduce the number of conditions: the average number of legally binding conditions in fiscal 2003 was 18, compared

TABLE 13.1 Descriptive Statistics

Variable	Number of Observations	Mean	Standard Deviation	Minimum	1st Quartile	Median	3rd Quartile	Maximum
Ethnic Fractionalization	546	0.406	0.330	0	0.056	0.357	0.728	0.930
Political Instability	502	0.166	0.363	0	0	0	0	2
Democratically Elected	641	0.633	0.482	0	0	1	1	1
Time in Power	641	6.596	7.933	0.006	1.663	3.652	7.609	44.334
Initial GDP per Capita (log)	574	7.709	0.897	5.804	6.955	7.655	8.455	9.512
Initial Population (log)	597	16.440	1.464	11.198	15.466	16.278	17.415	20.820
Preparation Costs (log)	640	12.567	0.821	8.337	12.228	12.685	13.116	14.424
Supervision Costs (log)	639	11.890	1.051	5.935	11.364	12.063	12.612	13.998
Finance Conditions (%)	633	0.183	0.257	0	0	0.091	0.235	1
Macroeconomic and Fiscal Conditions (%)	633	0.188	0.172	0	0.067	0.143	0.260	1
Sectoral Conditions (%)	633	0.586	0.294	0	0.417	0.632	0.821	1
Trade Conditions (%)	633	0.100	0.179	0	0	0	0.133	1
Number of Legally Binding Conditions	633	28.262	18.635	1	15	24	38	136
Loan Size (log)	643	18.422	1.098	14.914	17.728	18.421	19.337	21.822
Expected Duration of the Adjustment Operation	641	668.410	391.202	29	398	605	836	2777
IDA Dummy Variable	624	0.497	0.500	0	0	0	1	1
End of Cold War Dummy Variable	643	0.656	0.475	0	0	1	1	1

Sources: Beck, Levine, and Loayza 1999; Banks 2001; Europa Yearbook, various issues; World Bank ALCID; and staff estimates.

with the fiscal 1990 average of 34. At the same time, the share of single-tranche operations has increased significantly; in fiscal 2003, 27 of 45 total approved operations were single tranche, as compared with fiscal 1990, when none of 31 approved operations was single tranche. This trend is accompanied by a slight reduction in average preparation costs of adjustment operations, the respective amounts being $425,349 (fiscal 2002) and $431,995 (fiscal 1990). The bulk of conditions in the average operation were sectoral (58 percent of total legally binding conditions), trailed by finance as well as macroeconomic and fiscal conditions, each at 18 percent.[6]

Specification

Using this new database, we seek to address the following questions:

1. Is the success of adjustment operations explained by political-economic variables?

2. Do variables under the World Bank's control have any effect on the probability of success of its adjustment operations?

Our model can be outlined as follows: Let y_i^* be the probability of success of adjustment operation i. This probability is not directly observable. Instead we observe a dummy variable that indicates the success, y_i. Our model can be expressed as

$$y_i^* = c_y + b_i' \beta_y + d_i' \delta_{yp} + \varepsilon_{yi},$$

where c_y is a scalar, b_i is a $m \times 1$ vector of variables reflecting country conditions at the time of approval of adjustment operation i, β_y is a $m \times 1$ vector, d_i is a $l \times 1$ vector of variables under the World Bank's control associated with adjustment operation i, δ_{yp} is a $l \times 1$ vector, and ε_{yi} is a scalar mean-zero error term.

If the variables under the World Bank's control are independent of the error term (that is, if all these variables are exogenous), then we can use probit to estimate the indicator of success. However, if they were correlated with the error term (that is, they were endogenous), then we would have to find instruments and use a two-stage procedure to estimate the model. The endogeneity of the variables under the World Bank's control will play a key role in determining whether the variables under the World Bank's control have any effect on the success rate of its adjustment operations. Dollar and Svensson (2000) make a key assumption that these variables are endogenous, and this assumption is behind their conclusion that there is no relationship between any of the donor-effort variables and the success of the operations. They based their assumption on the fact that an exogenous shock that reduces the probability of success is likely to influence the World Bank's allocation of resources. However, they did not test whether the data support their assumption.

Our experience from working in a central advisory unit that is closely involved with country teams during the reviews of the majority of the World Bank's adjustment operations suggests that good preparatory work and close cooperation between World Bank teams and government officials result in better operations. This led us to a hypothesis that additional World Bank effort corresponds to a higher probability

TABLE 13.2 Features of Successful and Unsuccessful Adjustment Operations

	Successful	Failed
Country Characteristics		
Democratically Elected	82%	18%
Political Instability (average number of government crises during reform period)	0.13	0.26
Ethnolinguistic Fractionalization	0.40	0.44
Length of Time the Incumbent Has Been in Power Prior to Reform	6.5	7.8
Average Initial Population	49,709,981	33,689,025
Average Initial GDP per Capita	$3,416	$2,473
Variables under the World Bank's Control		
Preparation Costs	$370,539	$346,699
Supervision Costs	$203,513	$284,769
Number of Conditions (legally binding and desired actions)	42.23	47.10
Number of Legally Binding Conditions	28.94	29.02
Number of Tranches (tied to disbursement of funds)	1.97	2.34
Loan Size (million $)	$184	$179
Sample Information		
Number of Operations	421	136

Sources: Beck, Levine, and Loayza 1999; Banks 2001; *Europa Yearbook,* various issues; World Bank ALCID; and staff estimates.

of success if all other factors remain equal. Hence, we were led to question the assumptions of Dollar and Svensson (2000) that result in the lack of evidence that variables under the World Bank's control have any real effect toward the success of an operation. We used the Smith-Blundell test of exogeneity to investigate whether these variables are endogenous and our data support the hypothesis that the relevant variables under the World Bank's control are exogenous (for a detailed discussion, see the next section).

Of the 643 total adjustment operations covered in the dataset, OED had rated 557 by April 2004; 421 operations (76 percent) were rated satisfactory in meeting their objectives, and 136 (24 percent) were rated unsatisfactory. Table 13.2 demonstrates that country-specific characteristics seem to have a large effect on whether an operation will be successful (that is, rated satisfactory). Successful operations are generally associated with democratically elected governments (82 percent of successful operations were in countries with democratically elected signing authority, compared with 18 percent of failures), and a newer government is more likely to complete the objectives of the reform program. Similarly, failed adjustment operations seem to be concentrated more heavily in politically unstable environments, where government crises occur more frequently. There is no noticeable difference in the average ethnolinguistic fractionalization between successful and failed operations. Because the political-economic literature suggests that this factor affects the probability of success of reforms, it will enter our specification in a nonlinear fashion. However, the literature does not identify the functional form of the relationship, and following Dollar and

Svensson (2000) we choose the quadratic form. In addition, operations in countries with larger populations and higher gross domestic product (GDP) per capita are on average more successful.

The average values of variables under the World Bank's control (for example, number of legally binding conditions and loan size) are remarkably similar for successful and failed operations. However, successful operations get on average nearly 7 percent more preparation resources than failed operations, while failed operations consume on average about 40 percent more supervision resources than the successful ones.

Results

In table 13.3 we report a series of probit models that are designed to estimate the probability of success of adjustment loans and credits. In model 1 we include only the political-economic variables. As expected, democratically elected government and political stability increase the probability of success, while the length of time that the

TABLE 13.3 Probit Regressions

	Dependent Variable: OED's Outcome Rating						
Regression No.	(1)	(2)	(3)	(4)	(5)	(6)	(7)
Number of Observations	424	408	408	401	401	388	404
Constant	0.357	−0.294	−0.324	0.591	0.953	2.876	2.566
	(2.10)	(−0.20)	(−0.23)	(0.28)	(0.52)	(1.29)	(1.93)
Ethnic Fractionalization	2.591	2.652	2.599	2.606	2.633	2.804	2.813
	(2.83)	(2.60)	(2.62)	(2.43)	(2.50)	(2.56)	(2.70)
Ethnic Fractionalization	−3.078	−2.775	−2.729	−2.752	−2.821	−3.037	−3.144
(squared)	(−2.93)	(−2.26)	(−2.29)	(−2.13)	(−2.27)	(−2.35)	(−2.57)
Political Instability	−0.811	−0.939	−0.939	−1.105	−1.083	−1.082	−1.173
	(−3.82)	(−3.81)	(−3.88)	(−4.16)	(−4.13)	(−3.88)	(−4.48)
Democratically Elected	0.469	0.561	0.555	0.547	0.546	0.312	0.298
	(3.19)	(3.34)	(3.37)	(2.95)	(3.06)	(1.54)	(1.50)
Time in Power	−0.006	−0.007	−0.007	−0.013	−0.013	−0.018	−0.020
	(−0.74)	(−0.68)	(−0.79)	(−1.33)	(−1.41)	(−1.71)	(−2.07)
Sub-Saharan Africa		−0.428	−0.488	−0.015			
		(−1.13)	(−1.81)	(−0.05)			
Latin America and Caribbean		−0.427	−0.534	−0.389	−0.408	−0.204	−0.230
		(−1.10)	(−2.39)	(−1.53)	(−1.68)	(−0.80)	(−0.96)
East Asia		0.065					
		(0.17)					
Europe and Central Asia		0.170					
		(0.39)					
Middle East and North Africa		0.093					
		(0.21)					
Initial GDP per Capita (log)		0.060	0.090	0.221	0.168	0.035	
		(0.42)	(0.74)	(1.43)	(1.36)	(0.20)	

(Continued)

TABLE 13.3 (*Continued*)

	Dependent Variable: OED's Outcome Rating						
Regression No.	(1)	(2)	(3)	(4)	(5)	(6)	(7)
Number of Observations	424	408	408	401	401	388	404
Initial Population (log)		0.020	0.014	0.079	0.025	−0.020	
		(0.32)	(0.23)	(0.75)	(0.43)	(−0.31)	
Preparation Costs (log)				0.447	0.432	0.440	0.451
				(4.10)	(4.18)	(4.16)	(4.40)
Supervision Costs (log)				−0.580	−0.620	−0.642	−0.619
				(−4.46)	(−5.41)	(−5.33)	(−5.39)
Finance Conditions (%)				0.176			
				(0.31)			
Macroeconomic and Fiscal Conditions (%)				−1.036	−1.346	−1.470	−1.438
				(−1.58)	(−2.72)	(−2.92)	(−2.94)
Sectoral Conditions (%)				0.325			
				(0.54)			
Trade Conditions (%)				0.105			
				(0.24)			
Number of Legally Binding Conditions				0.006	0.006	0.003	
				(1.31)	(1.18)	(0.70)	
Loan Size (log)				−0.101			
				(−0.68)			
Expected Duration of the Adjustment Operation				-1.01×10^{-4}			
				(−0.48)			
IDA Dummy Variable						−0.188	−0.217
						(−0.71)	(−1.22)
End of Cold War Dummy Variable						0.557	0.595
						(2.96)	(3.54)
Predicted Ability	0.731	0.757	0.757	0.766	0.768	0.791	0.782
Likelihood Ratio Index	0.061	0.081	0.081	0.185	0.182	0.196	0.203

Sources: Beck, Levine, and Loayza 1999; Banks 2001; *Europa Yearbook,* various issues; World Bank ALCID; and staff estimates.

incumbent has been in power has a negative effect on the probability of success—implying that new governments are more likely to carry out successful reforms than long-term incumbents. We assume that ethnic fractionalization influences the probability of success nonlinearly. The implication is that high degrees of fractionalization lower the probability of successful reform. However, ethnic homogeneity is also a bad sign for reforms. The turning points vary between 0.42 and 0.48. Using only the political-economic variables, the model correctly predicts about 73 percent of the observations.

In model 2, we add some additional variables: regional dummy variables, initial GDP per capita, and initial population. The results indicate that policy-based lending tends to be less successful in low-income countries, in Latin America, and in Africa. None of the other regional dummy variables seems to have a relationship with the probability of success. The probability of success increases with population size.

Model 3 reports the results after the elimination of the regional dummy variables except for Latin America and Africa. Once again we observe the significant influence of country-specific political-economic factors on the success of an adjustment operation. Model 3 correctly predicts almost 76 percent of the observations.

In model 4, we introduce variables that are under the direct influence of the World Bank. Specifically, we add the following explanatory variables under the World Bank's control to the specification: preparation and supervision costs, number of legally binding conditions, size of loan, expected duration of adjustment operation, and shares of conditions related to financial policy, to macroeconomic and fiscal policy, to sectoral policy, and to trade policy.[7] We recognize that there is a potential endogeneity issue with these variables and we later test their exogeneity.

Before moving on to the testing of the exogeneity of the variables under the World Bank's control, we use the simple correlation and the partial correlation in the probit regression to eliminate the variables that seem to have no relationship with the probability of success: regional dummy variable for Africa, size of loan, expected duration of adjustment operation, and share of conditions related to financial policy, to sectoral policy, and to trade policy. The eliminated variables will be used as instruments for the test of endogeneity of the variables under the World Bank's control. The resulting model 5 shows the probit estimation results after the removal of the aforementioned variables. Of the remaining variables under the World Bank's control, preparation costs positively influence the probability of success, supervision costs and the share of macroeconomic and fiscal conditions are negatively correlated with the probability of success, and the effect of the number of legally binding conditions is statistically insignificant. Model 5 correctly predicts almost 77 percent of the observations.

The results of model 5 seem to suggest that some of the variables under the World Bank's control have significant influence on the probability of success of the adjustment operations. To verify that our model is correctly specified, we have to address the potential endogeneity of some of the explanatory variables under the World Bank's control. Smith and Blundell (1986) devise a simple exogeneity test for models with limited dependent variables. Under the null hypothesis of the test, the model (in this case model 5) is appropriately specified with all explanatory variables as exogenous. Under the alternative hypothesis, the suspected endogenous variables (in this case, preparation costs, supervision costs, the number of legally binding conditions, and the share of macroeconomic and fiscal conditions) are expressed as a linear combination of a set of instruments. The residuals from the first-stage regression are then included as additional explanatory variables in the model and, under the null hypothesis, they should have no explanatory power.

We use share of conditions related to financial policy, to sectoral policy, and to trade policy, size of loan, expected duration of adjustment operation, and regional dummy variables for Africa, East Asia, Europe and Central Asia, and Middle East and North Africa as instruments in the first stage. To be valid instruments, they should be correlated with the suspected endogenous variables (preparation costs, supervision costs, the number of legally binding conditions, and the share of macroeconomic and fiscal conditions) and uncorrelated with the dependent variable (OED's outcome rating). Consistent with this requirement, we do not find evidence that these instruments are correlated with the probability of the success of the reform—when included in model 5, the instrumental variable remains statistically insignificant, while the coefficients of the suspected exogenous variables remain largely unchanged.

The Smith-Blundell test statistic for exogeneity is 1.278. This chi-squared statistic with four degrees of freedom is not significant at any conventional level (p value of 0.865), so we cannot reject the null hypothesis on the basis of this test. In addition, we tested different subsets of the suspected endogenous variables and different subsets of the instruments used with different specifications of the model, and we could not reject the null hypothesis for any of our specifications. Thus, there is no evidence that the suspected variables are endogenous to the probability of success, and in the rest of the chapter we assume that preparation costs, supervision costs, the number of legally binding conditions, and the share of macroeconomic and fiscal conditions are exogenous.

A possible explanation of exogeneity of preparation and supervision costs is that these costs are likely to be budgeted in advance, and exogenous shocks do not have influence over the allocation of the World Bank's resources. Moreover, the share of macroeconomic and fiscal conditions is likely to depend on the nature of the policy problems in the borrowing country and the government's desire to attack particular problems, while the number of legally binding conditions is dependent on the scope of the operation and on the comfort of the World Bank with the implementation capacities of the borrowing government.

The end of the Cold War had major implications for the operations of the World Bank.[8] As illustrated in figure 13.1, the average quality of adjustment lending operations as measured by the OED's outcome ratings improved significantly after fiscal 1990. Therefore, we wanted to test whether there was a structural change in the quality of adjustment lending after the end of the Cold War or if this improved quality is a result of other factors.

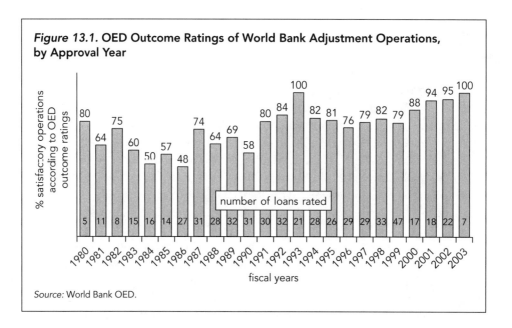

Figure 13.1. OED Outcome Ratings of World Bank Adjustment Operations, by Approval Year

Source: World Bank OED.

To be able to test the effect of the end of the Cold War we introduced a dummy variable with values equal to one for operations approved in fiscal 1991 or later and zero if otherwise. The inclusion of this dummy variable also enabled us to use the information related to the Cold War–era operations for the estimation of the model rather than simply using only post–Cold War data.

In addition, we introduced a dummy variable for agreement type (that is, indicating whether the operation originates from the International Bank for Reconstruction and Development or IDA) to account for differences in the probability of success between mid- and low-income countries. Model 6 reports the results after the introduction of these dummy variables.

In model 7, we drop several statistically insignificant variables from model 6: initial GDP per capita, initial population, and the number of legally binding conditions. As expected, the effect of the end of the Cold War on the probability of success of adjustment operations turns out to be significantly positive, whereas operations in the low-income countries tend to have lower probability of success, but this relationship is not significant. Model 7 correctly predicts more than 78 percent of the observations.

Conclusions

The relationship between the included political-economic variables and the probability of success of the reforms is stable throughout the analysis—democratically elected government and political stability increase the probability of success, the length of time that the incumbent has been in power has a negative effect on the probability of success, and both low and high degrees of ethnic fractionalization lower the probability of successful reform. These results confirm the findings of previous studies: there are institutional, economic, and political factors that affect the probability of success. The analysis also implies that policy-based lending tends to be less successful in Latin American countries and in low-income countries, but the statistical relationship is not significant.

The major conclusion of our analysis is, however, that in addition to political-economic variables there are variables under the World Bank's control that are significantly related to the probability of the success of adjustment operations. This conclusion implies that the World Bank is able to influence the probability of success of its policy-based lending operations not only by exercising heightened selectivity, but also through the design of an operation (for example, appropriate use of conditionality) and appropriate level of resources for preparation and supervision.

Our analysis shows that preparation costs are significantly related to the probability of success: more resources devoted to the preparation of an operation are associated with a higher probability of success. Higher preparation costs mean more time devoted to dialogue with the borrowing government and nongovernmental organizations to ensure better understanding of the country needs and country ownership as well as more careful design of the operations. Country ownership and better design in turn increase the probability of success. However, further studies should investigate which components of the preparation effort are the most important for the success of an operation.

Supervision costs are another variable under the World Bank's control with significant relation to the probability of success: more resources devoted to supervision of the implementation of an operation are associated with a lower probability of success. This does not, however, mean that by decreasing the resources devoted to supervision the World Bank can increase the probability of success, but rather that devoting more resources to the supervision of operations likely to fail does not help to achieve better results. The negative relationship between supervision costs and the probability of success implied by the data is probably the result of having more supervision resources assigned to risky operations in the past, and because these resources did not increase the probability of success, high supervision costs were associated with failed projects. To improve the likelihood of success, resources should be directed toward the preparation and design of operations.

The share of macroeconomic and fiscal conditions is determined by the focus of the operation, which is determined by the nature of the policy problems in the borrowing country and the government's desire to attack particular problems. Therefore, the operational implication of the negative relationship between this variable and the probability of success is that operations focusing mainly on macroeconomic and fiscal policy issues should be prepared more carefully.

According to our analysis, the number of legally binding conditions is not significant in determining the probability of success of the adjustment operations. In other words, we did not find any evidence that attaching more conditions to an adjustment operation would have any effect on the likelihood of success of the reform program. However, our analysis does not account for other important factors. In particular, as other internal studies have shown, the number of legally binding conditions is an important factor influencing the borrowing countries' nonfinancial costs associated with dealing with the World Bank.

Annex 13.1 Definition and Source of Variables

Variable	Definition and Source
Expected Duration of the Adjustment Operation	Expected duration of the adjustment operation from the approval date to the original closing date (in days) [*Source:* OED, World Bank]
Democratically Elected	Binary variable taking the value one if the chief executive was put in power by a democratic election prior to the reform; zero otherwise [*Source: Europa Yearbook*, various years]
Political Instability	Average number of governmental crises during the implementation of the operation [*Source:* Banks (1994)]
Time in Power	Number of years chief executive has been in power [*Source: Europa Yearbook*, various years]
Initial Population (log)	Initial population (log) [*Source: World Development Indicators (WDI)*]
Initial GDP per Capita (log)	Initial GDP per capita – log (US$ current, purchasing power parity) [*Source: WDI*]
Loan Size	World Bank loan amount in US$ millions [*Source:* OED, World Bank]
Loan Size (log)	Logarithm of World Bank loan amount in US$ [*Source:* OED, World Bank]
IDA Dummy Variable	Binary variable taking the value one if agreement type is IDA; zero if otherwise

Annex 13.1 (*Continued*)

Variable	Definition and Source
End of Cold War Dummy Variable	Binary variable taking the value one if the operation was approved after the beginning of fiscal 1991 (that is, June 30, 1990); zero if otherwise
Sub-Saharan Africa	Binary variable taking the value one for countries in Sub-Saharan Africa; zero if otherwise
Latin America and the Caribbean	Binary variable taking the value one for countries in Latin America and the Caribbean; zero if otherwise
East Asia	Binary variable taking the value one for countries in East Asia; zero if otherwise
Europe and Central Asia	Binary variable taking the value one for countries in Europe and Central Asia; zero if otherwise
Middle East and North Africa	Binary variable taking the value one for countries in the Middle East and North Africa; zero if otherwise
South Asia	Binary variable taking the value one for countries in South Asia; zero if otherwise
Preparation Costs	Preparation costs of the adjustment operation in US$ [*Source:* Business Warehouse (BW), World Bank]
Preparation Costs (log)	Logarithm of preparation costs of the adjustment operation in US$ [*Source:* BW, World Bank]
Supervision Costs	Supervision costs of the adjustment operation in US$ [*Source:* BW, World Bank]
Supervision Costs (log)	Logarithm of supervision costs of the adjustment operation in US$ [*Source:* BW, World Bank]
Overall Number of Conditions	Overall number of conditions [*Source:* ALCID, World Bank]
Number of Legally Binding Conditions	Number of legally binding conditions [*Source:* ALCID, World Bank]
Ethnolinguistic Fractionalization	Index of ethnolinguistic fractionalization, which measures the probability that two randomly selected people in a country belong to different ethnolinguistic groups [*Source:* Easterly & Levine (1997) and Beck, Levine, and Loayza (1997)]
Finance Conditions	Proportions of conditions related to financial policy out of total conditions [*Source:* ALCID, World Bank]
Macroeconomic and Fiscal Conditions	Proportions of conditions related to macroeconomic and fiscal policy out of total conditions [*Source:* ALCID, World Bank]
Sectoral Conditions	Proportions of conditions related to sectoral policy out of total conditions [*Source:* ALCID, World Bank]
Trade Conditions	Proportions of conditions related to trade policy out of total conditions [*Source:* ALCID, World Bank]
OED's Outcome Rating	OED evaluation on adjustment operations—binary variable taking the value one if the operation is rated moderately satisfactory or better; zero if otherwise. The OED bases its ratings of operation outcomes on assessments of whether the reform design was appropriate in terms of reducing poverty and fostering growth in the private sector, and to what extent stated policy goals have been met [*Source:* OED, World Bank]
Number of Legally Binding Conditions per Tranche	Number of legally binding conditions divided by the number of tranches [*Source:* ALCID and BW, World Bank]

Annex 13.2 Classification of Conditions

Starting in fiscal 2002 a new two-dimensional measurement and reporting system of World Bank activities was instituted to more accurately reflect the Bank's operational activities. For our purposes we include an analysis based on sectoral and thematic involvement of our adjustment operations. Sector classifications used in the Bank are based on the United Nations classification of economic activities with slight changes made to allow our system to better mirror the Bank's complex range of involvement. Themes were mainly developed to observe the development goals behind our involvement, and are most often used to track progress toward the Millennium Development Goals. We chose to group the conditions into areas (due to the classification to themes and sectors, not necessarily mutually exclusive) we were most interested in, namely: finance, macroeconomic and fiscal, sectoral, and trade. The areas were grouped as follows:

Finance: Banking Subsector; Capital Markets Subsector; Housing Finance and Real Estate Markets Subsector; Noncompulsory Health Finance Subsector; Noncompulsory Pensions, Insurance and Contractual Savings Subsector; Micro- and Small and Medium Enterprise Finance Subsector; Payment Systems, Securities Clearance and Settlement Subsector; and General Finance Subsector.

Macroeconomic and fiscal: Analysis of Economic Growth Subtheme; Debt Management and Fiscal Sustainability Subtheme; Economic Statistics, Modeling and Forecasting Subtheme; Macroeconomic Management Subtheme; Other Economic Management Subtheme; Public Expenditure, Financial Management and Procurement Subtheme; and Other Accountability/Anticorruption Subtheme.

Sectoral: Agriculture, Fishing and Forestry Sector Group; Information and Communications Sector Group; Education Sector Group; Health and Other Social Services Sector Group; Industry and Trade Sector Group; Energy and Mining Sector Group; Transportation Sector Group; and Water, Sanitation and Flood Protection Sector Group.

Trade: Export Development and Competitiveness Subtheme; International Financial Architecture Subtheme; Regional Integration Subtheme; Technology Diffusion Subtheme; Trade Facilitation and Market Access Subtheme; and Other Trade and Integration Subtheme.

Endnotes

1. We thank Stefan G. Koeberle, Harold L. Bedoya, Bruce Fitzgerald, Jaime Jaramillo, Saloua Sehili, Vlad Manole, Jan Walliser, and Henry Chase for support, comments, and suggestions.
2. On the basis of the fact that an exogenous shock that reduces the probability of success is likely to influence the World Bank's allocation of resources, Dollar and Svensson (2000) assume that these variables are endogenous. However, they did not test whether the data support their assumption.
3. The number of observations for our regressions varied around 400 owing to missing data for individual variables. The exact number of observations for each regression is reported with the regression results.

4. Conditions listed in the legal agreement signed by the borrowing government and the World Bank. Types of conditions include prior actions (fulfilled before the time of approval of single-tranche operations) and legal conditions of effectiveness (prior or future actions linked to release of individual tranches, regular or floating, of multitranche operations). As defined, legally binding conditions do not include desired actions or triggers.

5. Actions, excluding triggers used only in programmatic loans, listed in the loan documentation but not included in the legal agreement. Client government compliance with these actions is not tied to the release of funds.

6. The definitions of each classification are available in annex 12.2. Broadly, sectoral conditions are composed of those that have economic sector involvement in agriculture, fishing and forestry, information and communications, education, health and other social services, industry and trade, energy and mining, transportation, or water, sanitation and flood protection sector groups. Finance conditions are those classified with any subsectors under the finance sector group. Macroeconomic and fiscal conditions are those coded with an economic management theme or specific subthemes under the public sector governance theme group. Trade policy conditions are those coded under a trade and integration theme.

7. The definitions of each classification are available in annex 12.2. Broadly, financial policy conditions are those classified with any subsectors under the finance sector group. Macroeconomic and fiscal conditions are those coded with an economic management theme or specific subthemes under the public sector governance theme group. Sectoral policy conditions are composed of those that have economic sector involvement in agriculture, fishing and forestry, information and communications, education, health and other social services, industry and trade, energy and mining, transportation, or water, sanitation and flood protection sector groups. Trade policy conditions are those coded under a trade and integration theme.

8. A number of countries from the former communist block became members of the World Bank, and all these countries experienced a period of large structural changes, which accompanied their political and economic transformation. The World Bank played a critical role in supporting these changes. Furthermore, the political pressure on the lending process weakened after the breakdown of the Soviet Union.

Bibliography

Banks, A. S. 2001. Cross-National Time-Series Data Archive.

Beck, T., R. Levine, and N. Loayza. 1999. "Finance and the Sources of Growth." *Journal of Financial Economics*.

Dollar, D., and J. Svensson. 2000. "What Explains the Success or Failure of Structural Adjustment Programs?" *The Economic Journal* 110 (October): 894–917.

Easterly, W., and R. Levine. 1997. "Africa's Growth Tragedy: Policies and Ethnic Divisions." *Quarterly Journal of Economics* 112: 1203–50.

Europa Yearbook: A World Survey. London: Europa Publications, various issues.

Ranis, G. 1995. "On Fast Disbursing Loans Policy-Based Loans." Photocopy, Economics Department, Yale University, New Haven, CT.

Smith, and Blundell. 1986. "An Exogeneity Test for the Simultaneous Equation Tobit Model." *Econometrica* 54: 679–85.

World Bank. *World Development Indicators* (*WDI*) database, Adjustment Lending Conditionality and Implementation (ALCID) database, and Business Warehouse (BW) database.

14

The Growth Experience: What Have We Learned from the 1990s?

BACKGROUND NOTE
World Bank Poverty Reduction and Economic Management

The World Bank is just completing a major review titled "Lessons from the Growth Experience of the 1990s," including the growth impact of the main policy and institutional reforms introduced in the 1990s. The review takes a broad perspective on the events, country experiences, academic research, and controversies of the 1990s, to reflect on how they alter our thinking about economic growth. Its conclusions benefit from contributions by Bank and non-Bank "practitioners in development"—a revival of the lectures by "pioneers in development" in the early 1980s. Twelve policy makers, who were at the forefront of policy implementation in the 1990s, have used their experience to draw lessons about economic growth during a one-year cycle of lectures at the Bank. Twelve former Bank country directors have similarly shared the lessons they drew from their work at the Bank in a series of papers to be published separately. The report also benefited from the outcomes of the May 2004 Shanghai Conference. (For information on the proceedings of this conference as well as access to the discussions and case studies, please visit: http://www.worldbank.org/wbi/reducingpoverty/) This chapter describes briefly the scope and findings of this work, which has relevance for the discussions on the approach to and content of conditionality.

An Understanding of What Causes and Sustains Growth

An institution whose primary business is finance and advice for poverty reduction needs to have a good understanding of what causes growth and what sustains it. Poverty declines rapidly where growth is rapid and sustained. Poverty stagnates where growth is tepid. A few exceptions notwithstanding, the unambiguous impact of rapid growth on poverty reduction was confirmed again in the 1990s and was a central theme of the May 2004 Shanghai Conference.

Economics is an imprecise science, and the nature of economic growth has changed over the course of history. It is hence no surprise that our understanding of growth is partial and incomplete. The growth experience of the past 50 years has abundant examples of economists' inability to anticipate *successes*, such as Botswana, China, India, Indonesia, the Republic of Korea, Mauritius, Singapore, and Thailand; economists' and markets' inability to predict *crises*, such as the financial crises of the 1990s; and *disappointments*, such as the unfulfilled growth potential of Latin American and African countries in the past two decades. Growth is difficult to predict because it implies transformation of society, a break with past trends, behaviors, and institutions that reflect deep forces in societies and how they organize themselves.

Absent definitive theories, our views on growth have been influenced by facts and have changed pragmatically in the face of experience. The successful reconstruction of Europe and Japan, and the financial turmoil that preceded World War II, gave reason to believe in the 1960s and 1970s that governments could address market failures effectively, be a positive force for growth, and accelerate capital accumulation, as the main force driving economic growth. However, starting in the 1980s, the costs of industrialization policies based on import substitution and extensive state interventions in the economy led to greater recognition that the costs of government failures could be larger than those of market failures. The focus of growth strategies hence shifted from policies aimed at expanding productive capacity and accelerating the accumulation of capital to policies improving efficiency in the use of existing capacity.

The Promise of Economic Reforms

We approached the 1990s with the shared conviction that economic reforms would not only reverse what for many developing countries had been the "lost decade" of the 1980s, but would also bring about the conditions for sustained growth. Best captured in the "Washington Consensus" and the 1991 *World Development Report,* macroeconomic stability, domestic liberalization, openness to international trade, and reducing the role of the state became the principles that guided economic policies in the 1990s in former communist countries in Eastern Europe and Central Asia, in Latin America, in South and East Asia, in Africa and, although to a much lesser extent, in the Middle East and North Africa. In parallel, democratization of former communist countries and the consolidation of democracy in Latin America, Africa, and some East Asian countries gave ground to optimism that free markets and free societies provided the basis for rapid and sustained growth.

The results were unexpected—they exceeded the most optimistic forecasts in some cases and fell well short of expectations in others. Although implemented in a manner that departed from conventional wisdom—in terms of speed and manner of reform, large presence of the state, and, until very recently, high levels of import protection—domestic liberalization and outward orientation were associated with spectacular successes in East and South Asia in terms of growth, poverty reduction, and social progress. At the same time, booms and busts continued in Latin America and extended to East Asia and other regions as well. There were sharp declines followed by a prolonged and as yet incomplete recovery in former communist countries;

a second decade of stagnation in Africa; and costly and frequent financial crises: Mexico in 1994, East Asia in 1997, Brazil and the Russian Federation in 1998, Turkey in 2000, and Argentina in 2002.

The report confirms and builds on the conclusions of an earlier Bank report: the 1993 "East Asia Miracle," which reviewed experiences of highly successful East Asian economies. It confirms the importance of fundamental principles for growth: macrostability, market forces in the allocation of resources, and openness. At the same time, it echoes the finding that these principles translate into diverse policy and institutional paths, implying that economic policies and policy advice must be country specific if they are to be effective. Valid general principles do not imply generic "best practice" policy or institutional solutions. It also echoes the finding that selective government interventions can contribute to growth when they address market failures, are carried out effectively, and are subject to institutional checks.

The Impact of Key Policy and Institutional Reforms

More specifically, the report examines the impact on growth of key policy and institutional reforms: macroeconomic stabilization, trade liberalization, deregulation of finance, privatization, deregulation of utilities, modernization of the public sector with a view to increasing its effectiveness and accountability, and the spread of democracy and decentralization. It draws lessons both from a policy and institutional perspective and from the perspective of country experiences about how reforms in each policy and institutional area have affected growth. Regarding macroeconomic policies, for example, the report stresses the importance of the institutions underlying macroeconomic stabilization, the risks associated with external financial liberalization, the disruptions associated with episodes of exchange rate appreciation, and the sometimes excessive focus on minimizing inflation in the short term, which then came at the cost of growth-enhancing public spending that might have both increased growth and made stability more durable. Regarding trade, it highlights the fact that countries that have successfully integrated into the world economy have followed different approaches and also adopted a range of complementary policies, which makes it difficult to pin down the exact relationship between trade integration and growth—but establishes a strong positive relationship while not making it clear whether openness is the cause of or result from rising incomes. Unambiguously, however, all successful countries (for example, India and China) benefited considerably from integration in the world economy and access to external markets. Across policy reform experiences in different areas common themes also emerge regarding the importance of institutions, to which, for example, the chapter on finance attributes the main reason for results below expectations, and for effective checks on predatory behavior by the state and by the private sector. These are all important in explaining the outcomes of privatization, the performance of the public sector in the delivery of services, and the quality of the investment climate.

In addition to the impact of specific policies on growth, the report also draws lessons about growth considering the entire spectrum of policies and institutional reforms. It concludes that the emphasis of the 1990s on reforms improving efficiency in the use of existing capacity, while warranted at a time of extremely large distortions, did not balance it with sufficient focus on the forces driving expansion of that capacity. Whereas efficiency gains can bring about short-term growth, sustained long-term growth can only be achieved through expansion of capacity: accumulation of physical and human capital and technology improvements. This highlights the importance of the investment climate and of the confidence with which economic agents can forecast returns in the future.

The Lesson of Lessons

More important, perhaps the lesson of lessons of the 1990s is that we need to *get away from formulae* and realize that economic policies need to address the *binding constraint* to growth, instead of any constraint, at the right time, and in the right manner. This requires recognizing *country specificities,* and also requires more *economic and social analysis and rigor* than a formula-based approach to policy making. So, while recognition that there is no unique path to growth that can be known in advance introduces more flexibility and options, it also demands more rigor in the evaluation of these options than is the case in the application of formulae.

While they confirm the importance of market incentives for resource allocation, of openness, and of macrostability, the lessons drawn in this report highlight the diverse ways in which these principles can translate into concrete policy choices. They also echo Albert Hirschman's view that "development depends not so much on finding optimal combinations for given resources and factors of production as on calling forth and enlisting for development purposes resources and abilities that are hidden, scattered, or badly utilized." The lessons have implications for the understanding and practice of economic policies and advice and, in particular, for the Bank's analytical, strategic, and operational work, including for the formulation of growth strategies focused on relaxing the most binding constraints instead of making all policies "*best practice.*" The lessons also imply the need to temper technical expertise with humility and flexibility. And last but not least the lessons highlight the need for a better understanding of noneconomic factors, such as history, culture, and politics, in growth processes.

Bibliography

World Bank. 2001. *World Development Indicators.* Washington, DC.

15

Unsuccessful Adjustment Operations: Common Factors and Lessons Learned

SALOUA SEHILI[1]
World Bank

This chapter reflects on the World Bank's experience to present the most commonly occurring factors that have contributed to unsatisfactory reform outcomes of adjustment operations and the lessons learned from experience. The review draws mainly on country assistance evaluations and on project performance assessment reports undertaken by the Operations Evaluation Department (OED), primarily for countries with a high number of unsuccessful adjustment operations. It finds that, on the country side, the most common factors are lack of ownership and inadequate institutional quality (including corruption, limited absorptive capacity, and other institutional vulnerabilities such as weak financial systems, weak fiscal capacity and discipline, and rigidities and other weaknesses that increase the country's vulnerability to natural and exogenous economic shocks). On the Bank side, the common factors are inadequate assessment of ownership, and of the nature and quality of institutions (sometimes resulting from or leading to overly optimistic Bank assessments), which result in project design flaws such as weak conditionality, an insufficient implementation time frame, and poor tranching.

Case studies as well as econometric approaches to the analysis of policy-based lending performance have highlighted its sensitivity to sociopolitical as well as economic factors, and have provided some evidence for the effect of Bank effort (particularly with respect to project design and supervision inputs) on such performance.[2] Country ownership of the reform program—including the role of various stakeholders in such ownership, political instability, ethnic fractionalization, and the electoral process—and the nature and quality of country institutions and their capacity to implement reforms, have been found to affect the performance of policy-based lending.[3] These complex and dynamic sociopolitical and economic factors are difficult to measure, predict, or hedge against with a high degree of accuracy.[4] The success of reforms is also subject to the vagaries of natural or exogenous economic shocks, which have been known to bring reform programs to a halt. For example, the past decade has seen several financial crises: Mexico in 1994–5; Indonesia, the Republic of Korea, Malaysia, and Thailand in 1997–8; Brazil and the Russian Federation in 1998; Turkey in 2000; and Argentina in 2001–2. Significantly, however, crises can also give the impetus for new reforms: recent evidence suggests that a large number of good reformers during 1999–2003 were crisis and transition economies (World Bank 2004a).

Demographics of Unsuccessful Adjustment Operations

During fiscal 1980–2003, the Board approved 643 adjustment operations in 112 countries. Of these operations, 557 were rated by the OED,[5] of which 136 (24 percent) were rated as having marginally unsatisfactory, unsatisfactory, or highly unsatisfactory outcomes.[6] Significantly, almost two-thirds of these unsatisfactory loans were approved during fiscal 1980–90 (see figure 15.1).[7] The average unsuccessful loan amount was $180 million, ranging between $3 million and $2.5 billion. About 50 percent of the unsuccessful loans amounted to less than $100 million (see figure 15.2).

Regional Distribution

Figure 15.3 depicts the regional distribution of unsatisfactory adjustment operations: the Africa Region bore the brunt of unsatisfactory adjustment loans at 49 percent,

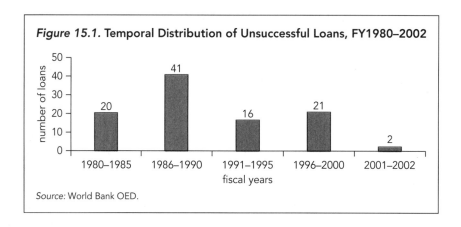

Figure 15.1. Temporal Distribution of Unsuccessful Loans, FY1980–2002

Source: World Bank OED.

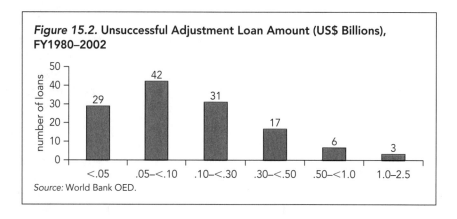

Figure 15.2. Unsuccessful Adjustment Loan Amount (US$ Billions), FY1980–2002

Source: World Bank OED.

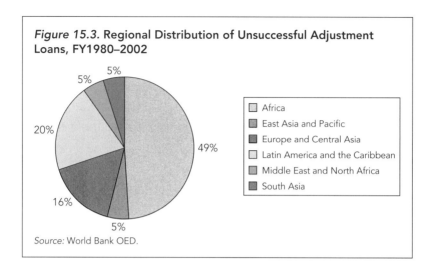

Figure 15.3. Regional Distribution of Unsuccessful Adjustment Loans, FY1980–2002

- Africa
- East Asia and Pacific
- Europe and Central Asia
- Latin America and the Caribbean
- Middle East and North Africa
- South Asia

Source: World Bank OED.

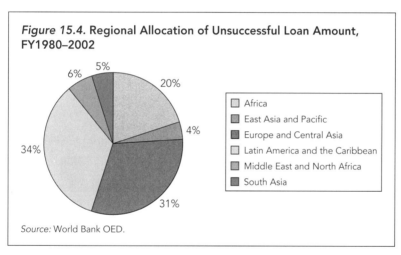

Figure 15.4. Regional Allocation of Unsuccessful Loan Amount, FY1980–2002

- Africa
- East Asia and Pacific
- Europe and Central Asia
- Latin America and the Caribbean
- Middle East and North Africa
- South Asia

Source: World Bank OED.

followed by the Latin America and Caribbean Region at 20 percent,[8] and Europe and Central Asia at 16 percent. When weighted by loan amounts, Latin America and the Caribbean and Europe and Central Asia take the lead at about one-third each, with Africa bearing one-fifth (see figure 15.4). Unsatisfactory loans were spread over 65 countries, with Argentina having the highest number (6), followed by Bangladesh (5), Burundi, Jamaica, Niger, Russia, Togo, Turkey, and Uganda (4) (see Annex 15.2). When weighted by loan amount, Argentina bears 17 percent, followed by Russia at 16 percent, and Turkey at 6 percent. Bangladesh accounts for only 4 percent, Uganda just over 1 percent, and Burundi, Jamaica, Niger, and Togo less than 1 percent.

Country Conditions

Country Performance and Institutional Assessment (CPIA) ratings began in fiscal 1996 and are available through fiscal 2002. During these years, 83 percent of the unsuccessful loans were extended to countries with a CPIA rating of better than 3.0 (that is, relatively favorable country conditions), with the highest proportion (56 percent) extended to countries with CPIA ratings of better than 3.5 (see figure 15.5). Notwithstanding this, the correlation between successful adjustment lending and CPIA is positive, indicating that successful adjustment lending tended to be extended to countries with good or improving policies. The figures cited simply underscore that a high CPIA rating is not a sufficient condition for successful adjustment lending.

Tranching and Conditionality

During fiscal 1992–2002, most unsatisfactory adjustment loans had four to five tranches (60 percent), while a third had two to three tranches (see figure 15.6). Seven percent were single-tranche operations. Thirty percent of the unsatisfactory loans had 1–15 conditions per tranche, while 56 percent had 16–44 conditions per tranche (see figure 15.7). Furthermore, the average number of conditions per tranche increases with the CPIA rating (see figure 15.8).[9]

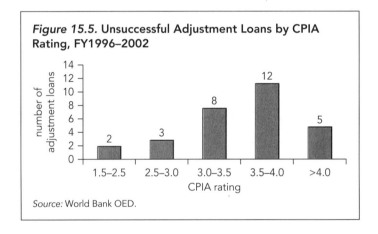

Figure 15.5. Unsuccessful Adjustment Loans by CPIA Rating, FY1996–2002

Source: World Bank OED.

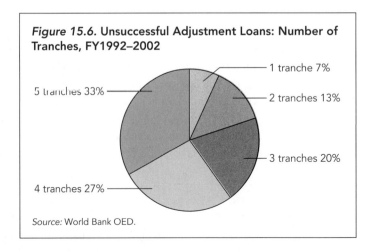

Figure 15.6. Unsuccessful Adjustment Loans: Number of Tranches, FY1992–2002

1 tranche 7%
2 tranches 13%
3 tranches 20%
4 tranches 27%
5 tranches 33%

Source: World Bank OED.

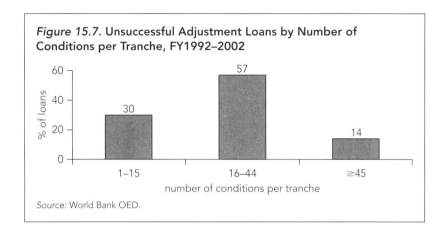

Figure 15.7. Unsuccessful Adjustment Loans by Number of Conditions per Tranche, FY1992–2002

Source: World Bank OED.

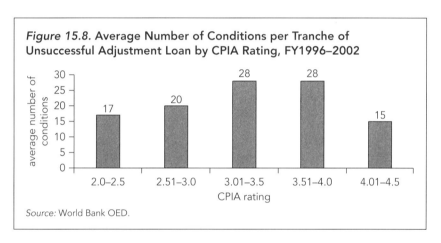

Figure 15.8. Average Number of Conditions per Tranche of Unsuccessful Adjustment Loan by CPIA Rating, FY1996–2002

Source: World Bank OED.

During fiscal 1980–2002, conditionality focused primarily on finance, industry and trade, and law and justice and public administration, averaging six to eight conditions per loan in each of these sectors (see figure 15.9). At least during the 1990s, trade and financial liberalization and privatization—two of the areas emphasized by the conditionality of unsuccessful adjustment operations—were not effective in promoting growth, in part because of a failure to ensure sound institutional underpinnings, good sequencing, or appropriate speed for the reforms (World Bank 2004b). For example, lack of transparency and competitiveness during the privatization process often led to capital capture by the elite. In the case of Argentina, there was lack of institutional development in the sense that the government's hands were tied through the Currency Board, which in turn increased the country's vulnerability to exogenous shocks. The lessons from China's success in achieving rapid growth, in spite of its deviation from the usual formulae for reform, and of Bolivia's lack of success, in spite of the fact that it applied all the reform formulae during the 1990s, further strengthen the message that reforms need to be tailored to country circumstances (World Bank 2004b).

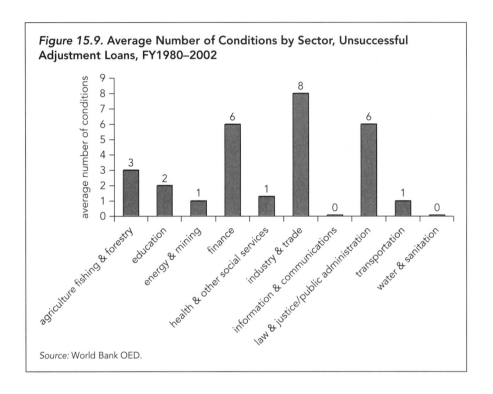

Figure 15.9. Average Number of Conditions by Sector, Unsuccessful Adjustment Loans, FY1980–2002

Source: World Bank OED.

Country and External Factors

Lack of ownership and inadequate institutional quality—including corruption, limited absorptive capacity, weak financial systems, weak fiscal capacity and discipline, and rigidities and other weaknesses that increase the country's vulnerability to natural and exogenous economic shocks—are the most frequently cited factors in unsuccessful adjustment operations.

Ownership

The Bank has defined ownership along four dimensions, so that it is more or less indirectly observable through a process that would signal ownership: "the locus of initiative of the reform program must be in the government; key policy makers must be convinced of the reform program; there must be support from the top political leadership; and there must be broad-based stakeholder participation, i.e., significant effort towards consensus-building." Ownership of reforms thus depends on the dynamic interplay of various actors (not all of whom are from the government) who seek to maximize their own objectives. These objectives may or may not be aligned with the welfare of the country or of the international community; these congeries of interest make ownership one of the most difficult factors to assess ex ante.[10]

Weak ownership. This review found that lack of borrower ownership of, and commitment to, the reform program was the most common and most important factor cited as having contributed to the failure of adjustment operations. An earlier review of a sample of unsatisfactory adjustment projects also found that weak borrower commitment was cited as a failure factor in 88 percent of the reviewed projects (World Bank 2002a). Lack of ownership can be on the part of the government, or it can be the consequence of dissent between different levels of government (as was the case, for example, in unsuccessful adjustment operations in Bangladesh, Jamaica, Niger, and Russia). For instance, during the transition, Russia witnessed a period of frequent turnover of senior-level government officials, which made it difficult to achieve and sustain consensus within the government on reforms. Furthermore, those who favored the proposed reforms were located mainly in core economic ministries and could not convince those in some line ministries (for example, energy and agriculture) to support the reforms (World Bank 2002b). In Zambia, the chief executive alone could place reforms into effect (these have been dubbed "stroke-of-the pen" reforms), and though this form of ownership was sufficient in the case of price, interest rate, and exchange rate liberalization, such was not the case with privatization and civil service reform, which were opposed by interest groups whose buy-in was not secured (World Bank 2002c). Dissent by special interest groups also undermined privatization, labor, and civil service reforms in Bangladesh, Georgia, and Niger. During the early 1990s in Ecuador, "core reformers" were derailed by opposition from the legislature and major stakeholders, a risk that the Bank was faulted for ignoring, given its knowledge of Ecuador's political instability and resistance to reform (World Bank 1999a). Even when the reforms are owned by the government, lack of support by the voters can adversely impact the reform programs (for example, in Argentina, Russia). Political instability can also have a negative impact on reform ownership as in the case of Bangladesh and Georgia, and in Niger, where fragmented political power rendered a willing government unable to implement reforms. This was further exacerbated by the high turnover of policy officials. Ownership of reforms can also be undermined by internal political conflict as was the case in Guinea, Niger, and the Philippines.

Bank shortcomings. Often, the Bank culpably failed to recognize the lack of ownership: for example, in Bangladesh, Jamaica, and Niger there was a clear absence of government communication with various stakeholders such as unions and student organizations, and hence a clear lack of consensus building for reforms (World Bank 1990b, 1998a, 1998b, 2003a). Although it is not always possible to accurately assess ownership ex ante, once a lack of commitment became apparent, as in Niger, the Bank was faulted for not having downsized its lending program until consensus for the reforms was secured (World Bank 2003a). In Russia, the dynamics were different: in 1997, although the lack of Russian commitment to the reforms supported by the Bank was unmistakable, the Bank was under intense international pressure to lend to Russia, and did so, hoping that financial support would ensure country ownership. This behavior, however, had a perverse disincentive effect, because the Russians inferred that international financing would be sustained in spite of poor reform implementation (World Bank 2002b). At the opposite end of the spectrum, during the 1990s under the Salinas administration, Mexican officials exhibited such strong ownership for reforms that discussions with the Bank revolved around timing and technical issues, rather than broad economic goals. This allowed the Bank to be flexible in terms of which policy actions would be included as explicit conditions and which would be left as implicit agreements; this in turn allowed the government to choose conditions that would not generate political opposition (World Bank 2001e).

Institutions

The nature and quality of institutions was the second most commonly cited factor as having undermined reform progress. Institutions have been defined as the formal and informal rules and norms that govern personal, socioeconomic, and political behavior, such that adherence to these rules and norms provides the predictability needed for societies to function, and helps solve problems such as agency and collective decision-making problems (World Bank 2004b). Recent evidence suggests that sound institutions are crucial for sustainable development, and that the reform efforts to date have overly focused on policy at the expense of the development of institutions (Rodrick 2003; World Bank 2004b). Institutional weaknesses have taken the form of corruption and inadequacies in the financial, corporate, and public sectors that have contributed to limited absorptive capacity, limited supply response, and increased vulnerability to internal and exogenous shocks. To at least some extent, when institutional weaknesses are recognized as having contributed to the failure of adjustment operations, it should also be recognized that the design of the operation was inadequate in tailoring the assistance to the country's circumstances.

Corruption. Corruption hindered reform implementation in many borrowing countries, including Argentina, Bangladesh, Côte d'Ivoire, and Guinea, where allegations of corruption in Bank projects also surfaced (World Bank 1990b, 1996, 1998a, 1999b, 2000a, 2003b). In Azerbaijan, corruption had a pervasive effect on the business climate and even hindered the operations of the International Finance Corporation (World Bank 2000b). Similarly, in Russia during the 1990s, corruption was cited as one of the factors that discouraged enterprise development and foreign direct investment and hindered activities by the International Finance Corporation and the Multilateral Investment Guarantee Agency (World Bank 2002b). In Argentina, the emergence of corruption scandals during the 1990s had an adverse impact on the impetus for reform (World Bank 1996, 2000a). In Uganda, corruption was proclaimed as one of the main risks to growth and poverty reduction because it was endemic in the public sector, interfering with the effective implementation of donor-assisted reforms and investment projects and adversely affecting the investment climate (World Bank 2001d). Ghana was also characterized as having widespread small-scale corruption in the public sector, which highlighted the need for civil service reform (World Bank 2000c). In Kenya, after the death of President Kenyatta in 1978, corruption pervaded the public sector as it became part of a patronage system in support of the ruling political party. The country ranked as one of the highest on the corruption perception index, and allegations of corruption in Bank-financed projects surfaced (World Bank 2000d). And corruption and cronyism in Indonesia during the Asian crisis were partly blamed for the sluggish progress in policy reform (World Bank 2003c).

Bank efforts in corruption. In several cases, the Bank has been faulted for failing in its assistance strategy to acknowledge and address corruption. In Russia and Uganda, for example, reduction of corruption did not become part of the Bank's assistance strategy until 1999 (World Bank 2001d, 2002b). In Côte d'Ivoire, the Bank was faulted for having extended broad support to the government without an adequate dialogue on the issue of corruption (World Bank 1999b). A recent review of the Bank's anticorruption initiatives has found that, notwithstanding a significant improvement in the relevance of Bank activities to address corruption in borrower countries, success has been limited because of the novelty and sociopolitical complexity of this dimension of governance (World Bank 2004a).

Institutional capacity. Failing to account for, and address, inadequate capacity has undermined Bank efforts across all Regions, though notably more often in the 1980s than at present.

- In Bangladesh, during the 1980s, reform delays were attributed to administrative weaknesses, further exacerbated by political events and frequent changes of top government and agency administrators. Macroeconomic, industry, trade, finance, and agriculture policy reforms were less than satisfactory in promoting sustainable growth. In part, this was attributed to deep-seated institutional and cultural characteristics that hindered the development of an institutional framework that could effectively design and implement appropriate policies. The Bank was faulted for being overoptimistic, having overestimated the country's institutional and delivery capacity, and for failing to place sufficient emphasis on medium-term institutional capacity building (World Bank 1990b).

- The Bank extended three structural adjustment loans to Jamaica during the early 1980s, raising the Bank's per capita commitments in Jamaica to the highest in the Latin America and Caribbean Region. This taxed the country's institutional capacity and burdened Jamaica with heavy debt. Furthermore, lack of supply response to the attempted reforms, rising unemployment, and deteriorating living standards undermined what support there was for the reforms (World Bank 1998b).

- In Ecuador and Malawi during the 1990s, systemic weaknesses in public, corporate, and financial institutions were cited as having contributed to a sluggish pace of reforms. Given the poor policy environment and systemic lack of institutional capacity in Malawi, the Bank was faulted for relying too much on supply responses and on traditional capacity-building measures (World Bank 1999a, 2000e).

- Similarly, the sluggish pace of Russia's transition (as well as that of other transitional economies) was partly attributed to weak institutional capacity (a legacy of the command economy) and to a low degree of trust in state institutions, which resulted in limited ownership of reforms by Russian citizens (World Bank 2002b).

Exogenous shocks. Institutional weaknesses can increase the vulnerability of an economy to exogenous shocks, which in turn can undermine reforms.

- During the 1990s Argentina was extremely vulnerable to exogenous shocks because of a weak banking system with a large number of insolvent banks, a large fiscal deficit, a lack of fiscal discipline in the provinces, and a high rate of unemployment, which resulted from the downward rigidity of nominal wages. All of this was exacerbated by the country's rigid real exchange rate (Currency Board System), which could not accommodate external shocks, such as the 1995 crisis. The devastating effects of the crisis undermined domestic confidence in the stabilization plan, which led to its demise. Although the government was later able to reduce the vulnerability of the financial system, labor reform to introduce flexibility in the labor market met with political opposition (World Bank 1996, 2000a).

- The devastating effects of the Asian financial crisis on Indonesia were largely attributed to the country's vulnerable banking system and volatile capital flows (World Bank 2003c).

- Besides the effects of limited institutional capacity as highlighted above, the sluggish pace of reform in Bangladesh during the 1980s was also attributed to the country's vulnerability to devastating natural calamities, the second oil price shock, and the international recession, which led to a sharp deterioration in the country's terms of trade, while external aid also declined (World Bank 1990b, 1998a).

- During the same period, the Philippines under the Marcos administration attempted to liberalize trade and the financial sector and promote export and investment incentives. The reforms, however, were hindered by the same adverse external environment, corruption, and political instability (World Bank 1999c).

- In the early 1990s in Malawi, the reform agenda was derailed in large part because of two severe droughts and deteriorating terms of trade for major exports (tobacco and maize), exacerbated by a lack of fiscal and monetary discipline (World Bank 2000e).

- Similarly, Russia's stabilization and adjustment reforms collapsed in 1998, in large part because of low world prices for its exports, especially oil, and a fixed exchange rate, which in turn led to increased external borrowing and heavy debt. Ripple effects from the 1997 East Asia financial crisis further exacerbated the situation by undermining investor confidence (World Bank 2002b).

Crisis and reform. Crises can undermine and derail a reform program, but they can also provide the impetus for reforms because they highlight the need for new measures to address the dire situation. For example, in response to the economic crisis caused by the second oil shock in the early 1980s, Turkey harnessed support for a new development strategy, pursued stabilization and then a successful structural adjustment program, and then initiated reforms in finance, trade, energy, and agriculture (World Bank 1993). During the 1990s, some 21 countries undertook reforms after they were hit by financial crises, natural disasters, or political conflicts, and 13 of them experienced increases in their CPIA over the subsequent four years (World Bank 2004a). Russia is another notable case. After disappointing progress in implementing various reform programs during the early 1990s, the years following the 1998 crisis saw significant progress in fiscal adjustment, incentive regime, legislation of structural reforms, and the strengthening of public institutions, all of which restored Russian trust in government institutions (World Bank 2002b).

   Fiscal capacity. Weak fiscal capacity or discipline is another factor commonly cited as significantly undermining a country's effort to reform, because it leads to severe macroeconomic instability. When combined with external shocks, it produces devastating effects on the economy. For example, in Argentina, President Alfonsin's Plan Austral and two subsequent stabilization plans were largely unsuccessful owing to the large public sector deficit which, in 1989, resulted in a severe bout of hyperinflation (World Bank 1996). During the 1980s, Ghana undertook deep exchange rate and trade reforms and removed price and distribution controls. The fiscal situation was rationalized, inflation and poverty were reduced, and growth rates and social indicators had improved by the early 1990s. However, in 1992, in spite of ample support from the Bank, the IMF, and other donors, Ghana experienced large fiscal deficits that continued through most of the decade, exacerbated by fiscal excess during election years. This resulted in high government borrowing, high rates of broad money growth, and high inflation. Increased government competition for savings led to periodic negative real interest rates and increased interest rate volatility. This, compounded with governance weaknesses and corruption, inhibited private investment and growth. The lack of fiscal discipline was ascribed to a lack of government ownership and commitment to achieving macroeconomic targets. Subsequently, in 1996 and early 1997, the Bank and the IMF interrupted their support (World Bank 2000c). In the case of Russia, inadequate fiscal adjustment combined with external shocks to bring the stabilization and structural adjustment program to a halt in 1998. Subsequently, Russia defaulted on its debt, floated the ruble (which depreciated by more than 60 percent), and saw its output drop by more than 5 percent (World Bank 2002b).

Bank Factors

Bank inputs in terms of economic and sector work (ESW), policy dialogue, project design, and supervision can also affect the outcome of policy-based lending. For example, an earlier review of a sample of unsatisfactory adjustment projects found that weaknesses in project design (such as overoptimism in terms of the scope and complexity of objectives or the time frame) were cited as a factor in all the reviewed projects (World Bank 2002a).

Economic and Sector Work

The factor under the Bank's control that has most often contributed, directly or indirectly, to unsuccessful adjustment operations is poor ESW. Especially when undertaken with participation of domestic talent, ESW helps identify and appropriately address important determinants of ownership, such as the various constituencies and stakeholders and how they might be affected by the proposed reforms.[11] ESW promotes better understanding of institutions and their implementation capacity and better building and strengthening of institutions (see box 15.1). Understanding the particular and specific workings of the economy in question is a prerequisite to fitting the reforms to country circumstances, identifying the binding constraints that guide selectivity and sequencing, and designing reforms that spur and sustain growth and reduce poverty (World Bank 2004b). Rigorous analysis increases the Bank's knowledge and understanding of the recipient country, which in turn helps tailor reform design to country circumstances.[12] Thus, it can be argued that where lack of ownership contributed to the failure of reforms, so did weak ESW. Where the Bank was overly optimistic in terms of the implementation capacity of the recipient country, there was a lack of appropriate ESW.

- An extreme example of lack of appropriate ESW occurred in the case of adjustment lending to Guinea during the 1990s for public sector, financial, and public enterprise reforms, when the only economic report issued was the 1990 Country Economic Memorandum (World Bank 2003b).

- In the case of adjustment lending to Bangladesh during the 1980s, it was argued that while the Bank did well in identifying the areas for reform, its reform proposals emphasized efficiency and did not pay sufficient attention to equity aspects, ignoring the different behaviors and conditions of the various socioeconomic groups, which in turn undermined support for the reforms. This was the direct consequence of weak analysis, which failed to account for the cultural and socioeconomic dynamics of Bangladesh (World Bank 1990b, 1998a).

- Potential crises can also be anticipated or mitigated with appropriate prior analysis; in the cases of Georgia and Russia better knowledge by the Bank might have placed it in a better position to mitigate the effects of crisis.

Poor program design. The lack of appropriate ESW and appropriate engagement[13] also underpin design flaws, such as broad loan objectives and a large number of conditions relative to government capacity (for example, Niger, at a time of high political instability), irrelevant loan objectives (Georgia, where endemic corruption and the need for poverty alleviation were ignored), unrealistic expectations about the length of time reforms would take (Kyrgyz Republic, Russia), and general overoptimism (Argentina, Bangladesh). Overoptimism tends to lead to inadequately rigorous analysis of economic and political risks and to insufficient attention being given to governance issues, as was the case in the Kyrgyz Republic during the 1990s. The Bank had unrealistic expectations in terms of the economy's response to structural changes and underestimated the effects of corruption, social and ethnic discord, drug trafficking, and the country's dependence on Russia. The Bank also overestimated the government's implementation capacity; and some Bank efforts mimicked operations in other transition economies rather than being tailored to the country's specific conditions: "The new policies and prices did provide incentives to restructure, raise productivity, and create wealth. But the new and old power structures, in combination with old clan loyalties, have given rise to competing and often countervailing incentive structures that made it more attractive, for example, for enterprise managers to strip assets than to enhance them, for farmers to slaughter millions of sheep than to tend to them, and for civil servants to extort and exploit private sector entrepreneurs than to assist

---

BOX 15.1 The Importance of Country Fit

Even when country ownership of reform is strong, a mismatch between the Bank's strategy and the country's policy-making styles can create tensions and lead to poor results for Bank assistance. In Uruguay, for example, the Bank had sought prior to the 1997 Country Assistance Strategy (CAS) to support policy reform through heavily conditioned multitranche adjustment loans. The authorities were genuinely committed to reform and initially shared the Bank's enthusiasm for ambitious, detailed programs. It quickly became clear, however, that the Bank's program was premised on a pace of reform more rapid than could be handled by the Uruguayan system, where a slow but steady pace of reform reflects a consensus style of policy making in a traditionally democratic society. As a consequence, the policy dialogue deteriorated.

Recognizing that the dialogue was bogging down, the Bank moved to single-tranche adjustment operations that recognized policy achievements as and when they materialized. This strategy permitted the government to pursue agreed objectives at a pace and by the means dictated by the domestic policy process rather than as prespecified by Bank lending operations. The country assistance evaluation finds this strategic switch to have been critical to the success of the Bank's program. Such flexibility led to good results because the government assumed full ownership of its program. *The lesson here is that the Bank and the government should agree on broad indicators of the effectiveness of development initiatives. But the government itself should have greater rein to decide how best to achieve the agreed reform objectives.*

In Costa Rica, the Bank's phasing and design of its program in the 1993 CAS jeopardized what had been a productive relationship. The lessons of experience at that time showed that Costa Rica had always been a slow reformer—with the pace of reform dictated by the complicated politics of consensus in a pluralistic, democratic political system. An adjustment loan taken to the Board with the 1993 CAS required the passage of legislation as a condition of loan effectiveness. This was a mistake. The Bank had to extend the effectiveness deadline six times while waiting for the required passage of legislation, and ultimately had to cancel it two years after Board approval. The policy dialogue deteriorated and adversely affected the 1993–99 lending and nonlending program.

Source: Adapted from World Bank 2004a.

---

them" (World Bank 2001f, 15). Overoptimism is not limited to the Bank; the IMF was also faulted for being overoptimistic in its design of an assistance package to Indonesia after it was hit by the 1997 Asian crisis, because the Fund underestimated the country's governance problems, especially in the financial sector. Consequently, the assistance program had to be revised twice during 1998 (World Bank 2003c).

Communications failures. Inadequate timeliness and dissemination of ESW has also limited its impact on the design of reforms.[14] For example, in the Philippines during the 1990s, high-quality ESW contributed significantly to developing the reform agenda and facilitating policy dialogue. However, key players in the government, parliament, cabinet, and business and academic communities were often unaware of the content of some Bank ESW, and some strategic decisions were made before the reports were completed. The Bank was particularly faulted for providing inadequate input to policy reform with regards to the judicial system and gender issues (World Bank 1999c). In

India during the 1990s, however, the limited dissemination of Bank reports and policy recommendations reflected not so much Bank failure as the government's resistance to policy advice from external sources (World Bank 2001g, 15). Similarly, in Indonesia during the Asian financial crisis there was insufficient time to assess government ownership, analyze the country's institutional capacity, or even identify appropriately the counterparts that would be responsible for project management of the banking reform loan that the Bank prepared (World Bank 2003c).

Conditionality and Tranching

Conditionality that is overly general, or that involves studies rather than actions, or ignores fundamental reforms in the rush to transfer resources has also contributed to unsuccessful adjustment operations (including in Guinea, Indonesia, Jamaica, Russia, and Zambia).

- Although the conditionality for release of tranches in three credits in Bangladesh during the 1980s was performance oriented, it was too general, not having addressed major sectoral and macroeconomic issues supported by the credits (World Bank 1990b, 1998a). When conditionality is too general, tranching is unable to support proper progress in reform implementation, as was seen in this case in Bangladesh.

- Similarly, diffuse conditionality and the limited ability of the Bank to leverage its resources in the context of lending for banking reform to Indonesia during the Asian crisis might have been a consequence of the fact that the Bank had already made the commitment to help bail out Indonesia, which resulted in less than satisfactory banking sector reform (World Bank 2003c).

- In several cases (for example, Argentina and Bangladesh during the 1980s, Indonesia during the 1990s), when a country had a dire need for foreign exchange and budgetary resources, the resource transfer objective took precedence over the fulfillment of the range of conditions tied to the loans, as specific and performance oriented as they might be, diluting the focus on the policy reform agenda.

Use of single-tranche operations when a country does not have a record of policy performance was also reported to have had an adverse impact on adjustment lending (for example, in Guinea). In Morocco (1999), a single-tranche loan did not prove effective in supporting needed reforms, partly because it lacked focus, and many of the prior actions consisted of studies or plans, rather than substantive, concrete actions (World Bank 2001h). In some cases, the Bank was faulted for having issued waivers, undermining the proposed reforms (for example, in Georgia).

Caveat

Of course, strengthening any one of the country and Bank factors reviewed above would not necessarily have resulted in better reform outcomes, nor has the presence of adverse factors necessarily resulted in unsatisfactory reforms. Rather, the examples highlight the complex and dynamic interplay of various factors. For example, strong borrower ownership is insufficient to ensure satisfactory progress in reforms, if the pace of reforms or the specific policy actions are not well tailored to the country's circumstances—and poor pace or tailoring can be attributed to limited institutional capacity or inadequate project design. Exogenous shocks can combine with existing institutional weaknesses to produce devastating effects on the economy and derail reforms; however, they can also provide the impetus for new reforms. International and time pressures can provide a strong incentive to overlook the lack of borrower ownership or institutional capacity. These factors simply highlight the degree of risk and uncertainty to which adjustment operations are subject. Nonetheless, accounting for these factors when designing an adjustment operation can only serve to increase the likelihood of its success.

Lessons Learned

The lessons derived from this review are neither new nor surprising and have been highlighted in many other reviews and analyses,[15] which have emphasized the importance of country ownership and country-specific programs—an approach that the Bank has already operationalized through the Comprehensive Development Framework. Recent research further emphasizes the need for adjustment operations to focus more on institutional development, an aspect that was somewhat neglected during the 1990 reforms, which focused primarily on policy reform while leaving institutional development to evolve naturally as a consequence of good policies (World Bank 2004b).

Country Ownership

The most generic, yet still highly relevant, lesson is that sustained country ownership and commitment to reforms are prerequisites to reform success. Neither large amounts of lending nor conditionality can "buy" or "enforce" ownership and commitment. Furthermore, it is important to identify the various agents whose ownership of the reforms is important (for example, different levels of government and interest groups). Sound and timely ESW and its dissemination as well as policy dialogue can help identify the various players, how they might be affected by the reforms, when a "critical mass" of ownership has been achieved, and how to tailor the reforms so that buy-in (or simply lack of opposition) can be secured. When lack of ownership is apparent or becomes apparent over time, the Bank should consider downsizing its adjustment lending program until a sufficient consensus for the reform has been achieved.

Country-Specific Design

Reforms should be designed and tailored to country circumstances, with particular attention to institutional characteristics and vulnerabilities, implementation capacity, and governance issues, including control of corruption. Here again, ESW (strengthened with local participation), policy dialogue, and sustained Bank engagement play a crucial role.

Defined Objectives

Loans should have narrowly defined and specific objectives, with realistic implementation timetables and actions that are within the borrower's implementation capacity. The loan's objectives should also draw a clear distinction between the resource transfer objective and the specific reform objectives.

Conditionality

Conditionality should not be used as a substitute for ownership and commitment. In this sense, it should not (and, indeed, cannot) "coerce" actions to which the reformer is not committed. When borrower ownership and commitment are present, conditionality can be viewed as an "instrument of mutual accountability," where the Bank commits to a resource transfer for the completion of actions to which the borrower is already committed and for which it simply needs support (Branson and Hanna 2000). From the perspective of a committed borrower, conditionality can also be used as a vehicle to signal its commitment to reforms to potential investors (Dhonte 1997).

Annex 15.1 Adjustment Lending: Lessons of Experience

Experience shows that adjustment programs have a better chance of success in countries with an appropriate macroeconomic policy framework and a high degree of borrower ownership. Programs did not fare well in countries with heavy debt burdens. Exogenous shocks such as natural disasters and deterioration of terms of trade also adversely affected the outcome of adjustment. The main lessons that emerged from the OED study are as follows:

Macroeconomic Policy

A sound macroeconomic policy framework is a critical element of adjustment programs and it is difficult for countries to make progress without it. An appropriate framework can produce internally consistent policy targets, contribute to program credibility, and minimize policy reversals. It also provides the basis for successful sectoral reforms.

Typically, stabilization is needed when a country has high inflation, is losing foreign exchange reserves, and has an unsustainable current account deficit. Tightening the overall fiscal position is a central element of macroeconomic adjustment programs. Countries still with an unsustainable debt burden need continued access to concessional lending, and, possibly, debt reduction or restructuring.

Sequencing Reforms

The sequence of reforms is crucial to the design of an adjustment program. While country-specific sequencing is optimal, some general rules can be derived from past experience.

In countries with acute macroeconomic problems, *structural adjustment* should follow, or at least be accompanied by, *macroeconomic stabilization*. However, some components of structural reforms complement macrostabilization and could therefore be initiated early on. Examples include fiscal reforms, which improve tax administration and expenditure control, and institutional reforms, which need time to take effect.

Trade Policy Reform

Meanwhile, trade policy reform may either complement or undermine *stabilization*, depending on whether it increases or reduces tax revenue. Because many adjusting countries rely heavily on trade taxes for revenue, the first phase of reform should concentrate on improving the transparency of the trade regime. This can be achieved by converting import quotas to tariffs, which helps to raise revenue and contributes to stabilization. The second phase involves reducing the tariff level.

Countries that first converted quotas into tariffs, and later lowered the tariff level, generally succeeded (Ghana, Indonesia), whereas those that did not had reversals (Morocco). In Ghana and Indonesia the stabilization programs were well under way before trade taxes were reduced. Morocco attempted simultaneous stabilization and revenue-losing trade reform, but had to reverse the process when revenue loss began to undermine stabilization. In Colombia and Jamaica, conversion of import quotas led to an increase in total tax revenue, contributing to the stabilization effort. Although both these countries failed to carry out the second phase of the trade reform, the initial progress was sustained.

In general, *trade liberalization* needs to be accompanied by *reforms in industrial and agricultural regulation*—such as the removal of barriers to entry and exit—and reforms in input and output pricing policies. In countries with highly distorted factor and product markets, *financial liberalization* should follow reforms in the *real sector*. Deregulating the financial sector while allowing the real sector to operate with distorted prices could result in significant misallocation of credit.

Supply Response

When the appropriate macroeconomic framework was in place, policy reforms, particularly trade liberalization, induced a strong and positive supply response in the real sector, as shown by faster growth of industrial output and a resurgence of exports, especially of manufactures.

In more than half of the 42 sample countries, growth rates of industrial value added and manufactured exports increased during the postadjustment period. But many of the initial gains were largely due to a more efficient use of capacity and better allocation of existing resources. More dynamic gains from increases in productivity have yet to be achieved.

In the remaining adjusting countries, supply response was sluggish despite progress in liberalizing trade. Apparently the response was held back by lack of macroeconomic stability; lack of reforms in domestic regulations; decline in public investment in infrastructure; and lack of well-functioning factor and product markets, essential for sustained growth.

High on the remaining agenda for reforms are domestic regulations that hinder competition and factor mobility. Public investment in infrastructure needs to be encouraged in order to improve the conditions for private and foreign investment. Long-term economic growth depends heavily on technical change. Market forces alone may not provide socially acceptable levels of investment in technology; government assistance may be needed here.

Financial Sector Reforms

Generally, financial sector reforms that followed macroeconomic stabilization were successful, whereas countries that deregulated interest rates too early had frequent policy reversals. This suggests that financial reforms need to be deliberately sequenced with regard to other reforms, and realistic time frames should be allowed for financial sector adjustment. While certain components of the reform program—institutional and competition reforms, for instance—could begin early in the adjustment process, widespread financial liberalization should wait for macroeconomic stabilization and liberalization in the real economy.

Public Enterprise Reform and Privatization

In many adjusting countries, public enterprise reforms are necessary to improve allocative efficiencies and reduce the burdens these enterprises typically place on government budgets. Experience suggests the following lessons:

- Because public enterprise reforms require detailed knowledge of the public enterprise sector, adequate preparation, based on the Bank's ESW and, where needed, technical assistance, is essential.

- The main goal of public enterprise reforms should be to enhance efficiency. Excessive emphasis on reducing the fiscal burden that enterprises place on the government may have undesirable consequences for efficiency. For example, it would be inappropriate to reduce the fiscal burden by freeing up the prices of public enterprise monopolies, such as in Turkey and Jamaica. In some extreme cases, monopoly pricing could contribute to inflation, thus undermining macroeconomic stabilization, as happened in Turkey.

- Governments' financial relations with public enterprises need to be transparent. Public enterprises should not receive preferential access to credit, tax exemptions, or government loans.

- In the area of divestiture, great care must be taken in choosing which public enterprises to privatize. Generally, it is preferable to start with those that have few legal or financial disputes to settle and are attractive to private investors. Privatized enterprises also should not be given special treatment or privileges.

- Where privatization is not feasible, alternatives such as leases or management contracts need to be actively explored.

Social Dimensions

Some social groups are bound to suffer from adjustment programs, at least in the short run. But there is ample room for better design of programs to mitigate the social costs of adjustment and safeguard people who are already disadvantaged. These costs can be reduced by relying on expenditure-switching policies, such as exchange rate devaluation, rather than expenditure-reduction policies, and by redirecting social expenditures toward areas such as primary education and health.

Comparing the two phases of adjustment in the Philippines, for example, expenditure-switching policies had less adverse impact on the poor:

- During the first phase, 1980–85, adjustment focused on reducing government expenditure. It successfully turned the fiscal account from a deficit of 4 percent of gross domestic product (GDP) in 1981 to a surplus of 2.4 percent in 1986. Real GDP growth, however, dropped from 3.8 percent in 1981 to −6.5 percent in 1984, and unemployment and urban poverty rose.

- The second phase of adjustment had a greater emphasis on expenditure-switching policies. While government expenditure was steadily increased, the exchange rate was significantly devalued, benefiting the poorest 40 percent of the population who produced labor-intensive exportable goods and consumed very few imports. Poverty declined significantly during the second phase of adjustment.

When designing adjustment programs, emphasis should be placed on basic, long-term issues of poverty and human development, rather than solely concentrating on compensatory measures. Targeted projects and programs addressing problems of both the "new poor" and the "chronically poor" should accompany, not substitute for, more basic reforms such as restructuring government expenditures. Further efforts should be made to help countries develop the ability to analyze the social impact of alternative policy mixes and to monitor changes in social indicators.

Environmental Dimensions

Adjustment policies have both positive and negative implications for the environment. For example, trade liberalization, exchange rate depreciation, or changes in taxes or subsidies may induce changes in the structure of production, which inevitably affects the environment.

Environmental issues received little attention in early adjustment operations, but more recent programs have begun to address these issues. More emphasis is needed. The probable impact of proposed adjustment policies on the physical environment should be identified and, when negative, appropriate action should either be incorporated in program design or addressed through separate investment projects.

Source: Adapted from World Bank 1993.

Annex 15.2

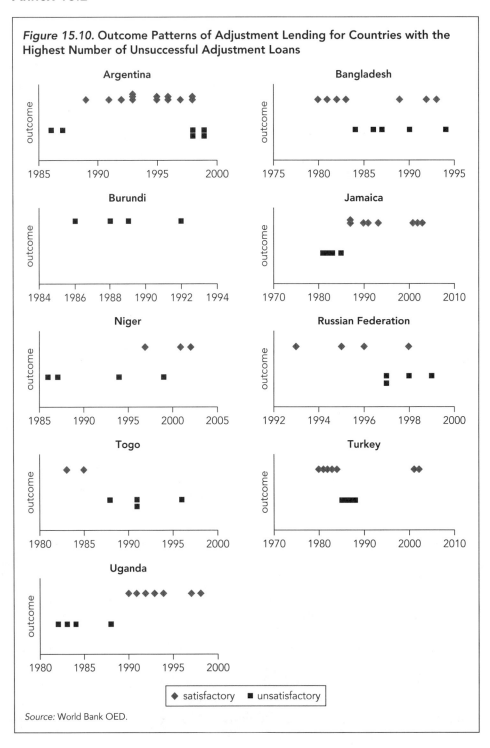

Figure 15.10. Outcome Patterns of Adjustment Lending for Countries with the Highest Number of Unsuccessful Adjustment Loans

Source: World Bank OED.

Endnotes

1. This chapter benefited from input, comments, and suggestions from Stefan Koeberle, Thaddeus Malesa, Victoria Elliott, Henry Chase, and attendees at the Conditionality Concept Review Meeting, May 11, 2004, World Bank, Washington, DC.

2. See, for example Ranis (1996), World Bank (2002a, 2004a), Boughton and Mourmouras (2002), Malesa and Silarszky (chapter 13 of this book). However, Dollar and Svensson (2000) found no such evidence.

3. Adjustment lending outcomes have also been found to be more sensitive to country conditions than those of investment lending (World Bank 2002a).

4. See, for example, Dollar and Svensson (2000), Killick (1998), World Bank (2004a).

5. OED outcome ratings have been shown to have a strong correlation with some of the objectives of reform, namely, inflation reduction and budget control, indicating that the outcome ratings tend to capture reform outcomes (Dollar and Svensson, 2000). A reviewer from the OED indicated that there is a possibility that adjustment operations are more likely to be rated favorably relative to investment operations, because adjustment loan objectives tend to be more general and adjustment operations are more likely to be judged on "process" as opposed to "results."

6. In this chapter, these loans will be referred to as "unsatisfactory" or "unsuccessful" loans.

7. Adjustment lending was introduced in 1980 to finance short-term balance-of-payments support, as well as to achieve short-term macroeconomic stabilization and to eliminate price distortions. Over the 1990s, it evolved further in support of longer-run institutional, social, structural, and sectoral reform, and incorporated lessons of experience. (See, for example, World Bank [1986, 1990a, 1992, 1994, 2001a, 2001b, 2001c, 2002a], Mosley, Harrigan, and Toye [1995], Thomas and others [1991], Burnside and Dollar [2000], Dollar and Svensson [2000], Koeberle [2003], Structural Adjustment Participatory Review Initiative [2002].)

8. The two Regions with the highest concentration of unsuccessful adjustment operations, Africa and Latin America and the Caribbean, are also those whose growth performance has been the most disappointing in this period.

9. Data limited to fiscal 1996–2002.

10. See, for example, Boughton and Mourmouras (2002) for a review of the theoretical and empirical analyses of ownership. They also note that one of the International Monetary Fund's (IMF) definitions is: "Ownership is a willing assumption of responsibility for an agreed program of policies, by officials in a borrowing country who have the responsibility to formulate and carry out those policies, based on an understanding that the program is achievable and is in the country's own interest." Concepts such as "willing" and "understanding" and "interest" highlight the difficulty to directly observe ownership.

11. See, for example, World Bank 2004b.

12. See, for example, World Bank 2002a, 2004a.

13. Lack of Bank continued engagement, such as in the cases of Georgia, Guinea, and Mexico (and to a lesser degree in Ecuador) seriously disrupted Bank lending, undermined client trust and dialogue, and hindered the Bank's ability to tailor reforms to specific country circumstances (World Bank, 1999a, 2001e, 2003b, 2003d).

14. See, for example, World Bank 2004a. The report also highlights the fact that the Bank's ESW risks becoming less relevant in countries with significant or growing technical skills, such as China and Mexico.

15. See, for example, World Bank 2002a, 2004a, 2004b; Boughton and Mourmouras 2002; and references therein.

Bibliography

Boughton, J. M., and A. Mourmouras. 2002. "Is Policy Ownership an Operational Concept?" IMF Working Paper WP/02/72, International Monetary Fund, Washington, DC.

Branson, W., and N. Hanna. 2000. "Ownership and Conditionality." OED Working Paper Series, No. 8, Operations and Evaluation Department, World Bank, Washington, DC.

Burnside, C., and D. Dollar. 2000. "Aid, Policies, and Growth." *American Economic Review* 90 (4): 847–68.

Dhonte, P. 1997. "Conditionality as an Instrument of Borrower Credibility." IMF Working Paper PPAA/97/2, International Monetary Fund, Washington, DC.

Dollar, D., and Svensson, J. 2000. "What Explains the Success or Failure of Structural Adjustment Programs?" *The Economic Journal* 110 (October): 894–917.

Killick, Tony. 1998. *Aid and the Political Economy of Policy Change.* London: Routledge.

Koeberle, S. 2003. "Should Policy-Based Lending Still Involve Conditionality?" *The World Bank Research Observer* 18 (2): 249–73.

Mosley, F., J. Harrigan, and J. Toye. 1995. *Aid and Power: The World Bank and Policy-Based Lending.* New York: Routledge.

Ranis, G. 1996. "On Fast-Disbursing Policy-Based Loans," CSIS Task Force on Multi-Lateral Development Banks, Center for Strategic and International Studies, Washington, DC.

Rodrik, D. 2003. "Growth Strategies." Manuscript, John F. Kennedy School of Government, Harvard University.

Structural Adjustment Participatory Review Initiative. 2002. "The Policy Roots of Economic Crisis and Poverty." World Bank, Washington, DC.

Thomas, V., A. Chhibber, M. Dailami, and J. de Melo, eds. 1991. *Restructuring Economies in Distress: Policy Reform and the World Bank.* New York: Oxford University Press.

World Bank. 1986. "Structural Adjustment Lending: A First Review of Experience." Operations Evaluation Report 6409, Washington, DC.

———. 1990a. "Report on Adjustment Lending: Policies for the Recovery of Growth." R90-57 IDA/R90-49, Washington, DC.

———. 1990b. "Bangladesh: Review of the Experience with Policy Reforms in the 1980s." Washington, DC.

———. 1992. "Third Report on Adjustment Lending: Private and Public Resources for Growth." R92-47 IDA/R92-29, Washington, DC.

———. 1993. "Adjustment Lending: Lessons of Experience." Washington, DC.

———. 1994. *Adjustment in Africa: Reforms, Results, and the Road Ahead.* World Bank Policy Research Report. New York: Oxford University Press.

———. 1996. "Argentina Country Assistance Review." Washington, DC.

———. 1998a. "Bangladesh: Country Assistance Review." Washington, DC.

———. 1998b. "Jamaica Country Assistance Note." Washington, DC.

———. 1999a. "Ecuador Country Assistance Evaluation." Washington, DC.

———. 1999b. "Côte d'Ivoire Country Assistance Review." Washington, DC.

———. 1999c. "Philippines: From Crisis to Opportunity—Country Assistance Review." Washington, DC.

———. 2000a. "Argentina Country Assistance Evaluation." Washington, DC.

———. 2000b. "Azerbaijan Country Assistance Evaluation." Washington, DC.

———. 2000c. "Ghana Country Assistance Evaluation." Washington, DC.

———. 2000d. "Kenya Country Assistance Evaluation." Washington, DC.

———. 2000e. "Malawi Country Assistance Evaluation." Washington, DC.

———. 2001a. "Adjustment from Within: Lessons from the Structural Adjustment Participatory Review Initiative." Washington, DC.

———. 2001b. "Adjustment Lending Retrospective." Operations Policy and Country Services, Washington, DC.

———. 2001c. "Supporting Country Development: Strengthening the World Bank Group's Support for Middle-Income Countries." Washington, DC.

———. 2001d. "Uganda Policy, Participation, People." Washington, DC.

———. 2001e. "Mexico Country Assistance Evaluation." Washington, DC.

———. 2001f. "Kyrgyz Republic Country Assistance Evaluation." Washington, DC.

———. 2001g. "India Country Assistance Evaluation." Washington, DC.

———. 2001h. "Morocco Country Assistance Evaluation." Washington, DC.

———. 2002a. "2001 Annual Review of Development Effectiveness: Making Choices." Washington, DC.

———. 2002b. "Assisting Russia's Transition: An Unprecedented Challenge." Washington, DC.

———. 2002c. "Zambia Country Assistance Evaluation." Washington, DC.

———. 2003a. "Project Performance Assessment Report: Niger Economic Recovery Credit, Public Sector Adjustment Credit, Public Finance Reform Credit, Public Finance Recovery Credit." Washington, DC.

———. 2003b. "Project Performance Assessment Report: Guinea Second Structural Adjustment Credit, Public Enterprise Sector Rationalization and Privatization Technical Assistance Credit, Financial Sector Adjustment Credit, Third Structural Adjustment Credit, Fourth Structural Adjustment Credit." Washington, DC.

———. 2003c. "Project Performance Assessment Report: Indonesia Banking Reform Assistance, Policy Reform Support Loan I, Policy Reform Support Loan II." Washington, DC.

———. 2003d. "Project Performance Assessment Report: Georgia Structural Adjustment Credit I, Structural Adjustment Technical Assistance Credit I, Structural Adjustment Credit II, Structural Adjustment Technical Assistance Credit II, Energy Sector Adjustment Credit." Washington, DC.

———. 2004a. "2003 Annual Review of Development Effectiveness: The Effectiveness of Bank Support for Policy Reform." Washington, DC.

———. 2004b. "Lessons of the 1990s." Draft report, Washington, DC.

16

Part 3 Discussion Summary

The presentations of the second session focused on the analytical work of the World Bank Operations Evaluation Department, the question of objectives and conditionality, and adapting the latter to the particular environment of the target country. This effort involves selectivity and a thorough understanding on the donor side of what the borrowing country needs and is capable of doing.

Benchmarks for Conditionality and Ownership

One point raised during the discussion was that of international benchmarks for process conditionality and ownership. The representative from the European Bank for Reconstruction and Development (EBRD) suggested that it would be difficult to establish benchmarks, because it would result in exclusion of those countries that most need the aid provided by loans. These countries do not have access to external resources through the markets; they may also be unable to access expertise or external advice owing to weak domestic political institutions. Countries that need external data, financing, or expertise are generally in trouble, cannot help themselves, or are in a mess. It was noted, however, that countries with good institutions, policies, and political leadership could also be in a mess as a result of exogenous causes such as conflict in neighboring countries or natural or public health disasters. The speaker from Oxford University countered that some level of minimum standards should be required, not only for the sake of consistency, but also because programs designed on an ad hoc basis where the donor fixes this and that would create a nightmare. Using a system of minimum standards would be an important step toward depoliticizing the process. The standards would have to be able to shift as necessary and in a transparent fashion.

It was suggested that the concept of "country ownership" was misleading and obfuscating. The representative from the EBRD pointed out that the political systems of countries where donor agencies are operating are frequently unrepresentative and repressive—ranging from mildly authoritarian to brutally repressive—and have political leadership that is corrupt and economically illiterate. In such instances, the individuals responsible for program implementation are weak, and there is little buy-in from civil society. In fact, it is in such countries that civil society is weakest at a time when it is needed the most. In three cases, the EBRD is conducting only private sector programs and is no longer working with the state. The donors should be more selective and perhaps refrain from operating in countries where their actions are more likely to worsen an already desperate situation because the minimal standards of political institution and governance are not satisfied. It was noted that although the EBRD does not lend large amounts of money, it is actively involved in promoting change and building capacity for change; to this end the EBRD encourages narrowly focused reform programs with quick payoffs (two to three quick payoff reforms).

A representative from Vietnam discussed the psychological aspect of conditionality, noting the natural opposition to the external imposition of conditionalities. The main objective should be to help the partner country to develop and implement its own development agenda rather than have it undertake the donor's agenda.

Selectivity was also discussed with reference to the extent to which lending programs are focused. Selectivity amplifies differentiation and, when applied to middle-income countries with a high probability of success, it can serve as a role model and significant incentive for the countries at the bottom to change.

A number of questions were raised about the Country Policy and Institutional Assessment (CPIA) rankings, focusing primarily on the transparency of the ratings and the components that go into determining a country's score. The concern is that while a number of the criteria are sensible, some areas could be considered controversial, such as privatization and creating an enabling environment for the private sector. At present, the CPIA is a World Bank internal rating system; the decision not to make it public was taken by the Board of Directors in an effort to prevent it from becoming a political negotiation. The World Bank speaker commented that the CPIA weighting could be adjusted to place a greater emphasis on results, but noted that, ultimately, the information coming from within countries makes the difference.

Ownership and Sovereignty

A number of participants discussed ownership and sovereignty as central to effective lending; however, positions varied greatly on these two issues. While some suggested that ownership must come from all levels of society, it was noted that this is just not possible in some countries where the political system is authoritarian or totalitarian. A related topic was the focus on accountability and whether it should be upwards or downwards. Accountability upwards tends to come at the expense of accountability downwards. The speaker from Oxford addressed the question as to whether the push for downward accountability affected sovereignty. He suggested that it's not the government but the people of a country that are sovereign; therefore, there is no contradiction of sovereignty.

The question was raised regarding the potential for low or no conditionality support with incipient turnaround for low- or poor-performing countries in order to provide some support to facilitate the reform process. It was suggested that this step might increase aid effectiveness. The speaker from Oxford University referred to Uganda as an excellent example, because the donors were able to start prereform with small levels of aid and were then able to ramp up the volume of aid as the reform program progressed. By contrast, the reforms in Zambia started out with huge volumes of aid, eliminating the ability of donors to ramp up the aid; consequently, large amounts of aid were pumped into weak environments.

The representative from the African Development Bank commented that the Low-Income Countries Under Stress seem to perform worse than the middle-income countries in the CPIA rankings. Not only are these countries subject to a greater number of conditionalities, but they also tend to have weaker institutional and policy-making capacities. This, consequently, makes it more difficult for them to engage as equal partners and, in some cases, makes them less inclined to implement the policy changes because they do not feel ownership for them. The African Development Bank representative suggested that more emphasis be placed on the linkage between conditionality and capacity with the aim of further developing the latter. The minister of state from Ethiopia added that many African countries have agreed to the International Network for Peace and Development in Africa Initiative and most are committed to bringing about economic transformation, so donors should leave it to the African governments and people to articulate what they mean by political and corporate governance.

Another component of the capacity issue, raised by the representative from the Ministry of Planning and Investment in Vietnam, is that as the governments and the donors get more involved in the process, the role of the government in coordinating becomes more time consuming. It was suggested that the resources of the government be increased to better cope with the coordination of the development agenda and that the project channel be reduced to a manageable level.

Minimum Standards

On the subject of minimum standards, one view was that ex post conditionality could get around the problem of donors being motivated by disbursement, and that aid recipients would do enough to stay above the minimum and have less incentive to perform. The difficulty with establishing the minimum standards line is that it needs to be drawn in the right place, and drawing it too high runs the risk of excluding a number of countries with significant populations of poor people. Conditionality was also discussed with respect to the notion of process conditionality and the benefits/detriments thereof. On the one hand, process conditionality was seen as beneficial in that it could motivate countries to accelerate reforms; on the other hand, it was seen as posing more practical operational challenges, and this is one of the reasons that the Poverty Reduction Strategy Paper processes have been unsatisfactory—in effect they are a one-size-fits-all condition.

Although there is a need for consistency with the basic elements of reform programs, such as the Poverty Reduction Strategy Paper/Poverty Reduction Support Credit, this must be balanced by an appropriate focus on the country particulars and its capacity to implement any reforms. The manner in which a lending program and its associated conditions are structured can have a tremendous impact not only on the success of the program from a donor perspective, but also on the partner country's ability to develop ownership for the reform initiatives and thereby give it a greater chance of success.

Part IV
Toward Country-Owned
Approaches: Do We Still
Need Conditionality?

17

Introduction

MASOOD AHMED
Department for International Development

Toward Country-Owned Approaches:
Do We Still Need Conditionality?

This session will focus on some of the elements of the emerging approaches to policy-based lending and will discuss how conditionality relates to country-based approaches and country situations.

One issue is how conditionality and ownership relate, particularly in a country that is coming out of a financial crisis. Many of the earlier chapters have been focused on long-term partnerships and Poverty Reduction Strategy Papers, and there has been some discussion about middle-income countries and countries coming out of crisis. The next chapter, by Kemal Dervis, addresses this issue of conditionality and ownership in more detail. Dervis, who lived through and managed this crisis in Turkey, is ideally placed to offer a broad assessment because he was previously in charge of the work on poverty and economic management with the World Bank.

The next chapter is by Gilles Hervio, who is also knowledgeable about conditionality and ownership. He has been working on these issues with the European Commission for many years. He discusses the use of outcome-based conditionality as a way to move forward, beyond focusing on inputs toward making disbursements based on outcomes. In many ways the European Commission has led the way in experimenting with this approach.

18

The Turkish Experience with Conditionality

KEMAL DERVIS
Former Minister of the Economy, Turkey

Skewing the Enforcement of Conditionality

During my tenure as an economic minister in Turkey, one of the key issues I dealt with was the banking crisis. With support from the Bretton Woods institutions, in particular the legal and economic work performed by the World Bank, Turkey had created a banking supervision agency, an agency that was supposed to be independent, and indeed legally was so.

At the time, however, there was a coalition government consisting of three parties, and each party leader had appointed two of the seven Board members, with one other being nominated from the largest party. It was soon discovered that every one of those Board members was loyal to a party leader. The relationships were quite informal—formally the Board members were independent, yet in fact the Board was highly politicized, which was exactly what the establishing law was initially trying to avoid.

As a result, one day at midnight, the reformers who had supported the independence of the banking supervision agency rushed a motion into parliament when most deputies had left or were sleeping, managed to field a quorum, and fired all except one of the seven supervision members. They then appointed six others who were true professionals and independent personalities not beholden to any special group or interest. The one remaining Board member was kept on because he had too much political support. Although the move was a necessary step to get the banking supervision agency to truly behave independently, it was a gross violation of the explicit condition set by the World Bank, and hence should have been a matter of contention.

The Case for Conditionality

If we are going to continue to be in a constrained aid resource environment where there is selective allocation of aid resources, there is always going to be some form of conditionality. There must be some sort of rules on which aid allocation is based, and these rules, whatever they may be, form some kind of conditionality.

Allocation of Aid Resources

If the rules on how to distribute aid are as impartial as possible (in other words, as technically and economically driven as possible, as opposed to being driven by geostrategic, military, or other interests), we are better off as a world. Recognizing that there are going to be allocation rules, there is something to be said for making them as economic and as socially biased as possible, rather than the big powers giving money to whoever happens to be their ally at the time. The most recent example of this situation is Iraq's debt reduction, which has been the largest in recent history, not for any particular economic reason except that it is politically important.

The Need for a Comprehensive Program

It is important to maintain a comprehensive and coherent economic program, the concept of comprehensiveness being distinct from the multiplicity of actually binding legal conditionalities. Drawing a parallel with the Turkish experience, the government's economic reform program for 2000 was in many ways a macroeconomically fairly well-designed and carefully thought-out program. The program relied on an exchange rate regime that was going to become more flexible with time, and because Turkey had had strong inflation for 20 years, it was important to deflate. However, the program missed some key points, including the banking system supervision system. When a country has a weak banking system and then experiences a run on the banks, it can easily result in an attack on the currency, which is what happened in Turkey. So, weak banking supervision in many ways was one of the key causes of the failure of the whole macro program and of the crash Turkey experienced in 2001. It illustrates that the program was not comprehensive enough.

Streamlining: A Universally Positive Good?

When we focus on streamlining, it is important to try to focus on what is critically important and what is not vitally important, but we should also keep in mind that economies are interdependent. If we miss one important point in the picture, we are likely to pay for it, and therefore we cannot push streamlining too far.

Conditionality and Ideology

We need to rid conditionality and policy advice of ideology. A lot of the policy advice in the past, especially in the 1980s, was driven by the influences of the Reagan/Thatcher conservative revolution where certain ideological buzzwords were more important than the actual substance of the policy. The World Bank and others have distanced themselves from such practices, but it is important to keep reminding ourselves that policy advice should be based on analysis and empirical facts, rather than on knee-jerk ideology.

As an example, the International Monetary Fund made this mistake early on during the Asian crisis, when it immediately jumped to a knee-jerk reaction: fiscal restraint should be the number one priority, whereas in fact the nature of the Asian crisis was quite different. The mistake was, however, corrected fairly quickly.

Quality of Fiscal Policy

The quality of fiscal policy is as important in a medium-term framework as the actual size of the deficit or of the primary surplus. To many economists it is clear that a government expenditure that actually creates net wealth for the government, in other words a good investment, is something quite different in terms of long-term fiscal sustainability than a simple current expenditure or social transfer. Lumping these two types of expenditures together in International Monetary Fund conditionality and focusing solely on the overall deficit is a big mistake, as opposed to making sure that the fiscal policy is conducted in a truly growth-supporting way.

International Codes and Standards

We still view the world too much through a framework of nation states, state actors, developing countries, developed countries and international institutions, while the reality is much more complex. There are divisions within states, there are reformers and conservatives, there are vested interests everywhere. Thus, the move within the Poverty Reduction Strategy Paper framework, and within the Comprehensive Development Framework, to really have all partners involved in the debate is a most welcome move.

In this context, the building of standards and codes internationally is an important part of the picture. Standing by certain codes of conduct is not a conditionality imposed on any particular country by others or by international institutions, but rather an attempt by the world community to make rules together by which everyone should play and stick to.

One of the biggest problems in this type of scenario is that oftentimes some powerful countries break the rules first. In parallel, big corporations and big interests have often managed to capture the agenda in the past and have been able to draft the rules to their advantage. One of the clearest examples of this is the Uruguay Round Agreement on Trade-Related Aspects of Intellectual Property Rights; some of what was included was really put there in response to intense lobbying from the pharmaceutical lobby by the United States and other rich countries.

However, the World Trade Organization in theory is a democratic organization, because small, poor, developing countries can actually block an agreement, which is not the case in many other international organizations. The accommodating rules permit such countries, which were previously thought to be at a disadvantage, to stand in defense of their agenda. This is a point that is often overlooked by the protestors who fancy themselves as champions of the poor.

19

Toward Multiyear Outcome-Based Conditionality

GILLES HERVIO
European Commission

The European Commission (EC) has provided budget support since the beginning of the 1990s. For 10 years it used traditional policy-based conditionality, combining World Bank and International Monetary Fund conditionality with some specific conditionality. At the end of the 1990s, the EC decided to change its approach because of a number of concerns, namely, the high level of subjectivity involved in setting conditions and in assessing their fulfillment; the evidence of the fact that policy conditionality led us far from looking at the result and the reality in the country, and of the often disproportionate impact of nonfulfillment of conditionality (not enough or too much); and finally the negative impact on the ownership of reforms.

Respecting Ownership

What does ownership mean? What does respecting ownership mean? Respecting ownership means, first of all, respecting national processes rather than developing parallel processes. Respecting ownership also means to agree to disagree and sometimes to disagree to agree.

Donors have to accept a difference of views on policy action needs and timing, as well as the need to support national debate and accept democracy. Donors have to accept political choices different from their beliefs.

The donor community has a long history of mistakes in the advice it gives (for example, privatization and user fees in education and health). Thus, humility is extremely important. Furthermore, the separation of policy dialogue and capacity building from lending and grant conditionalities becomes essential.

The consequence of respecting ownership in those cases when we do not agree on a policy is that we have to move to monitoring results. We have to accept that the political choices are not the ones we believe in, and therefore we have to look at what changed in the reality.

Sometimes, we also have to disagree to agree. It is good to remember that ownership does not mean accepting everything. For example, violation of human rights and corruption are unacceptable and disqualify a country from receiving any aid from the EC. These issues have to be part of the political dialogue donors have with developing countries. In addition, the EC has some eligibility conditions for providing budget support, including macroeconomic stability, improvements in public finance management, commitment to poverty reduction, and capacity to monitor results. However, rather than applying standards the EC is trying to look at trends, that is, whether things are improving or not.

The EC has to move away from some current practices, which did not change reality much. Even in the second generation of Poverty Reduction Support Credits (PRSCs) we find incredibly long lists of conditions and long policy matrices. For example, in PRSC 4, 5, and 6 in Burkina Faso there are 17 pages listing 211 indicators and conditions. It is fair to say that they are not strictly conditions (the number of "prior actions" is about 30); however, the EC asks the government and the task team to negotiate and monitor every indicator. It is a similar situation in Uganda—the policy matrix there includes 241 indicators. These numbers are remarkably stable. The structural adjustment program for Burkina Faso in 1998–2000 included 189 indicators and that for 2000–2 included 236. Thus, the number has remained about the same over time and it needs to be changed.

The EC also has to move away from the current epidemic of action plans. For example, the program for Burkina Faso requests 18 action plans from the government. The EC needs to focus instead on results and dialogue. A policy dialogue with the government needs to be informed by results and reality rather than by ideology.

The EC Approach

The EC has tried to change its approach since the end of 1999. A new way of providing budget support is now being applied in 30 countries—mainly in Africa to support poverty reduction budgets and Poverty Reduction Strategy Papers, but now also in Latin America and Asia to support sectoral policies (for example, sectoral budget support). The amount of disbursements is about €500 million annually.

One of the objectives of this effort is to reduce volatility and subjectivity. The approach is based on three-year programs, which include fixed tranches and additional performance tranches. There is supposed to be only limited conditionality attached to the fixed tranches: ideally, the only conditionality should be related to macroeconomic stability (but the EC is actually reviewing if it has succeeded in limiting the number of conditions for these fixed tranches). Additional performance tranches for variable amounts are linked mainly to service delivery (for example, a change in the life expectancy of the population). The EC has no other indicators and no matrix.

The EC is also trying to use service delivery indicators: they are monitorable, drawn from the government strategy (including the Poverty Reduction Strategy Paper when available), and have the potential to change rather quickly. The EC takes into account corrective government actions, if any, and external factors that can influence the service delivery. Examples of indicators that may move quickly include attendance at primary health service, prenatal health care, immunization rates, and net growth of the enrollment rate in the first year of primary school.

Difficulties

This innovative approach is not without problems. For instance, it is not always easy to define and agree on the indicators to be used because they are not always included in the Poverty Reduction Strategy Paper. There is also an issue in setting the target values—sometimes they are overoptimistic, sometimes too low. However, the assessment process is much easier than the assessment of policy conditionality.

There have been few cases where there was a good reason for missing the target. But if, as happened in Mozambique, the government argues with good reason that the nonachievement of a target is due to the impact of a flood, the EC may neutralize the indicator. To use service delivery indicators within the policy dialogue is still quite difficult. The support from other donors is limited. And on the government side, it is not always easy to have the time to analyze the results—the move toward this approach requires a cultural change, which is not easy to achieve, including within the EC staff.

Availability of data is another problem. It is, however, more the result of a long-standing lack of interest rather than a technical problem. If we are able to go to Mars, it should be possible to monitor these basic data.

Going Forward

Donors should move from matrix reality to matrix revolution. The capacity-building policy dialogue may take a different form from these current long policy matrices. We should move toward result orientation, using more selectivity and less conditionality.

The EC may need to move to even more innovative approaches. For example, it is still in the mode of yearly conditionality, which made sense for structural adjustment programs with specific and quick objectives (macroeconomic suitability and structural reform). But it has not changed its instruments to support poverty reduction and the Millennium Development Goals. It may make sense to move from yearly conditionality to multiyear conditionality in order to support longer-term reform.

The EC may be able to apply some of what it has learned from the Heavily Indebted Poor Countries experience. It first agreed to have a threshold, then to provide financial support (which is not far from budget support) during interim periods, and then, after some limited conditionality was agreed upon, to provide long-term support. The EC should start to think about a similar innovative mechanism with multiyear conditionality for delivering support for achieving the Millennium Development Goals.

20

Conditionality and Country Performance

HAROLD BEDOYA
World Bank

This chapter attempts to analyze the effect of policy-based lending conditionality on country performance, as measured by gross domestic product (GDP) per capita growth two years after loan approval. The effect of conditionality is analyzed in four broad policy areas, represented by the four main clusters comprising the World Bank's Country Policy and Institutional Assessment (CPIA) rating: (a) macroeconomic policy performance (macro), (b) policies for social inclusion/equity (social), (c) public sector management and institutional performance (PSM), and (d) structural policy performance (structural).[1]

The objective is to test whether, two years after loan approval, conditionality leads to improved country performance. It is expected that the factors influencing improved country performance include initial income, conditionality mapped to one of the four CPIA clusters, and macro and fiscal effects. The effects two years after loan approval are analyzed to determine the short- to medium-term impact of loan conditionality on GDP per capita growth.

Before-After Approach

A before-after analysis was undertaken of 217 loans in 80 countries approved between fiscal 1996 and fiscal 2002[2] and of the corresponding 6,077 legally binding conditions[3] out of the 8,113 total conditions (binding and nonbinding) associated with the loans. Figure 20.1 shows the distribution of loan conditionality after each condition is mapped to one of the four CPIA clusters; annex 20.1 shows how this mapping is done.

Legally binding conditionality during fiscal 1996–2002 is found to focus mostly on structural policy: about 45 percent of all legally binding conditionality focuses on structural conditionality, followed by 25 percent on public sector management and institutions, and 21 percent on social sector policies. However, when one examines trends for each of the four policy areas, the use of structural conditionality appears to be declining while that of public sector management conditionality appears to be

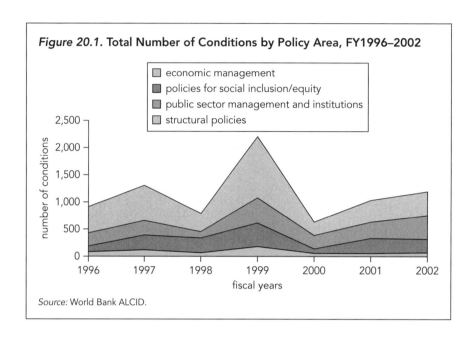

Figure 20.1. Total Number of Conditions by Policy Area, FY1996–2002

Source: World Bank ALCID.

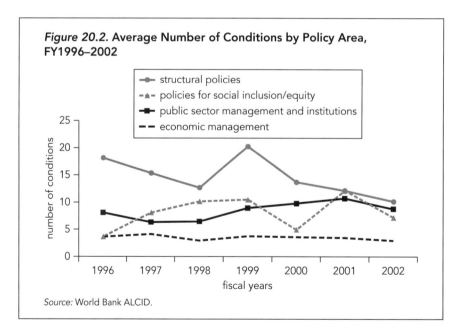

Figure 20.2. Average Number of Conditions by Policy Area, FY1996–2002

Source: World Bank ALCID.

slowly increasing and that of macroeconomic management conditionality has been essentially stable (see figure 20.2).

Based on the yearly average of the total CPIA rating (the rating representing all 20 policy and institutional reform areas) for fiscal 1996–02, and solely for the purposes of this chapter, countries with policy-based loans during this period have been grouped as high performers, good performers, and poor performers.[4] The CPIA rating prior to the year of approval of the policy-based loan is selected as the beginning period of observation because the bulk of loan preparation is undertaken in the year prior to loan approval, and the impact could thus be assessed without the influence of the loan in the CPIA rating. By comparing the change in the prereform CPIA cluster rating with the two- to three-year average postreform CPIA cluster rating one can broadly assess the relative strengths and weaknesses of specific loan conditionality.

The before-after analysis shows that, on average, adjusting countries with better policies in the macro, social, and PSM areas have grown faster two to three years after the approval of a policy-based loan than have their poor-performing counterparts. Figure 20.3 shows this relationship for fiscal 1996–2001. The exception is for structural

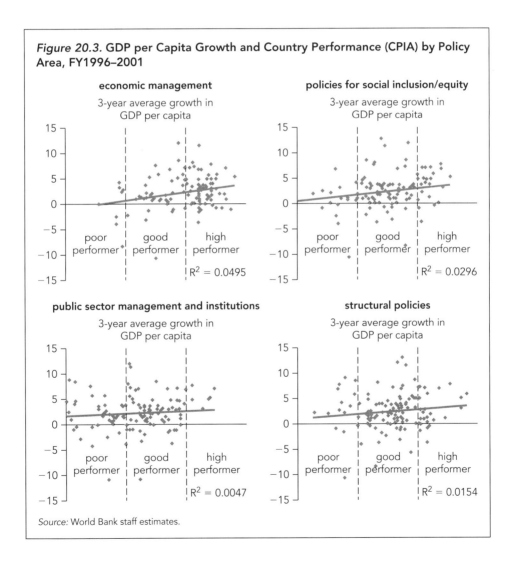

Figure 20.3. GDP per Capita Growth and Country Performance (CPIA) by Policy Area, FY1996–2001

Source: World Bank staff estimates.

TABLE 20.1 Average GDP per Capita Growth 2–3 Years after Loan Approval by Country Groups

Loans Approved in FY 96–02 Avg. CPIA Ratings	Poor Performer	Good Performer	High Performer
Economic Management	−0.8	2.1	2.5
Policies for Social Inclusion/Equity	0.6	2.4	3.1
Public Sector Management and Institutions	1.7	2.3	5.5
Structural Policies	3.0	2.2	2.5

Source: Author's estimate.

performance, where GDP per capita growth has been on average higher in poor-performing countries than in good- or high-performing countries (see table 20.1). One explanation for this apparent anomaly is the positive impact on GDP of higher oil prices in certain poor-performing oil economies.

Empirical Analysis

The empirical analysis in this section attempts to determine whether conditionality causally influences country performance.[5] Data for the analysis are drawn from 134 World Bank–supported policy-based loans approved in 69 countries between fiscal 1996 and fiscal 2000. The time series panel is mostly composed of data from the World Bank's World Development Indicators database, the Adjustment Lending Conditionality and Implementation Database (ALCID) maintained by Operations Policy and Country Services, and the *Europa Yearbook,* which provides data on country governments and their political arrangements.

Econometric Model and Application

Variants of the following equation are used to address the conditionality-performance link:

$$p_{it} = p_{it(init)}\beta_p + a_{it}\beta_a + b_{it}\beta_b + y_t + \varepsilon^p_{it}, \qquad [1]$$

where i indexes countries, t indexes time, p_{it} is the change in the logarithm of GDP per capita in 1995 prices two years after loan approval, $p_{it(init)}$ is the initial dependent variable, a_{it} is an $m \times 1$ vector of dummy variables that take the value of one if the loan carries conditionality on the four m CPIA cluster and zero otherwise, b_{it} is an $n \times 1$ vector of variables that might affect country performance, y_t are fixed effects, and ε^p_{it} is the zero scalar.

A fixed-effects-pooled-least-squares is used to estimate equation 1. The equation variants use White heteroskedasticity-consistent standard errors and covariance. They are estimated using a panel of policy-based loans approved between fiscal 1996

TABLE 20.2 Selected Summary Statistics: Common Sample

Policy-Based Loans Approved in FY96–00	Mean	Median	Maximum	Minimum	Std. Dev.
	in Number of Conditions				
GDP per Capita	2.4	2.3	28.0	−11.8	4.7
Total Legally Binding Conditions	35.9	28.5	160.0	4.0	26.3
Macro Conditions	3.7	2.5	16.0	0.0	3.8
Social Conditions	7.0	3.0	66.0	0.0	10.5
PSM Conditions	6.8	4.0	38.0	0.0	8.3
Structural Conditions	18.3	14.5	98.0	0.0	17.9
Number of Loans	134				
Number of Countries	69				

Source: Author's estimates

and fiscal 2000 (the fiscal year is July–June). Conditionality observed in a loan approved in fiscal 1996 is grouped with 1996 data.

The country performance equation 1 is specified to account for a small range of institutional and policy conditions that can help explain country performance. To capture the convergence effects of the dependent variable, country performance during period t is allowed to depend on the logarithm of p_{it} at the beginning of the period. The specification to account for macroeconomic and structural exogenous variables, b_{it}, follows some elements of the empirical growth literature: inflation, the current account balance as a percentage of GDP, and government consumption as a percentage of GDP.

Table 20.2 provides summary statistics for the main variables that are the focus of the analysis—conditionality and country performance. The mean number of legally binding conditions was 35.9 for the full set of 134 loans, with a maximum of 160 conditions in a 1999 loan to Indonesia. The mean annual improvement in country performance was 2.4 percent, with the largest improvement at 28 percent in a European country (1997) and the largest deterioration at 11.8 percent in an East Asian country in the context of the East Asian crisis (1998).

Results

Table 20.3 summarizes the results of applying the data to the model. Column 1 shows equation 1 specified without the interest variables, to determine the most significant variables—it shows that all four exogenous variables are significant. All five regressions use this same set of variables, because they represent elements of economic and fiscal factors that might affect country performance.

Once conditionality is considered, and using a fixed-effects-pooled-least-squares, social sector conditionality shows a statistically significant (at the 1 percent significance level) positive effect on GDP per capita growth two years after loan approval (see column 3), together with inflation and government consumption negative effects. Column 6 shows the regression when all four conditionality groups are included.

TABLE 20.3 Effect of Conditionality on GDP per Capita

Method: Pooled Least Squares
White Heteroskedasticity-Consistent Standard Errors & Covariance

Dependent Variable: Change in GDP per Capita (t+2)	(1)	(2)	(3)	(4)	(5)	(6)
Initial GDP per Capita in 1995 Constant Prices (in logs)	−0.0991***	−0.0545	−0.0674	−0.0520	−0.0679	−0.0277
Inflation, Consumer Prices (annual %)	−0.0001***	−0.0001***	−0.0001***	−0.0001***	−0.0001***	−0.0001***
Current Account Balance (% of GDP)	0.0019***	0.0007	0.0006	0.0005	0.0006	0.0005
General Government Final Consumption Expenditure (% of GDP)	−0.0033***	−0.0064***	−0.0074***	−0.0067***	−0.0065***	−0.0077***
Macro Conditions		0.0097				0.0182
Social Conditions			0.0188***			0.0211***
PSM Conditions				−0.0064		−0.0132
Structural Conditions					−0.0030	−0.0001
Adjusted R-Squared	0.33	0.33	0.37	0.32	0.32	0.35
Number of Observations	319	110	110	110	110	110

Source: Author's estimates.

***Significance at the 1 percent level.

Loans with social sector conditionality tend to have a positive effect on GDP per capita growth two years after loan approval. Conditionality on macro, PSM, and structural areas does not seem to have a positive effect.

Conclusions

Findings from a before-after analysis indicate that, on average, adjusting countries with better policies grew faster two to three years after loan approval compared with poor-performing countries, and that conditionality focused mostly on structural and public sector management actions. The results of the empirical model further suggest that an increase in social sector conditionality in policy-based loans tends to be strongly associated with GDP per capita growth two years after loan approval. However, conditionality in the other three policy areas does not seem to have an effect on country performance. These latter results may reflect the short time period studied. They point to the need for more focused research in specific reform areas, such as exploring the effect of conditionality addressing fiduciary and procurement systems on the quality of public financial management performance. Such focused exercises could yield more reliable or more informative results for individual reform areas than those provided by this analysis of the four broad reform areas. There is scope for further research focusing on the impact of conditionality on more specific micro reform areas.

ANNEX 20.1. Mapping Loan Conditions with Country Performance: Thematic and CPIA Categories

Thematic Classification of Loan Conditions (ALCID Database)	Country Policy and Institutional Assessment (CPIA) Categories (2003 Guideline)
Economic Management • Analysis of Economic Growth • Debt Management and Fiscal Sustainability • Economic Statistics, Modeling, and Forecasting • Macroeconomic Management	**Economic Management** • Management of Inflation and Macro. Imbalances • Fiscal Policy • Management of Public Debt • Management and Sustainability of the Dev. Program
Financial and Private Sector Development • Corporate Governance, Standards, and Financial Reporting • Infrastructure Services for Private Sector Dev. • Regulation and Competition Policy • Small and Medium Enterprise Support • State Enterprise/Bank Restructuring and Privatization • Municipal Finance (Urban Dev.) • Rural Markets and Rural Finance (Rural Dev.)	**Structural Policies** • Trade Policy and Foreign Exchange Regime • Financial Stability • Financial Sector Depth, Efficiency, and Resource Mobilization • Competitive Environment for the Private Sector • Goods and Factor Markets • Policies and Institutions for Environmental Sustainability
Trade and Integration • Export Development and Competitiveness • International Financial Architecture • Regional Integration • Technology Diffusion, Trade Facilitation, and Market Access	
Environment and Natural Resources Management • Biodiversity and Climate Change • Environmental Policies and Institutions • Land Management • Pollution Management and Environmental Health • Water Resources Management	
Social Protection and Risk Management • Natural Disaster Management • Poverty Strategy, Analysis, and Monitoring • Social Risk Coping, Mitigation, and Reduction • Vulnerability Assessment and Monitoring • Access to Urban Services for the Poor (Urban Dev.)	**Policies for Social Inclusive/Equity** • Gender • Equity of Public Resource Use • Building Human Resources • Social Protection and Labor • Monitoring and Analysis of Poverty Outcomes and Impacts
Social Development, Gender, and Inclusion • Participation and Civic Engagement • Conflict Prevention and Postconflict Reconstruction • Gender and Indigenous Peoples • Social Analysis and Monitoring	

(Continued)

ANNEX 20.1. (*Continued*)

Thematic Classification of Loan Conditions (ALCID Database)	Country Policy and Institutional Assessment (CPIA) Categories (2003 Guideline)

Human Development
- Child Health, Nutrition, and Food Security
- HIV/AIDS and Other Communicable Diseases
- Education for All, Education for the Knowledge Economy
- Health System Performance
- Population and Reproductive Health
- Noncommunicable Diseases and Injury

Public Sector Governance
- Administrative and Civil Service Reform
- Decentralization
- Public Expenditure, Financial Management, and Procurement
- Tax Policy and Administration
- Other Accountability/Anticorruption
- Municipal Governance and Institution Building (Urban Dev.)
- Rural Policies, Services, and Institutions (Rural Dev.)

Public Sector Management and Institutions
- Property Rights and Rule-Based Governance
- Quality of Budgetary and Financial Management
- Efficiency of Revenue Mobilization
- Quality of Public Administration
- Transparency, Accountability, and Corruption in the Public Sector

Rule of Law
- Access to Law and Justice, Legal Services
- Judicial and Other Dispute Resolution Mechanism
- Law Reform and Legal Institutions for a Market Economy
- Personal and Property Rights

Endnotes

1. The CPIA exercise assesses the quality of a country's policy and institutional framework on the basis of observable policies, with "quality" defined as the degree to which the framework fosters poverty reduction and sustains growth and the effective use of development assistance. World Bank staff assess and rate 20 policy and institutional performance areas, which are then grouped and averaged into the four clusters identified above.

2. Note the difference in periodization (fiscal 1996–2002, 217 loans, 80 countries) and, hence, the number of conditions in this section compared with those in the Empirical Analysis section (fiscal 1996–2000, 134 loans, 69 countries). Data for all the variables in the empirical analysis are more limited than those available for the before-after analysis.

3. Legally binding conditions are recorded in the legal agreements (the text is confidential and undisclosed) and are the basis of the commitment between the World Bank and the borrower on a program of cooperation throughout the period of a policy reform program.

4. A CPIA rating of 4.000 and above is designated "high," a rating of 3.000 to 3.999 is designated "good," and a rating less than 2.999 is designated "poor." Two things about this classification should be stressed at the outset: (a) no such groupings are in use today at the

World Bank, and (b) neither the CPIA ratings nor the countries they represent are disclosed by the Bank.

5. There are two problems with this use of country performance regressions. First, the country performance regressions may suffer from parameter homogeneity—the assumption that the variables used to describe country performance are identical across countries. This assumption implies that a set of loan conditionality in similar policy areas has the same effect on country performance across countries. This assumption of parameter homogeneity may be invalid because country circumstances are so heterogeneous. By allowing for fixed effects (i.e., constant terms differ across countries) this problem is addressed, but the approach may be of limited value in this study because the time dimension employed in the country performance regressions is relatively short. Country performance during fiscal 1996–2000 may be a function of actions and policies taken in periods prior to the one studied in this chapter, and the data may contain business cycle factors; consequently, it is difficult to see how long-term country performance can be affected by such short time periods. The second analytic issue is the question of causality. Many of the variables used to explain country performance are drawn from economic and social dimensions that also affect performance—the endogenous problem.

21

Adjusting Conditionality: Prescriptions for Policy-Based Lending

DANIEL MORROW[1]
The George Washington University

There seems to be growing acceptance of three key ideas related to World Bank policy-based lending (also called adjustment lending).[2] First, country ownership is a sine qua non for successful, sustainable reforms, and therefore conditionality associated with policy-based lending should be, in Tony Killick's words, "pro forma," consensual conditionality rather than "hard core," coercive conditionality. Second, in place of coercive loan conditionality, the Bank should exercise country selectivity, providing policy-based lending only if and when a country has already taken adequate ownership of the reforms that the Bank believes are essential for accelerating growth and poverty reduction. Third, as recognized for more than a decade, policy-based lending is now used mostly to support second- or third-generation reforms rather than macroeconomic adjustment programs. These second- and third-generation reforms are institutionally and politically complex, and for these sorts of reforms the utility of conditionality is especially uncertain and its design is problematic.

The Bank has begun to come to grips with the implications of these ideas for its policy-based lending operations. Its recent efforts to write new guidelines and define good practice for policy-based lending reflect these ideas in some important ways. But in its common practice the Bank still needs to accept their implications more fully in order to increase the likelihood that policy-based lending will generate net benefits. In addition, the Bank needs to address directly the question of under what circumstances, if any, policy-based lending is appropriate in supporting reforms that have no net fiscal cost. More generally, it needs to revisit the broad question of what policy-based loans (PBLs) are in fact financing and to develop clearer guidelines on the appropriate amounts of each PBL and on how those amounts should be adjusted in response to delays or deviations in implementation of the associated reform program.

This chapter explores several remaining conceptual problems of World Bank policy-based lending when such lending is used to support second- and third-generation reforms rather than to assist countries in responding to macroeconomic or financial crisis.[3] It begins with an elaboration of the points noted above, which then leads to a discussion of the potential nonfinancial benefits and costs of policy-based lending in terms of their contribution to the design and implementation of good reforms. Finally, the chapter makes recommendations for the guidelines and good practices for Bank policy-based lending.

This chapter makes assertions about common patterns of Bank policy-based lending in recent years on the basis of a thorough review of IBRD PBLs during fiscal 2000–2, a more limited review of IDA PBLs during that period, on selected Country Assistance Strategies (CASs) from that period, and on my own experience as a former Bank staff member. However, the validity of the analysis and recommendation should be further examined using a larger and more recent sample of policy-based lending, including especially IDA credits and more recent CASs.

Current Doctrine and Reality about the Bank's Policy-Based Lending

It is now widely held that it is wrong and futile to use lending conditionality to compel a government to do that which it is not convinced it should do. In the case of many creditworthy, especially middle-income, countries, this reflects a simple reality. These countries have reasonable access to international capital markets, and IBRD lending typically provides only modest financial advantages. Therefore, the Bank does not have any significant financial leverage over these countries' policy making (except possibly during periods of financial crisis when access to alternative financing is severely constrained). In the case of noncreditworthy, mostly low-income, countries that remain dependent on continuing flows of IDA credits and other official development assistance, the Bank might be able to exercise considerable leverage. But it is now official doctrine that conditionality should not be compulsive. Paul Collier and Tony Killick laid the basis for this new doctrine in their early critiques of conditionality, and the new doctrine is now widely expressed in World Bank documents, if not yet fully reflected in Bank practice. The Bank's well-known study on *Assessing Aid: What Works, What Doesn't and Why*, stated: "In its own internal reviews the World Bank has come to the same conclusion—'ownership,' or strong domestic support of reforms, is essential for adjustment lending to succeed" (World Bank 1998, 52). The Bank's recent draft note on designing policy-based lending—which uses the term "development policy operation" as the new name for policy-based lending—states: "Conditionality should complement ownership, not substitute for it. Conditions for development policy operations need to be agreeable to the government and the Bank. When conditional lending is used to induce a government to undertake reforms that it does not wish to do, it is unlikely that these reforms will be fully implemented and sustained. Furthermore, the prospects for improving governance and the accountability of a government to its own citizens will likely be undermined" (World Bank 2004, 3).[4]

It is still true that PBLs involve "money for policy." The Bank's proclaimed justification for each of these loans is that it "supports" the government's reform program. The disbursements of the loans are explicitly conditional upon the government's implementation of agreed measures within those reform programs. But under the new doctrine these conditions are, in the vocabulary of Tony Killick, "pro forma" rather than "hard-core" conditions:

> Pro forma conditionality [is] described as policy commitments written into aid agreements for the convenience of both parties. These are consensual, included in order to set out systematically and clearly a mutually-agreed package of measures, codifying what should be done and in what sequence; serving as a kind of institutionalized memory against the possibility of changes among key ministers, officials, perhaps even the government itself; providing a vehicle through which agencies can undertake their program lending, and for persuading the management and/or Boards of aid agencies of the adequacy of the policy program. Hard core conditionality, by contrast, [is] seen as coercive: actions, or promises of actions, made only at the insistence of the lender or giver, measures that would not otherwise be undertaken, promised involuntarily by governments in urgent need of money. (Killick 1998, 188)

In his 1998 study, Killick advocated the use of pro forma conditionality and went on to say: "The question may well be asked: why . . . bother with the modalities of conditionality at all? The answer is that, for the reasons just suggested, these may make life easier for both parties, may smooth the path for policy reform, make it more orderly, more assured" (Killick 1998, 188). Although the Bank has not adopted the term "pro forma" conditionality, it has in principle adopted the concept. The draft note on policy-based lending answers Killick's question in this way:

> A development policy operation [the new term for a PBL] can complement ownership in several ways. The process of preparing the Program Matrix of relevant actions and outcomes generates a dialogue among various parts of the government—and often with nongovernmental stakeholders—that can improve the design of the reform program and help build broader support for the reforms. Bank staff can play a useful role during the design phase by providing analysis and advice, drawing on experience in other countries, and by facilitating communications among stakeholders within the country. Once agreement within the government and between the government and the Bank has been reached, the formal conditionality associated with development policy operations can complement country ownership:
>
> • The Program Matrix can help keep the program on track during its implementation, in particular by creating a timetable and incentives for completing actions.
>
> • The formal agreement to the conditions and triggers that are part of the Program Matrix signal to the broader government and to the public that the government is committed to carrying through the reform program, generating momentum in the reform process and strengthening expectations that the reform will be sustained. This is often important in inducing a positive private sector response to a policy change.
>
> • The agreement between the government and the Bank on conditions and triggers also provides assurance to Bank Management and shareholders that the reform program will be sustained and will generate benefits that justify the loan, credit, or grant.

If the reforms associated with Bank PBLs are consensual rather than coercive, this does not mean that the Bank has no influence at all on the content of the policy reforms. During the course of dialogue associated with the preparation and negotiation of a PBL, including related economic and sector work, the Bank staff may very well persuade the government about what reforms are needed and may significantly influence the details of the reform program. And the government might equally persuade the Bank to change its initial ideas and positions. In any particular instance it would be difficult to determine which party has exercised more influence over the other in deciding on the details of policy reforms. But, to the extent that the Bank follows its new doctrine, it is appropriate to say that conditionality is not coercive even if the Bank has been influential in designing the reform program associated with a PBL.

Selectivity as a Substitute for Hard Core Conditionality

The doctrine that the Bank should use policy-based lending only to support reforms that enjoy country ownership does not imply that the Bank should be willing to finance any sort of reform or to finance a country-owned program that involves no substantial effort to address the country's remaining policy and institutional impediments to development. Instead, the prevailing wisdom is that the Bank should provide PBLs selectively to those countries that have already taken ownership of a set of reforms that the Bank agrees are useful for its further development. The draft note on policy-based lending states the principle in this way: "Ownership is a necessary but insufficient condition for Bank support. The Bank should finance development policy operations to support reform programs that have adequate ownership and, in the Bank's judgment, contribute to the country's development goals. Collaborative analytic work and policy dialogue help define the set of reforms that meet these dual criteria." The draft goes on to say:

> Designing a development policy operation is a two-stage process. First, the Bank's Country Assistance Strategy (CAS) sets the strategic context with which all of the Bank's individual lending operations should be consistent. It also defines the country outcomes, which the Bank expects to positively influence and to which the individual lending operations should contribute. In the CAS the Bank exercises judgments about *country selectivity* in the allocation of Bank resources and about the broad conditions in which a development policy operation would be appropriate. Through the CAS and its updates, the Bank makes clear the general direction of the reform program to which the government should be committed prior to active preparation of each possible development policy operation.
>
> • Inclusion of a development policy operation in a CAS's base-case lending scenario reflects a judgment that such an operation is justified by the country's current level of policy and institutional development, its needs for Bank financing, its creditworthiness, and its general commitment to move forward in appropriate reform areas.
>
> • In some cases, a development policy operation may be included only in a high-case lending scenario—that is, after an improvement in specific dimensions of the country's policy and institutional framework or a demonstrable increase in the government's commitment to move forward with a reform program in specific areas.
>
> When a government has achieved the relevant thresholds indicated in the CAS, including a sufficient indication of ownership of the associated reform program *in broad terms,* the country and Bank begin to design and negotiate the details of that operation. The amount and the timing of the operation may be adjusted relative to that envisioned by the CAS in response to (a) the quality and cost of the policy and institutional changes that the government decides to pursue, and (b) any significant changes in the country's economic environment (such as terms of trade shocks that affect the fiscal balance).

In one important respect, such selectivity is similar to hard-core conditionality: access to the financial resources of a PBL depends on the government's acceptance of a set of reforms that the Bank considers useful for the country's development. Nonetheless, there are important differences between this concept of selectivity and the traditional application of hard-core conditionality. First, and most important, from the government's perspective, the primary challenge is no longer reaching agreement with the Bank on a set of reform measures but building sufficient support for the reforms within the country. Second, with respect to timing, selectivity implies that at least a reasonable level of ownership for a particular set of reforms has been achieved before the Bank begins to work with a country on the detailed definition of a reform program and the conditionality for an associated PBL. Such prior ownership implies a much higher likelihood that the reforms will be implemented and sustained. And, third, following the selectivity approach, the nature of the Bank's dialogue and engagement with the country is likely to be different than in the case of traditional policy-based lending based on hard-core conditionality. In some cases, the Bank may be absent from the internal dialogue through which a government develops ownership for a reform program. This is more likely to be the case in a country in which the Bank has not earned a reputation as an objective, constructive partner. In other countries, the Bank may have actively engaged in both analytical work and policy dialogue about these reforms and have been an agent in building country ownership. In this latter circumstance, the dialogue is likely to be a noncoercive give-and-take in which the Bank can function as a partner in policy analysis and formulation rather than as a dictator of policy reforms. Through such dialogue, the Bank can learn about the country's circumstances and the government's point of view so that the details of the reforms are more "home grown" and less driven by ideas from Washington.

There are, however, two problems in applying this vision of selectivity. First, for noncreditworthy countries that desperately need Bank policy-based lending to cover fiscal needs, there is strong pressure to accept—or at least pretend to accept—the reforms that the Bank has indicated are necessary if the country is to be selected as eligible for additional policy-based lending. Critics of the Poverty Reduction Strategy Paper (PRSP) process have noted this problem frequently. They argue that governments put into their PRSPs those policy reforms that they assume the Bank and the IMF prefer. It might be the case that the Bank could detect such "fake ownership." This would require a rather careful assessment of the domestic politics surrounding a potential reform program, and the Bank may not be well situated or even motivated to undertake such an assessment.

Second, applying a selectivity approach in lieu of hard-core conditionality for policy-based lending requires that the Bank provides clear and timely information to a country on what reforms are considered necessary to merit Bank financial support. Doing so would require that the Bank's criteria for evaluating a country's policy and institutional environment and for allocating loan resources are fully understood by the governments concerned. This would need to be done at a Bank-wide level and, more important, for each individual country. Thus far, the Bank has partly embraced this idea. The substance of the Bank's Country Policy and Institutional Assessment (CPIA) and its related system of performance-based allocation of IDA lending resources have been made more transparent. Since 2000, for IDA countries, Bank staff have disclosed and discussed an IDA country's CPIA ratings and the performance-based allocation system with the government authorities, and the CPIA ratings for all IDA countries are posted in quintile format on the Bank's Web site. For IBRD countries, country creditworthiness rather than the CPIA plays a key role in the lending decisions, and the CPIA scores for IBRD countries are not disclosed. Improving transparency at a systematic level would need to be matched at the country level by clarity in the CAS. Ideally, according to the draft note cited above, "Through the CAS and its updates, the Bank makes clear the general direction of the reform program to which the government should be committed prior to active preparation of each possible development policy operation." But, in practice, this is not always the case. CASs sometimes provide only vague indications about what a country would need to do to qualify for additional policy-based lending.

Institutionally and Politically Complex Reforms

The reforms that the Bank supports through recent PBLs are usually quite different from the sorts of reforms associated with policy-based lending in the 1980s and even in the early 1990s. They are usually second- or third-generation reforms that do not involve major macroeconomic policy changes designed to achieve stabilization or additional major shifts toward a more market-oriented and open economy.[5] As summarized in the Bank's recent "Adjustment Lending Retrospective" report, "The content of [PBLs] has evolved in line with the changing development context . . . it focused in the 1980s on fiscal adjustment in response to external shocks and on removing obstacles to growth . . . the Bank's adjustment operations in the 1990s changed along a number of dimensions, with increased attention to poverty reduction, institutions, and complex social and structural reforms . . . As many countries have removed economic distortions, [policy-based lending] is now increasingly supporting reform agendas associated with medium-term institution building" (World Bank 2001a, xi, xiv).

Often the reforms now associated with policy-based lending involve efforts to improve the provision of basic public services within a sustainable fiscal framework and to improve core government functions, such as the regulation of banking. Following are two examples of the type of reforms on which PBLs are often conditional: (1) The Colombian Social Sector PBL supported, among many other things, "the expansion of the subsidized health insurance coverage of the poor, issuance of regulations to implement the new methodology for allocating health transfers to territorial entities, strengthening the Health Superintendency, . . . establishment of performance and monitoring agreements between the national and selected governments/Education Secretariats . . ." (2) The Second Economic Restructuring Loan to the state of Karnataka in India required administrative reforms focused on "civil service reform, freedom of information, service agency reforms, measures to reduce corruption, decentralization, and e-governance, with the objectives of improving the efficiency and transparency by which government transacts its business and delivers services."

Such reforms are very different from the sort of "stroke-of-the-pen" measures often associated with early structural adjustment programs—decreasing tariffs, increasing a tax rate, or eliminating a subsidy for electric power. For the most part, they involve changes in the behaviors of government institutions that are intended to improve the efficacy and efficiency of public services.[6] Such reforms may seem unambiguously good and hence uncontroversial. That may be true for the broad intentions. But, in fact, such reforms are institutionally and politically complex. The core interests of many groups are often at stake, and the devil is truly in the details. In many ways, these second- and third-generation reform programs are more difficult to adopt and, once formally adopted, harder to implement than earlier reforms.

Such reforms are institutionally and politically complex because they involve four sets of obstacles, as described by Nelson (1999) in her analysis of education and health sector reforms:

- **Multiple vested interests and stakeholders.** Many groups within and usually outside government must cooperate to implement these sorts of reforms. As Nelson says, ". . . simply overriding their objections may be unwise even where reformers have sufficient power."

- **A long timetable.** Changing institutional arrangements and behaviors of large government bureaucracies and large groups such as tax administrators or teachers takes time. According to Nelson, "this means that political battles do not stop after reforms are approved but are re-cast and re-fought at both national and local levels, often diluting or derailing the reforms."

- **No blueprint for reform.** Although there may have been a "Washington consensus" among international financial institutions and many borrowing governments about first-generation structural adjustment programs, there are no technical models for public administration reforms or for reforming the education and health sectors that command wide consensus. What can be made to work in one setting is not likely to work elsewhere in just the same way. Bureaucratic cultures differ, and that matters a lot in institutionally complex reforms. As Dani Rodrik puts it, "institutional innovations do not travel well" (Rodrick 2002, 3)

- **Little apparent urgency.** Poorly run, even corrupt, public services are a well-recognized problem. But, unlike hyperinflation or other macroeconomic crises, they can be tolerated for a long time by societies and their political elites. In the face of opposition from vested interests (who face concentrated, often immediate losses), politicians often find it easiest to postpone reforms that have widely diffused, incremental, and long-term benefits.

Paul Collier and Joan Nelson predicted that this shift in the reform agenda in many countries would substantially complicate and perhaps reduce the use of policy-based lending. In writing about whether or not policy conditionality might be redesigned to avoid past failures in promoting reforms, Collier based his negative conclusion partly on the observation that ". . . the reform agenda has largely moved on from macro-economic policies to sectoral policies, such as civil service reform and privatization.

These policies are intrinsically more complex, both politically and administratively, and so less suited to timetabled conditions than the earlier generation of reforms" (Collier 2000, 305). Nelson also stressed the shift in the reform agenda of borrowing countries and, because of this and other factors, predicted (wrongly, or at least prematurely) that "the outlook is for further shrinkage in the relative and absolute levels of policy-based loans" (Nelson 1996, 1552).

More specifically, the characteristics of the types of reforms now most commonly associated with Bank policy-based lending have these important implications:

• These reform processes cannot be well designed primarily by an external agency. Because good design requires intimate knowledge of the local setting and institutions and because implementation requires some degree of consent from the many stakeholders, such reforms must truly be "homegrown." Imported designs will not carry much credibility.

• The process of designing reforms becomes much more complicated, involving not only the executive ministries but often also the national parliament, autonomous implementing agencies, subnational governments, and nongovernmental actors.

• Implementation of these reform programs usually involves some trial and error to discover what works best, and some give-and-take to maintain support from the various interest groups as implementation unfolds. This makes it hard, if not counterproductive, to specify and commit to the detailed steps of the reform program for two or three years in advance.

• These sorts of reforms almost never depend on a few key measures, but require a host of small steps and behavioral changes. It is true that design and approval of a new law or major regulation is often important. But *implementation* of that law or regulation is the key and often more difficult challenge.[7] Outlining a program of implementation involves a lot of detail.

• A related implication is that the process of reform has, in the words of Paul Collier, "fairly low observability—their operation depends upon behavior at the local level, or within the bowels of various ministries, over a long period of time" (Collier 2002, 8). This means that monitoring implementation of behaviors that matter and enforcing meaningful conditions by an external party is difficult, if not impossible.

No Net Fiscal Costs for the Reforms

In many cases, the reform programs associated with policy-based lending in recent years do not involve a net fiscal cost to the government—even in the short run. Furthermore, the reforms are not undertaken in order to adjust to some exogenous shock to the country's fiscal or external balance.

This distinguishes many recent PBLs from most of the early policy-based lending. In the early 1980s, especially in Latin America, the intention of policy-based lending was to provide financial resources during a transitional period in which the government took policy measures so that the country's economy could adapt to the sudden increase in oil prices and interest rates during that era. Often these adjustment policies would involve short-term costs, but also, it was hoped, long-term benefits to the government's treasury and to the economy. The money from PBLs was intended to help bridge the gap. For example, reducing import tariffs would in theory help the economy to improve its international competitive position and eventually its growth rate and external balance. In the short run, however, lower tariffs meant lower government revenues and higher imports. A PBL would at least partly compensate for the shortfalls in fiscal revenue and net foreign exchange earnings. In these circumstances, the money provided by the loan had an important role in cushioning the impacts of adjustment.

Subsequent to the early 1980s, policy-based lending was increasingly used to "support" reform packages that were designed to improve the government's fiscal position from day one: the reforms involved no short-term net costs either to the treasury or the economy as a whole.[8] In these cases, the formal justification for the Bank loan was that the country as a whole had an external financing need, not that the reforms themselves had any short-term costs. Until the early 1990s, the Bank economists needed only to establish that the country faced a current account deficit and therefore a need for capital inflows. In 1992 the Bank formally relaxed its macroeconomic criteria for PBLs, requiring only that a country had an "actual or anticipated external financing gap with balance of payments or fiscal origins." This placed the focus primarily on the government's need for financing for its overall fiscal program, including its debt service, rather than on the costs of the associated reform program.[9]

Among recent PBLs, many are associated with reform programs that do not increase the government's overall expenditures, decrease its revenue stream, or increase its financing requirements. According to the Bank's "Adjustment Lending Retrospective" report, only about 60 percent of the fiscal 1998–2000 adjustment operations even estimated the cost of reforms, implying that in at least 40 percent of the cases financing the near-term cost of the reform was not a rationale for the loan and indicating that the reforms probably had no significant fiscal costs. Many of the policy changes are designed to improve efficiency rather than expand programs—and therefore save money. Many others require changes in the behaviors or rules of existing government agencies, and the costs of such changes in terms of incremental expenditures for consultants or new staff are small relative to the amounts of the loans. Here are two examples of reforms that involve little or no net fiscal costs. (1) The Decentralization PBL to Mexico in 1999 had four main objectives: imposing hard budget constraints on federal resources provided to states and municipalities; reducing moral hazard in subnational borrowing; increasing the transparency and public accountability of subnational fiscal and financial management; and setting up pilot mechanisms to enhance efficiency in decentralized expenditures in the environment and health sectors. (2) The reforms supported by Tunisia's Third Economic Competitiveness PBL involved: enhancing the private investment climate by improving the business environment and corporate governance and developing private sector participation in infrastructure; strengthening banking regulation, accelerating development of the capital markets, and reforming the insurance sector; and improving international communications technology regulations.

Among recent PBLs, there are important exceptions to the observation that many reform programs have no short-term cost to the government.[10] Recent loans for financial sector restructuring in Mexico and Brazil explicitly provide financing for the government to, in effect, buy bad loans from banks as part of a program to restore solvency to the banking system and reactivate commercial lending.[11] In a few cases, the reform program may increase costs to the central government but induce savings among subnational governments. For example, in the case of the Russian Fiscal Federalism and Regional Fiscal Reform Loan, part of the loan was used to finance a facility that gives grants to provincial governments that are successfully implementing programs of fiscal reform. Also, pension reform programs often involve high front-end costs.

For those reform programs that do not need incremental financing, the logical question is: what is the money from the PBL actually used for? The common jargon of Bank policy-based lending obscures this question. The operative word, as cited frequently above, is that the loan "supports" the reform program. The fuller formulation is equally vague: "[PBLs] provide quick-disbursing financing to member countries with external financing needs in developing and implementing policy measures and institutional reforms" (World Bank 2002b, 2). Although this might be mistakenly interpreted to mean that the PBL actually finances the incremental costs of a reform program, this is often not the case.

In some cases, the Bank loan does not expand the financial resources available to the government, but simply substitutes for some other source of financing. A few loan documents are explicit about this. The PID for the Brazil Energy Sector Reform Loan explains: "The proposed loan does not increase the resources available for public sector spending. Under Brazil's fiscal regime, a PBL from the Bank substitutes for financing from alternative, more expensive debt sources and substitutes foreign for domestic lending." The PID for the Mexico Programmatic Environment Structural PBL is equally explicit: after repeating the exact wording quoted above from the Brazil loan, it adds "[The loan] does not increase aggregate fiscal resources available to environment and other sectoral agencies since the fiscal envelope is defined by the binding fiscal surplus targets."

Even if the availability of Bank financing would allow the government to expand its borrowing and expenditure programs at the margin but the associated reform program has no net fiscal costs, then, of course, the Bank typically has no influence over or perhaps even no knowledge about how these incremental resources are used. Even in the case in which the reform program has a net fiscal cost, it is not at all certain that the activities of the reform program itself would be in fact the marginal activity. If the reform program is part of the core of the government's program, as expected if the program is truly owned by the government, then the incremental financing from the loan money actually goes to some other, unidentifiable activity. In the case of policy-based lending and in contrast to project lending, this fungibility of money is tacitly recognized by the absence of any pretense of linking the Bank's disbursements to any particular set of expenditures.

The fact that the funds from a PBL often cannot be linked directly to any set of expenditures—incremental or otherwise—begs the question of how the size of a

PBL is determined. There are no clear guidelines within the Bank about how to set the amount of a PBL. The current Bank operational directive for policy-based lending states: "there is no simple rule for determining the size of an individual [PBL]." It suggests that the costs of the reforms to be supported may be a helpful indicator of the appropriate size of the loan, but adds that "such costs are hard to measure with precision . . . Generally speaking, the appropriate size of an adjustment operation is a matter of judgment based on a number of factors, including the actual or expected external financing gap, the scope for burden sharing with other donors and lenders, and the size of the overall lending program. Decisions on loan size are also influenced by the country's creditworthiness (for IBRD countries) . . ." (World Bank 2001b, 70).

In traditional Bank practice, explicit consideration has usually been given to three factors—the amount of total financing that the country needed from the Bank to close its external "financing gap," the importance and political difficulty of the associated reforms themselves, and informal norms about the size of loans relative to the size of the country's economy. The financing gap is notionally the amount of borrowing that the government needs from the Bank to complete its borrowing requirements—which may be defined by the overall balance of payments needs of the country or by the public sector borrowing requirement. However, in the case of most IBRD borrowers, when the government has access to private capital markets, the notion of a financing gap becomes meaningless. How much the government should borrow from the IBRD rather than other creditors is indeterminate, and the concept of a financing gap provides no real guidance about the appropriate size of an IBRD loan. Even for most IDA countries that do not have many other financing options, the gap is subject to large estimation errors. Hence, in discussions within the Bank, considerable weight is often given to the equally ambiguous concept of the importance or difficulty of the associated reforms. Because the mindset of "buying reforms" has often dominated within the Bank, the key question has often been whether the Bank is—in a very subjective sense—"getting its money's worth." Finally, there are some rough norms or rules of thumb within the Bank. Almost any PBL for a large economy such as Brazil or Mexico is set in the range of $400–$600 million. PBLs for small economies such as Bulgaria, Jamaica, or Tunisia would typically be set in the range of $50 million–$150 million.

However, at least implicitly within the Bank and probably explicitly in the minds of the government officials concerned, the size of PBLs has often been set keeping in mind a desired level of net disbursements from the Bank to the government and hence the desired direction and pace of change in the government's total debt outstanding (TDO) to the Bank in the context of its overall debt management strategy. The case of Mexico illustrates the point: from 1990 through 2002, Mexico's TDO was held within a rather narrow range of $10.9 to $12.1 billion. A recent CAS argued that the TDO should be kept at about $12 billion. This stability was maintained primarily by adjusting the amounts of the steady stream of PBLs. In the case of Brazil, a recent CAS suggested that over the latter half of the 1990s there was an understanding that, subject to reasonable policy directions, the Bank would increase its TDO to Brazil, and the sizes of PBLs were set accordingly. For Morocco, a recent CAS noted that the government was gradually reducing its external indebtedness, taking advantage of large concessional inflows (largely from the European Union) and privatization receipts, and that the Bank's TDO would continue to decline. Given this debt management objective, the next PBL was set at $65 million, and sectoral PBLs in the pipeline were anticipated to be less than $50 million.

Implications for the Potential Nonfinancial Benefits and Costs of Policy-Based Lending

Taking into account these dominant characteristics of many recent policy-based loans—consensual conditionality associated with institutionally and politically complex reforms, which often involve little or no net fiscal costs, what can be said about the potential nonfinancial benefits and costs of the Bank's policy-based lending? In this discussion, nonfinancial benefits and costs are assessed in terms of the likely impact of the PBL on the design and implementation of a good reform program.[12] The government concerned intends to implement the reforms anyway. The reforms by their nature need to be designed and implemented by the domestic stakeholders largely on the basis of intimate knowledge of local circumstances. And, if the government does not need extra money to implement them, why should the Bank provide a loan to "support" such reforms? What are the pros and cons of the Bank's involvement?

The nonfinancial potential benefits and costs of Bank policy-based lending fall into four categories: analytical contributions by Bank staff to policy formulation; value added to the bureaucratic decision-making process; value added to the political decision-making process; and value of the Bank loan as a signaling or commitment device.[13] Consider each in turn.

Analytical Contributions by Bank Staff

The Bank and its sympathetic observers claim that the design of the policy reforms associated with policy-based lending is improved through the analytical contribution of Bank staff. During the dialogue leading up to the loan, the staff may bring to bear their own analysis of the problems and policy options facing the country. Such analysis may be usefully informed by the experiences of other countries with similar reform programs, of which the Bank staff are more likely to be aware than their counterparts within the borrowing government.

Indeed, there seem to be many compelling examples of the value added of the Bank's analytical work. In the case of the Programmatic Financial Sector Loan to Brazil, the PID claimed that "[The Bank] has maintained an active and fruitful dialogue on financial sector matters with the Brazilian authorities over the past years, including importantly through technical assistance lending to the Central Bank of Brazil (approved in 1997) and extensive analytical financial sector work carried out mainly in 2000." The Colombia Social Sector PBL also reportedly drew heavily on prior analytical work. According to the President's Report, the loan "represents the culmination of the Bank's program of social sector strengthening activities initiated with the [Government of Colombia] three years ago. This program consists primarily of three lending operations and two sector studies . . ."

There may be, however, two reasons to question the value of the analytical contributions of Bank staff to the design of policy reforms supported by PBLs. First, when the reforms are institutionally and politically complex as discussed above and there is no blueprint for successful reform, the knowledge and analytical skills brought to bear by Bank staff may be less relevant and, in the worst case, may crowd out more relevant local knowledge.[14] James Scott, in his book *Seeing Like a State: How Certain Schemes to Improve the Human Condition Have Failed*, discusses the differences between what he calls *metis*—local, practical knowledge—and *techme*—generic, theoretical knowledge. He argues compellingly that "true development" depends more on metis than techme. The same proposition may well be true for the sorts of reform processes now most commonly supported by Bank policy-based lending. In such circumstances, unless handled with great sensitivity, the involvement of outside "experts" from the Bank can easily do more harm than good by giving too much weight to the opinions of outsiders. As is expressed on the Global Development Network Web site: "New insights from social theory or new findings from cross-country studies can only be applied in a specific country with a detailed understanding of local context. Without sound local knowledge, imported policy knowledge may be irrelevant or, worse, backfire."[15] The likelihood of doing more harm than good will depend in part on the substance of the reforms themselves. For example, what works best in the realm of banking sector regulation is likely to be more universal than in the realm of education services or public administration. But it is clear that the Bank's PBLs are increasingly focused on domains in which the importance of local knowledge grows and the relevance of other countries' experiences diminishes. This means that the potential benefit of the Bank's analytical contribution will be much harder to realize and may involve greater risk that the Bank's analysis and advice will be wrong and damaging.

A second reason to wonder about the value of the analytical contributions of Bank staff is that, as their pool of human capital deepens, the technical quality of government staff and national researchers in most of the borrowing countries has probably improved substantially over the past couple of decades and continues to improve. In these countries, nationals increasingly improve their capacities to learn about the reform experiences in other countries and to interpret that experience without the intermediation of the Bank staff. Even if the Bank can do an excellent job of recruiting talented, highly trained, and experienced staff, their value added will necessarily decline relative to the value added to policy analysis, design, and implementation from nationals both inside and outside of government.

The Bank has certainly recognized both of these challenges. There is much that it has done and can do to ensure that its analytical contributions do have value added to borrowing governments. In particular, expanding the use of national staff in country resident offices and undertaking analytical work collaboratively with nationals have been pursued as means to ensure the relevance of the Bank's analytical work.

But the key question remains this: why not put the quality of the Bank's analytical contributions to a "market test" by unbundling it from lending? Bank staff has long recognized that the offer of a large loan serves to "buy a seat at the table" and differentiates the Bank from most other sources of advice. It ensures that government officials will at least listen to their advice about policy design, even if they do not finally accept that advice. Hence, the Bank argues that "Advice is often more acceptable and credible when linked to resource transfer" (World Bank 2002a, xxii). But the question should not be: is the Bank's advice accepted and credible? Instead, is it right? If, as suggested above, it is increasingly difficult for the Bank to provide quality advice and there is even a growing risk that its advice will be wrong, shouldn't the Bank have to *earn* a seat at the table on the basis of the quality of its analytical work? If so, then the potential analytical contribution of the Bank cannot be regarded as a benefit of policy-based lending per se but as a potential benefit of the Bank in its role as a "knowledge bank." In fact, the bundling of advice with lending probably increases the risk that the Bank will not have sufficient incentive to ensure the quality of its advice and that some governments will take bad advice just to get the money.

From the Bank's perspective, a substantial impediment to "unbundling" analytical work and policy advice from lending is that a loan is the primary means by which the Bank can recover at least part of the cost of staff and consultants involved in the analytical and advisory work. As expressed in an internal memo, "Clients have no way to engage the Bank on a sustained basis outside promising to borrow large amounts." Offering analytical and advisory services on a fee-based basis would not only put the quality of the Bank's work to a market test but also remove the distortions of incentives involved in linking policy advice to large loans.

Value Added of the Bank to Bureaucratic Decision Making

Focusing on the potential analytical contributions of Bank staff is in part motivated by the premise that designing and implementing policy reforms is primarily an intellectual task facing a government—as if the government were a rational, unitary decision maker. Of course, that is not the case. Policy is almost always made through a complicated bureaucratic and political game involving several parts of the central government administration, if not also parliament, subnational governments, and other stakeholders, on the basis of imperfect information and analysis. The process is usually burdened by bureaucratic and personal rivalries. Attention to the reform issues may be crowded out by the deluge of daily demands on senior players in the government. And there are often no deadlines for decision or action. Even putting political competition and interests aside, making policy is usually a messy, drawn-out process, and especially so for the sort of reforms described above.[16]

In such a milieu, it is possible that the Bank can play a catalytic role simply by virtue of its conveying power, its access to actors at all levels within the government and among civil society, its incentives for pressing toward closure, and perhaps its reputation as a relatively neutral, objective party. From this perspective, the Bank's involvement in the process of preparing and implementing the policy reforms associated with a PBL may facilitate the government's decision-making process by stimulating dialogue, especially among parts of the government that otherwise would not communicate well, and by imposing a greater discipline and timetable on the process of internal dialogue and decision making.

The documentation for recent PBLs occasionally, albeit vaguely, claims such a useful role for the Bank. In the documentation for the Colombia Social Sector PBL mentioned above, it is claimed that the Bank's sector studies have stimulated discussions of social sector reform issues within and outside of government circles. The PID for the Third Provincial Reform PBL in Argentina states: "Lessons from the ongoing experience suggests that the loan design for a direct relation between the Bank and the provinces is important in enabling the Bank to bring to bear its international experience and in providing a mediating influence between the federal and provincial stakeholders."

Obtaining credible evidence of the value added of Bank staff in the decision-making process associated with policy-based lending is difficult. The claims by Bank staff about such matters are likely biased. Occasionally, officials from borrowing countries comment directly on the matter. According to the Commission on the Role of the Multilateral Development Banks (MDBs) in Emerging Markets, "Officials from countries such as Brazil, Mexico, Turkey, Hungary, Thailand, and Korea repeatedly cite the services that are 'bundled' with MDB financing as a key reason for seeking MDB loans. They value the detailed, project, and sectoral analysis of MDB staff and the dialogue on tough internal policy and budget choices that the lending process catalyzes" (Commission on the Role of the MDBs in Emerging Markets 2001, 4).

Even granting the plausible claim that the Bank's involvement stimulates dialogue among various parts of the government and between the government and civil society, the question is again relevant whether or not this depends on the lending itself. Perhaps the Bank's potential role as a process facilitator could be unbundled from the loan and linked only to its analytical work. Such unbundling seems especially feasible because, in most cases, the line agencies involved in implementation of many of the reform programs often do not receive incremental financing from the loan in any case. However, perhaps the offer of the loan is crucial in legitimizing and strengthening the role of the Bank staff within the contentious process of policy debate. In particular, the offer of a loan might provide a crucially important ingredient to any difficult policy-making process—an incentive to come to closure and take decisions. The value of a deadline to the process of government decision making can be quite high. The pressure from Bank staff working toward agreement on a PBL—usually in response to the internal pressures within the Bank to bring forward loan proposals sooner rather than later—may therefore be helpful to governments. This may be especially true in dealing with reforms for which the pressure to act is not urgent—one of the characteristics of many of the reforms supported by recent loans.

But pressure to come to closure can be a double-edged sword for the sort of institutionally and politically complex reforms under consideration. It can short-circuit healthy, albeit time-consuming, processes of discussion and consensus building among the various stakeholders. It is this concern that underlies Joan Nelson's recommendation to "make haste slowly:"

> The intrinsic requirements for sustainable reforms in education and health and the durable internal constraints in both [the World Bank and the IDB] counsel a basic strategy of making haste slowly. The quickest road to major sustainable change may not be the most direct and shortest route, but instead a patient and circuitous journey that builds comprehension and recruits support. In many countries, the World Bank and the IDB should emphasize laying the groundwork and creating preconditions for future reforms rather than trying to press ahead immediately with ambitious measures. (Nelson 1999, xvii)

The risk that time pressure associated with a Bank loan may short-circuit healthy processes of decision making with respect to complex reforms may be increased when a government's ministry of finance wants the loan for the sake of its external borrowing program. Once the finance ministry has decided that it wants or needs the Bank loan, it may work aggressively with the Bank to complete agreement on the details of a reform program without sufficient regard to the quality of agreement among the other parties in the government. When the local knowledge of those other parties is needed for good design and their cooperation is needed for effective implementation, this can seriously threaten the eventual success of the reform.

The 1999 Mexico Decentralization Adjustment Loan illustrates such risk. In early 1999, the Mexican Ministry of Finance and the Bank agreed in principle that a $600 million loan would be approved by the end of that calendar year and hence six months ahead of a national election. This large loan was an important component within the ministry's annual external borrowing program and its strategy for strengthening the country's macroeconomic position going into the election period. Beginning in the spring of that year, the Bank and the government entered into an intensive period of analytical work and dialogue on the complex policies governing the fiscal relationships between the central government and the state and municipal governments throughout Mexico. According to the Bank's Operations Evaluation Department's "Mexico Country Assistance Evaluation" (2001), this was a productive dialogue, and the Bank's analytical contributions were well received. By the end of the year, the ministry had come to closure on a set of regulations that could be promulgated under the authority of that ministry, without congressional approval, and the loan went ahead on that basis. The loan documentation recognized the risks involved: "Making decentralization more efficient and accountable to democratic control will require a substantial set of reforms . . . The proposed loan will not directly address the full set of required reforms . . . and should thus be seen as a first but significant step . . . The Decentralization Adjustment Loan policy commitments do not require legislative action, with one exemption—the already scheduled budget submission for year 2000 . . . Even if the government and congress reach the necessary consensus, there remains a possibility that some states or municipalities would refuse to adopt recommendations that they may perceive as federal imposition." In other words, the tight timetable set for the lending operation, together with other factors, led to a process that did not fully include either the congress or the subnational governments. This may have increased the risk that the process would be undermined at later stages. It is quite possible that linking these Mexican decentralization reforms to the timetable for a large loan was the right thing to do under the circumstances. But this case illustrates a potential, generic problem: relying on large Bank PBLs to complete a government's external borrowing program puts the preparation and agreement on that loan on a timetable that may be incompatible with a process for healthy national debate and democratic approval. In that case, the Bank's involvement in the country's decision-making process may do more harm than good.

Value of the Bank to the Political Decision-Making Process

There is another possible way—long cited in the literature on the political economy of reform—in which the Bank's support for policy reform via PBLs might be regarded as helpful: the offer of a large loan contingent on certain policy reforms may tip the balance of political support in favor of the proreformers within the government. This is a subtly different justification than those presented above. It does not suggest that the Bank imposes its will on a government that is unified in opposition to the Bank's policies, that the intrinsic quality of the Bank's analytical work wins crucial support on its merits, or that the Bank's participation in the bureaucratic *process* facilitates decision making. Instead, it is based on the recognition that almost every policy change involves winners and losers—even when the country as a whole benefits—and that the distribution of political power between winners and losers may be quite finely balanced. In such a case, the contingent offer of the Bank loan itself might swing the balance in one of several ways. Possibly, the endorsement of the Bank will persuade some parties that this is in fact good for the country. More likely, the availability of the (at least supposedly) incremental financing from the Bank might be sufficient inducement for those who were otherwise neutral to support the proreform elements. In some cases, that incremental financing might even make possible expenditures that would at least partially compensate losers.

The Bank itself has used this argument to support policy-based lending. The Bank's "Adjustment Lending Retrospective" report notes: "Several country studies have identified a positive role for conditionality: reformers welcomed the conditionality and used the associated external commitment as a tool to push through the reforms . . ." (World Bank 2001a, 67). But without detailed case studies by politically knowledgeable observers of the circumstances of each loan, it is impossible to say how many recent Bank PBLs played such a role in the politics surrounding the associated reforms. The question has been studied in the literature on the political economy of reforms. Killick summarizes the issue and the evidence:

> A last-ditch defense of conditionality can be offered. This tacitly accepts the dominance of domestic politics but asserts that conditionality provides a means whereby donors can strengthen the position of reformers within government and can tip the balance in favor of change . . . But how often are the knife-edge situations favorable to effective intervention most likely to arise? Our own country studies drew a blank on this. That we were able to find little or no evidence bearing upon this question itself suggests that they may be rather rare occurrences . . . Overall, then, a defense of conditionality in terms of its ability to tip the political balance in favor of reforms bears limited weight. (Killick 1998, 156–58)

This negative conclusion about the political utility of the Bank's conditional loans for policy reforms is buttressed theoretically by two other considerations. First, the notion itself is most applicable to one-time, stroke-of-the-pen, and largely irrevocable policy decisions. That is certainly not the nature of the reform programs supported by many recent PBLs. As Nelson (1999) pointed out, the reforms of social sectors are played out over many years, and there are numerous points along the way at which political struggles between pro- and antireformers are waged. The provision of a contingent Bank loan in the initial period of reform is therefore unlikely to be helpful to the political sustainability of that reform. However, it might be argued that there is often a "tipping phenomenon" at play in the sense that, once the broad directions of reform are set in motion, subsequent political battles may modify the details of its implementation but not block or reverse it altogether.

Second, in some countries and political circumstances, the overt association of the World Bank with a particular reform is likely to be politically detrimental. It may generate more opponents than it neutralizes. As Collier has pointed out, the Bank's involvement may create the perception, regardless of the reality, that the reforms are not truly owned by domestic stakeholders. The loan's formal conditionality may raise doubts in the minds of the public that the reform program is indeed good for the country. Such a backlash is more likely in a country in which the Bank does not enjoy a favorable public image. This was likely a consideration in the minds of the Mexican government during the early 1990s. Because the World Bank was associated with the "imperialist forces" of Washington in the minds of many Mexicans, the government chose to associate the Bank loans only with reforms on which they already had strong political support and to keep the Bank's name away from the most controversial issues such as telecommunications and power privatizations.[17]

Value of the Bank Loan as a Signaling or Commitment Device

Finally, there may be circumstances in which the government's agreement with the Bank for a well-defined reform program is useful as a means to convince nongovernmental actors of the seriousness of the government's intentions and its resolve to implement the reforms. This may be particularly helpful if the effectiveness of the reforms depends on a change in the way the private sector views its incentives and opportunities. For example, domestic and international investors may consider that the government's commitment to maintaining fiscal discipline and reducing inflation is more credible if such commitments are conditions of Bank lending and therefore subject to Bank monitoring, and this may induce higher investment levels. Or it might be that reforms involve a new set of prices, and demand and supply will not adjust to those new prices unless private actors are persuaded that the pricing reforms will not be reversed. Also, the government's commitment to the Bank to implement the reform program might serve to weaken the resolve of domestic opponents of the reform.

The Bank itself often uses this "commitment device" argument in defense of conditionality. For example, a recent Bank document states: "By increasing the cost of backtracking on policies . . . commitments to donors can enhance the government's credibility in sticking to policies that face opposition from special interests or that have short-term costs but long-term benefits" (World Bank 2002c, 101).[18]

Although in theory conditionality could be valuable as a signaling or external commitment device, there are several reasons to doubt that this is important in most circumstances. First, as an empirical matter, in discussions about disclosure policy within the Bank's Board of Executive Directors, the representatives of borrowing governments have traditionally opposed any requirement for the public disclosure of the full documentation of PBLs. Prior to approval of a new disclosure policy in mid-2002, only the very general public information documents had to be disclosed on the Bank's external Web site.[19] Under the new disclosure policy, after much lobbying by nongovernmental organizations and some Organisation for Economic Co-operation and Development governments for greater transparency in Bank operations, there is a "presumption in favor of disclosure," but the full Program Document for Bank PBLs is made publicly available only after the borrower concerned gives its consent.[20] (As an exception to this general rule, the new policy requires full disclosure of the documentation for IDA Poverty Reduction Support Credits [PRSCs], which are based on a PRSP.) In short, the traditional attitude of most borrowing governments against required disclosure of PBL documents suggests that they do not typically regard PBLs as a useful commitment device.[21]

The utility of recent PBLs as signaling or commitment devices is also theoretically doubtful because the success of the sorts of reforms now commonly supported usually does not depend on the expectations and market-driven responses of nongovernmental actors. Furthermore, because most of the reform programs now supported by PBLs are rather prolonged processes of change, conditionality is likely to be useful as a signaling or commitment device only for brief periods when the intentions of a government are unclear and its track record is unproven.[22]

Another argument against the utility of PBLs as a signaling or commitment device is that the Bank's record of enforcing conditionality is not very strong, as argued by Killick (1998) and Collier (2000). Given its mixed track record on enforcement of conditions, the Bank may have already "debased the currency" and greatly weakened the potential utility of loan conditionality as a commitment device. It would take some years of visibly tough enforcement of conditionality to reverse this legacy. This is particularly unlikely in light of the nature of the reforms now supported by policy-based lending. As noted above, such reforms typically involve a myriad of small steps rather than a few key measures, and failure to implement some of these small steps would not logically cause the Bank to withhold disbursements.

Summing Up Potential Nonfinancial Benefits and Costs

The nonfinancial net benefits from Bank policy-based lending that are not associated with a macroeconomic or financial crisis depend on the circumstances surrounding the loan. Because they are typically subtle and hard to observe, assessing the net benefits in any particular case is likely to be difficult. For an individual loan, only one or two, if any, of the possible nonfinancial benefits cited above may be relevant. The

Bank's analytical contributions to the design and implementation of reforms can often be helpful. But the fact that the Bank is buying rather than earning the attention of the government may also have negative effects in terms of crowding out local knowledge that is especially relevant to the institutionally and politically complex reforms that countries are now pursuing. Other potential benefits—facilitating the government's decision-making processes, tipping the political balance in favor of reformers, or providing a signaling or commitment device—might arise from time to time. But it cannot be assumed that these potential benefits will be routinely significant. Given the nature of the reform programs now often associated with PBLs, there may be an equal number of circumstances in which the Bank's involvement in the reform process through its PBL—especially if done without great care—has adverse effects on either the politics of reform or the decision-making process. In particular, the time-pressured processes and detailed advance blueprints traditionally associated with Bank PBLs may do harm to healthy national debate and consensus building and to learning-by-doing that must underpin these sorts of reforms. Drawing heavily on the advice of outsiders and specifying relatively short time horizons for their implementation may lead to wrong designs and overly hasty implementation. Especially in those cases in which the reforms involve no incremental fiscal costs or the government has alternative access to financing, such harmful effects from the Bank's involvement might outweigh the financial benefits of the loan. When the PBL is needed to help meet overall financing requirements, these harmful effects might be overlooked or excessively discounted by the government and the Bank.

Recommendations for Noncrisis PBLs

The Bank could take—and, in many cases, seems to be taking—many steps to increase the likelihood that PBLs will do more good than harm. In many ways, the draft note already cited is aimed in the right direction. The recommendations below apply to PBLs for second- and third-generation reforms that are not designed to help respond to a macroeconomic or financial crisis.

In designing its new guidelines for PBLs, the Bank should give more attention to the point that the potential nonfinancial benefits and costs of PBLs depend to a large extent on the nature of the reforms to be promoted and on the institutional and political circumstances surrounding the reforms. The guidelines should require staff to talk with the government about the potential nonfinancial benefits and costs, should encourage discussions about how to maximize potential net benefits, and should explicitly discourage use of PBLs when circumstances are unfavorable to providing net benefits. This more cautious approach might lead to more sparing use of PBLs than currently anticipated by the Bank.

The Bank needs to clearly and repeatedly articulate to broad audiences, including within borrowing countries, its current doctrine that conditionality is used only as a complement to, not a substitute for, country ownership. To make that persuasive, it needs help from the borrowing governments, which must make their ownership of the reforms associated with PBLs clear and credible. The Bank also needs to improve guidance to and training for its staff in assessing ownership and should cite evidence of ownership in its documentation of PBLs. The draft note on policy-based lending takes a step in this direction.

The Bank also needs to further strengthen the capacities of its staff to contribute usefully as facilitators of a government's decision-making process. This nonfinancial benefit of PBLs can be important and useful in many circumstances, and the Bank needs to further legitimate this purpose of its work on PBLs and train staff explicitly for this role.

The Bank team working with a government on the design of policy reforms and the loan conditionality should aggressively seek to tap into local knowledge and should be seriously humble about the relevance of other country experience. This effort means forming partnerships with national think tanks and academics, using national consultants, and relying heavily on staff with deep country knowledge, including nationals of the country working in the resident mission. And it means a general tendency to defer to the judgments of government on issues of institutional design.

In recognition of the need for trial and error and for flexibility in the timing of reform programs, the Bank should in most cases use what it calls programmatic policy-based lending. Under this approach, a three-year program of expected reform measures is agreed upon in advance, usually with increasingly less detail for the second and third years. Loans are approved only on an annual basis. The exact preconditions for each loan are agreed upon only in the months before loan approval, and they may vary somewhat from the originally agreed-upon measures. This step is intended to encourage regular monitoring and evaluation of the reform program and its outcomes and to facilitate mutually agreed-upon modifications to the reform program as implementation proceeds. These advantages of programmatic policy-based lending are increasingly recognized within the Bank. The draft note on policy-based lending states: "A series of single-tranche loans, credits, or grants [that is, a programmatic operation] is usually the best approach for supporting a well-specified medium-term program." For IDA countries, the PRSC—the new "gold standard" for IDA policy-based lending—is almost always a programmatic operation.

The Bank should recognize that most PBLs will need a rather substantial set of "mini-conditions" and should reinterpret its publicly stated intention to simplify and streamline the conditionality associated with its PBLs. The Bank itself and outside observers have routinely advocated such simplification and streamlining.[23] But, given the nature of typical reform programs, this intention will be consistently frustrated. If the Bank wants an agreement with the government about what will happen "on the ground" rather than merely on paper, there needs to be a rather elaborate set of mini-conditions. In this connection, it would be helpful to create a clear vocabulary to distinguish between a few key measures, if any, that are regarded as essential to the reforms (for which failure to implement on schedule would likely trigger reductions in future loan amounts or withholding further disbursements of an ongoing loan) and other measures that would be regarded more flexibly (for which failure to implement on schedule would not even need formal "waivers" from the Bank). The former category of measures should become formal conditions, and the others could be retained in the program documentation as "milestones" or "benchmarks." The draft note on policy-based lending puts forward such a vocabulary and advocates the limited use of "conditions," but ample use of "milestones."

A related point is that, at least with respect to noncrisis PBLs, the Bank should avoid tough rhetoric about its intentions to strictly enforce its conditionality and develop practices that favor modulating loan amounts rather than all-or-nothing disbursement decisions.[24] It should accept the fact that the typical reform programs are not amenable to "get tough" approaches to enforcing conditionality.[25] The progress of the reform program as a whole involves many small steps, which are usually inputs rather than outputs. Monitoring overall progress is hard. Probably not one of the detailed steps and the associated mini-conditions by itself can be used as a make-or-break conditionality. This, together with the need for flexibility noted above, usually makes it hard for the Bank to completely withhold disbursements or new commitments because the program is demonstrably off track. Instead, the Bank needs to develop a practice of modulating the amounts of lending within a programmatic framework in response to delays in or deviations from the agreed-upon reform program.

The Bank ought to further amend its recent disclosure policy to require—not just encourage—that both the government concerned and the Bank publicly disclose the full documentation for PBLs, including the government's Letter of Development Policy. Getting agreement on such an amendment would likely require an effort by Bank management to persuade borrowing governments that, as stated in the draft note on policy-based lending, "the principle of country ownership of reform programs cannot be credible without such disclosure."

To pursue its intention to use selectivity as an alternative to hard-core loan conditionality, the Bank needs to be clearer about its criteria for determining whether a country qualifies for policy-based lending. Beyond disclosing its CPIA and performance-based assessment systems for IDA countries, this means ensuring that CAS documents are always clear about which reforms are considered essential for the country's development and would merit support through policy-based lending.

The Bank needs to keep the preparation of PBLs on very flexible timetables, resisting the internal pressures to get loans approved within a targeted fiscal year. This step will avoid short-circuiting the necessary processes of designing a home-grown reform and building country ownership.

The Bank should seek to expand its offer of fee-based consulting services for the sorts of reforms that are now often associated with PBLs. This effort would provide governments the option of seeking the Bank's analytical contributions and advice without having to take a loan, and it would allow Bank managers to offer such services without feeling that they must also push a loan in order to justify their use of staff time and budget.

Finally, the Bank needs to be clearer and more transparent—in its internal discussions and in public disclosures of its programs—about the factors determining the size of individual PBLs and the level of total PBL financing for each country. Unless there is greater clarity about the basis and rationale for PBL financing, there will be no basis for judging whether the financial benefits of the loan outweigh any potential nonfinancial costs. There are several possible approaches:

- One possibility is to require that policy-based lending is only used to finance reforms that have a near-term fiscal cost, and the size of each loan would be chosen to cover all or part of that cost over a certain period. This approach would have several important advantages. It would make clear that the Bank's involvement is warranted by the need to finance the costs of the reforms. It would lend credibility to a government's claim of country ownership of reforms because it eliminates the incentive for governments to adopt the Bank's recommendations on reforms for the sake of gaining uncommitted financial resources. In these ways, it would enhance the transparency and integrity of the instrument.

- A second approach would be to explicitly acknowledge and seek to legitimate the now-tacit objective of using PBLs to manage the level of a government's TDO to the Bank. In doing so, it would need to make the case within each CAS for the desired trend in the TDO—which implies making the case for the government's overall borrowing plans and the Bank's role within that plan—and also to discuss within the CAS to what extent the Bank might adjust the levels of PBLs to help the government cope with unexpected fluctuations in its demand for external financing. Furthermore, it would need to make clear within each CAS which areas of policy reform would be linked to possible PBLs, ensuring that the Bank is engaging on issues that are critically related to poverty reduction and sustainable development and not only on areas in which the government is already interested in reforms. To do otherwise would allow the lending objective to drive the policy dialogue rather than the other way around. If the Bank uses the offer of a PBL to buy a seat at the table, it should make sure that it is the right table.

- A third possibility, and probably the best approach, is to fully merge policy-based lending with budget support lending in the sense that loans would be linked both to an agreed set of policy and institutional reforms and a defined set of public expenditures within an agreed framework for overall public expenditures. In some respects, this is the direction in which the Bank has been heading in defining the approach to PRSCs.

Endnotes

1. The author is a former World Bank staff member and is now a part-time professor at the Elliott School of International Affairs, The George Washington University, as well as a consultant to the World Bank.

2. This chapter uses the term "policy-based lending" rather than "adjustment lending" for two reasons. First, "adjustment" is a misnomer for the sorts of reforms now commonly associated with quick-disbursing loans conditional on specified policy and institutional reforms. Second, the World Bank, following a recent review of its lending instruments, has retained policy-based lending using the name "development policy lending" and has dropped the name "adjustment lending." "Policy-based loans" is used in this paper to

refer to both International Bank for Reconstruction and Development (IBRD) loans and International Development Association (IDA) credits or grants, and "loan" refers to both IBRD loans and IDA credits and grants.

3. The arguments and recommendations put forward here relate to policy-based lending by the World Bank not related to macroeconomic or financial crisis. Furthermore, they do not necessarily apply to conditional lending by the International Monetary Fund (IMF). The IMF normally provides financing under different circumstances and deals with a different set of policy and institutional issues than the Bank.

4. This draft note, which is now posted on the Bank's external Web site for comment, is titled "Good Practice Note—Designing Development Policy Operations." Development Policy Operations is the Bank's new name for policy-based lending.

5. For one of the earliest discussions of the evolving nature of reform programs in middle-income countries, see Naim 1995. This shift in the reform agenda over time is well described in Nelson 1996.

6. There are exceptions in which recent adjustment loans support first-generation reforms. For example, Brazil's Programmatic Financial Sector PBLs involved privatization of state-owned public banks, and the Energy Sector Reform Loan required power tariff adjustments. The Tunisia Third Economic Competitive PBL included further privatization of state enterprises.

7. In February 1999, Kim Dae-Jung, president of South Korea, remarked: "Looking back on the past year of reform, I can draw one important conclusion. It is that introducing new laws and institutions alone is not enough. Reform can succeed only when these institutional changes are accompanied by changes in people's minds. This is the real test." Quoted in Santiso 2002.

8. On this point, see Gilbert and Vines 2000, 21–23.

9. On these issues, see especially World Bank 2001, 68.

10. However, some PBLs are associated with policy reforms that actually bring windfall gains to the government. For example, the Information Infrastructure Sector Development Loan to Morocco for $65 million was associated with privatization of the main telecommunications operator, which provided huge privatization revenues to the government.

11. For example, the program information document (PID) for the Mexico Second Bank Restructuring Facility Loan says that "Bank funds would help finance part of the IPAB's [Instituto para la Protección al Ahorro Bancario (IPAB; Mexico's deposit guarantee fund)] debt-servicing needs arising from the implementation of its bank resolution transactions, complementing other sources of funds available to IPAB . . ."

12. In the vast literature on adjustment lending, there has been much attention to the "social costs of adjustment," meaning the likely negative impact of adjustment policies on the welfare of various groups. In this chapter, "cost" means only a negative impact on the likelihood that a reform program will be well designed and successfully implemented.

13. Other possible nonfinancial benefits have been suggested by some but, in my judgment, do not deserve serious consideration. One argument in favor of policy-based lending is that it provides reformers within the government with the opportunity to blame the Bank for necessary reforms. Although this has probably often been true, it should not be encouraged because it undermines longer-term country ownership of reforms. Indeed, it probably should be regarded as a nonfinancial cost, not a benefit. On this point, see Collier 1997. Another possible argument is that PBLs provide a positive signal to global capital markets that the country's macroeconomic environment is judged stable by the Bank and that this might help induce capital inflows. However, given the number of occasions in which the Bank has provided PBLs in circumstances in which the macroeconomic situation turned out to be unsustainable, it is probably a more common view that the Bank gives PBLs primarily to countries in trouble.

14. A similar argument is that, in their analytical work, the Bank staff are too "purist," pushing for technically appropriate solutions that give insufficient weight to the country's political and institutional constraints.

15. See http://www.gdnet.org/subpages/aboutgdn.html.

16. See Grindle and Thomas (1991), Brinkerhoff (1996), and Crosby (1996) for excellent discussions of the processes of policy making and implementation in developing countries.

17. See Operations Evaluation Department 2001.

18. *Assessing Aid: What Works, What Doesn't and Why*, which strongly supports a shift from traditional conditionality to country selectivity, stated: "Conditionality still has a role—to allow governments to commit to reform and to signal the seriousness of reform . . ." (World Bank 1998, 19).

19. Among the fiscal 2002 PBLs by IBRD, the full Program Documents are available on the Bank's Web site only for the Colombia Social Sector PBL and the Mexico Programmatic Environment Structural Adjustment Loan. In some cases, it is even hard to find the required PID about PBLs on the World Bank public Web site. For example, the PBLs for Brazil do not show up in the list of lending operations accessible from the Brazil country page, but can only be discovered through a document search. Similarly, the loans to the Indian states of Karnataka and Andhra Pradesh cannot be found on the India country page, but only through a search of the Bank's entire Web site.

20. See World Bank 2002d, 7–8.

21. It might be argued that borrowing country governments have resisted public disclosure of Bank documents not because they want to avoid publicizing the Bank's support for the associated reform program but because those documents usually include a risk assessment that might be politically sensitive. If that were their primary motivation, however, it would have been logical to resist inclusion of such risk assessments in public documents rather than to suppress public release of the entire document.

22. This is an important conclusion of Devarajan, Dollar, and Holmgren 2001. See p. 34. Although this study used case studies of African countries, the point is likely to be valid among IBRD borrowers as well.

23. For example, the Bank's Strategic Framework paper says: ". . . we will streamline loan conditions—making them fewer, better targeted, and more realistic" (World Bank 2001b, 10). The issues paper prepared in anticipation of updating the Bank's PBL guidelines refers to the "Bank's continuing efforts to make conditionality more focused and selective" ((World Bank 2002b, 1). The Commission on the Role of the MDBs in Emerging Markets advocates that "To ensure that conditionality augments rather than undermines the effectiveness of MDB lending, the MDBs should simplify policy conditionality . . ." (Commission on the Role of the MDBs in Emerging Markets 2001, 11).

24. The Commission on the Role of the MDBs in Emerging Markets (2001, 11) also proposed that "Once conditions are agreed upon the MDBs should be prepared to halt disbursements if governments fail to honor commitments."

25. Even if IBRD had leverage because of the government's lack of alternative financing, Killick (1998, 190) argues that hard-core conditionally might be applied effectively only for policy changes that are simple, easily monitored, and amenable to treatment as a precondition. That is seldom true with respect to the elements of institutionally complex reforms.

Bibliography

Brinkerhoff, Derick W. 1996. "Process Perspectives on Policy Change: Highlighting Implementation," *World Development* 24 (9): 1395–1401.

Collier, Paul, 1997. "The Failure of Conditionality." In *Perspectives on Aid and Development*, ed. Catherine Gwin and Joan Nelson, Policy Essay No. 22. Washington, DC: Overseas Development Council.

———. 2000. "Conditionality, Dependence, and Coordination: Three Current Debates in Aid Policy." In *The World Bank: Structure and Policies*, ed. Christopher Gilbert and David Vines. Cambridge, United Kingdom: Cambridge University Press.

———. 2002. "Making Aid Smart: Institutional Incentives Facing Donor Organizations and Their Implications for Aid Effectiveness." Paper presented to the Forum Series on the Role of Institutions in Promoting Economic Growth, April 2002.

Commission on the Role of the MDBs in Emerging Markets. 2001. "The Role of the Multilateral Banks in Emerging Market Economies," Carnegie Endowment for International Peace and others.

Crosby, Benjamin L. 1996. "Policy Implementation: The Organizational Challenge." *World Development* 24 (9): 1403–15.

Devarajan, Shanta, David R. Dollar, and Torgny Holmgren, eds. 2001. *Aid and Reform in Africa*. Washington, DC: World Bank.

Gilbert, Christopher L., and David Vines, eds. 2000. The World Bank: Structure and Policies. Cambridge, United Kingdom: Cambridge University Press.

Grindle, Merille S., and J. W. Thomas. 1991. "Policymakers, Policy Choices, and Policy Outcomes: The Political Economy of Reform in Developing Countries." In *Reforming Economic Systems in Developing Countries*, ed. D. H. Perkins and M. Roemer. Cambridge, MA: Harvard Institute for International Development.

Killick, Tony. 1998. *Aid and the Political Economy of Policy Change*, with Ramani Gunatilaka and Ana Marr. London: Routlege.

Naim, Moises. 1995. "Latin America: The Second Stage of Reform." In *Economic Reform and Democracy*, ed. Larry Diamond and Marc R. Plattner. Baltimore, MD: Johns Hopkins University Press.

Nelson, Joan. 1996. "Promoting Policy Reforms: The Twilight of Conditionality?" *World Development* 24 (9): 1551–59.

———. 1999. *Reforming Health and Education: The World Bank, the IDB, and Complex Institutional Change*, Policy Essay No. 26. Washington, DC: Overseas Development Council.

Operations Evaluation Department. 2001. "Mexico Country Assistance Evaluation," World Bank, Washington, DC.

Rodrik, Dani. 2002. "After Neoliberalism, What?"

Santiso, Carlos. 2002. "Governance Conditionality and the Reform of Multilateral Development Finance: The Role of the Group of Eight," No. 7, G8 Governance, School of Advanced International Studies, Johns Hopkins University.

World Bank, 1998. *Assessing Aid: What Works, What Doesn't and Why*. New York: Oxford University Press.

———. 2001a. "Adjustment Lending Retrospective: Final Report," Operations Policy and Country Services, Washington, DC.

———. 2001b. "World Bank: Strategic Framework," Washington, DC.

———. 2002a. "The Role and Effectiveness of Development Assistance: Lessons from World Bank Experience." Paper presented to the United Nations International Conference on Financing for Development, March 2002.

———. 2002b. "From Adjustment Lending to Development Policy Support Lending: Key Issues in the Update of World Bank Policy," Operations Policy and Country Services.

———. 2002c. "Global Development Finance," Washington, DC

———. 2002d. "The World Bank Policy on Disclosure of Information," Washington, DC.

———. 2004. "Good Practice Note—Designing Development Policy Operations," Draft. www.worldbank.org under Consultations on the Update of Operational Directive (OD) 8.60.

22

Part 4 Discussion Summary

Forum participants discussed various aspects of country-owned approaches to conditionality, mainly focusing on several key, multidimensional issues, such as selectivity, minimum requirements and standards, the relevance of policy leveraging, outcomes-based conditions, and country context.

There was general agreement on the issue of selectivity and the need for donors to limit the number of lending conditions to a few, high-priority actions that are critical to the success of the government's reform program. Doing so would set clearer expectations and allow the government to focus its resources appropriately, as opposed to trying to meet a wide range of actions that are marginally important, such as action plans, or unrealistic, such as politically sensitive issues. Participants expressed broad concern over capacity constraints and the burden donors impose by overloading recipient governments with a large number of conditions. While understanding that numerous conditions may naturally reflect the complexity of modern economies and the linkages between policy areas, participants urged donors to reduce the burden through improved streamlining and harmonization. As the International Monetary Fund, the World Bank, and other multilateral development banks are working to improve the division of labor, bilateral donors also need to avoid duplication by restricting their conditions, particularly to areas of specialization.

Capacity constraints were a particular concern directed to the European Union and other donors that rely on outcomes-based conditionality to determine size and timing of budget support. The concern is that partner governments risk spending a disproportionate amount of time measuring outcomes that, in some cases, are difficult to track reliably and on an annual basis, rather than implementing core policy and institutional reforms. The representative from the European Commission countered that developing and monitoring outcome indicators should not be too difficult because the Millennium Development Goals provide a common, universal set of indicators that the development community has agreed to and is committed to monitoring. He noted that donor credibility (relative to taxpayers) ultimately depends on showing improved social indicators that should be at the core of poverty reduction programs. One participant proposed widespread publicity of social outcomes from the regional to the national level to reduce the incentive to overreport outcomes.

Another key issue related to who or which party was responsible for the selectivity of conditions. Several participants implied that, despite the much talked about country-ownership principle, donors are still "imposing" conditionality. However, some notable exceptions were mentioned. The Senegalese representative commented that his government has worked closely with all parties to derive a restricted list of indicators on which donors base their conditionality. He added that dialogue and donor harmonization was very important in this process. Others commented that country context greatly influences the type of dialogue and working relationship between donors and recipient governments. For example, in crisis situations, conditionality often takes on a much more traditional, prescriptive role in which donor aid can leverage painful stabilization-oriented measures. Nevertheless, a balance is needed to ensure sufficient social protection is in place during a crisis. At some point, conditionality should once again focus on growth, efficiency, and equity issues, and countries must take over and lead the development process.

The discussion over country context led several participants to postulate that conditionality in general is quite different in middle-income countries compared with lower-income countries and Low-Income Countries Under Stress. One participant pointed out that many middle-income countries do not engage in long-term relationships with donors to the same extent as lower-income countries, and when donors do lend to middle-income countries, it often entails stabilization. The question was then posed as to how one moves from crisis-type conditionality to one of long-term mutual accountability. One suggestion was to establish minimum conditions, such as macrostability, public sector governance, fiscal management, and anticorruption measures. Conditionality would then be scaled up as the program developed. Several participants tried to differentiate conditions from minimum "requirements." The latter entails certain prerequisites that must be met—some participants referred to them as eligibility requirements—and without which development assistance would almost certainly fail. It was noted that work on international standards is vital not only in establishing eligibility requirements but also in facilitating donor harmonization and pushing through with the results agenda.

Participants diverged on how international standards may impact development assistance. The distinction was drawn between the call for conditionality standards and the standardization of conditionality; the representative from Niger cautioned that the latter may result in countries losing ownership of the process. Moreover, while some general principles could be applied globally, the risk is that minimum standards overlook the local context and may not be realistic for certain countries. The Basel banking regulations were cited by one participant as a "dangerous promoter of systemic risks" in some areas. However, defining standards can actually result in greater transparency.

Participants discussed the assertion that ideological or political conditionality should be detached from development assistance. The representative from the African Development Bank suggested that the two ultimately cannot be separated, but that the issue is one of sequencing who does what and at what particular point in time. Agencies such as the African Development Bank, however much they would like to take the lead, are far less suited to judging elections than taking the lead on development issues once the political environment is set right. Corruption was cited as another example of a potentially difficult and politically sensitive issue that greatly impacts aid effectiveness. The European Union currently considers anticorruption as an essential element of its conditionality, and the representative from the European Commission added that the donor community needs to move toward a more robust instrument to measure public financial management, and that the work being done now on performance assessment framework programming is moving toward the right direction.

It was noted that concurrent with the efforts to harmonize donor conditionality, equal attention needs to be paid to the volatility of budget support and the potential for disruption of aid flows owing to underperformance by the country. For low-income countries, particularly Low-Income Countries Under Stress, such a disruption could be disastrous to the country itself. Donor coordination/harmonization should also include a policy for harmonious disengagement, and budget support instruments need to be designed to curtail volatility, particularly given the upcoming discussions to increase financial commitments in support of the Millennium Development Goals.

Part V
Partnerships in Policy-Based Lending

23

Introduction

RICHARD MANNING
Organisation for Economic Co-operation and Development

Partnerships in Policy-Based Lending

This session focuses on partnerships in policy-based lending and assesses the nature of these partnerships. It will discuss how partnerships can help to improve the use of conditionality in policy-based lending and how different approaches to collaboration can enhance predictability of aid. This session will address one key question: how to align donor and partner support when country performance is inadequate.

The real challenge in the context of partnership is what to do with the category of countries with which you cannot easily have a policy dialogue. For example, how can donors manage a partnership with the category of countries that Myanmar represents? It is important to remember that there are several heavily aid-dependent countries in this category and they are critical to the achievement of the Millennium Development Goals because a lot of poor people are living in these countries. We desperately need a partnership model for these countries. In particular, we have to make sure that harmonization and donor alignment improve partnership in such countries.

24

Policy-Based Lending and Conditionality: The Experience of Vietnam

DUONG DUC UNG
Ministry of Planning and Investment, Vietnam

The nearly 20-year reform process in Vietnam, which was initiated in 1986 and has brought about significant and renowned changes in the socioeconomic development of the country, has always been a well-acknowledged example of a country-led change process. Over the period, the economy has been able not only to maintain its stability but also to generate continued growth, even during the regional financial crisis in Asia in 1997 or the unfavorable conditions the world economy has faced in recent years. Noteworthy has been Vietnam's ability to retain a fairly high annual growth rate exceeding 7 percent over a long period, which is the second-highest level in Asia, just after China. There also has been remarkable progress in terms of social development, including a sharp drop in the number of poor households to just 12 percent in 2003.

Reform and Global Integration

The reform process has been going hand in hand with Vietnam's regional and global economic integration. Vietnam has now become a member of various regional and international institutions, such as the Association of Southeast Nations, Asia-Pacific Economic Cooperation, and Asia-Europe Meeting, and it is actively negotiating for accession to the World Trade Organization by 2005.

Vietnam's socioeconomic achievements during the course of reform are attributable to various factors, among which policy reform has played a decisive role. It should be noted that this overall reform in general and the socioeconomic policy reform in particular have been a truly locally rooted and internally driven process, rather than one implemented merely because of outside pressures. As such, the policy measures undertaken are really ones of the people and for the people, which explains why they are widely and strongly supported in the society.

The development and implementation of policy measures in Vietnam are also processes that reflect the multilateralism and diversification orientation of the government, which advocates a broadly consultative mechanism with the international donor and business communities. In terms of policy-based loans (PBLs), cooperative relations between Vietnam and international financial institutions such as the International Monetary Fund, the World Bank, or the Asian Development Bank date back to the early 1990s. More recently, a number of bilateral donors have also taken part in these relationships, either on a bilateral basis or through cofinancing schemes.

With the International Monetary Fund, Vietnam has worked out a number of PBLs, such as Stand-By Arrangements or the Systemic Transformation Facilities, which were based on economic structural adjustment measures in 1993 and 1994. An Enhanced Structural Adjustment Facility loan was then formulated on a three-year basis to help Vietnam achieve sustainable economic growth and strengthen the country's balance of payments. The Poverty Reduction Growth Facility in 1999 was a reform in PBL form that took place after the East Asia financial crisis that was described as seeking to help low-income member countries to fight effectively against poverty. In the case of Vietnam, as the country began to develop its own Comprehensive Poverty Reduction and Growth Strategy, these annual schemes focused much around this strategy.

With regard to the World Bank, the government of Vietnam has received a number of PBLs such as the Structural Adjustment Credit-1, with a policy focus on budget management state-owned enterprise reform, and reform in the financial and trading systems. The successful completion of the first Structural Adjustment Credit opened up the way for its continuation with the Structural Adjustment Credit-2 Program, which was later changed to the Poverty Reduction Support Credit. This scheme supplements well the Poverty Reduction Growth Facility of the International Monetary Fund and is being used to help Vietnam strengthen policy reforms in the areas of banking, state-owned enterprises, trade liberalization, public expenditure reform, and private sector development. In addition, the World Bank also provides PBL schemes in project form, such as the Rural Finance Project I that aimed at the development of the Rural Development Fund or Funds for the Poor. The fruitful implementation of these loans has allowed the two parties to enter into phase II of the project, which has two key components, namely, rural credit and capacity building for the project stakeholders.

As for the Asian Development Bank, Vietnam has worked out the Financial Sector Program Loan, a scheme aimed at creating favorable conditions to promote the development of the private sector, foreign direct investment, and state-owned enterprise reform. The second generation of this loan scheme focuses more on the banking and financial sector.

In addition, a number of other bilateral donors are participating in such PBL schemes. Among them is the Japan-initiated Miyzawa program, which is of notable significance because it aims to help Vietnam promote development of the private sector and especially small and medium enterprises in the wake of the regional financial crisis.

The Experience of Vietnam

Thus far, Vietnam's experience with PBLs has been positive, mainly for the following reasons: (a) the reform measures committed to by the government of Vietnam in the PBL schemes are also ones that are seriously being pursued by the government in the framework of the country's reform process; (b) the PBLs have played an important catalytic role for the policy reform progress in the country's transition period; (c) the PBLs have brought about a fast-disbursement source of finance to help enhance macroeconomic stability as well as the implementation of various important socio-economic programs in the country; and (d) the PBLs have also helped to strengthen human resource development In Vietnam via the associated training programs.

However, a number of improvements need to be considered for these PBL schemes: (a) the conditionality of PBLs reflects at times strong donor will to tie the recipient government to a pressing reform roadmap that is not necessarily adaptable to the country circumstances; (b) PBL measures are at times overly broad and scattered, involving too great a number of implementing agencies, thus reducing the necessary focus of the loan while increasing the time spent on negotiation and getting agreement; and (c) the policy measures are usually designed in a fixed manner, leaving little room to adjust to changes taking place during the implementation stage.

In conclusion, Vietnam's experience offers a number of key lessons for recipients of PBLs: (a) It is essential that the government take full ownership in the design of policy measures as well as a strong leadership role during the implementation of commitments; (b) all externally imposed conditionality will fail to effectively help the recipient partner; and (c) a constructive partnership that allows a frank and open consultative process between the government and the donors is a must for a successful implementation of PBL schemes.

25

Alternatives to Conditionality in Policy-Based Lending

OLIVER MORRISSEY
University of Nottingham

Conditionality has acquired meaning as a term to describe the mechanism of policy-based lending that has predominated in donor-recipient relationships, especially as practiced by the international financial institutions since the early 1980s. Interpreted literally, it simply means that aid (concessional lending) is given subject to the recipient country meeting certain conditions. In this literal sense, all aid is conditional (to a greater or lesser extent). However, *conditionality* has acquired a stronger meaning than this literal interpretation. First, it is applied to conditions on policy reform (as distinct, for example, from fiduciary conditions on accounting for the use of funds). Second, it refers to the use of financing to leverage policy reform, that is, to impose particular policies, which need not be the policies that would freely be chosen by the recipient. Third, the conditions tend to be many and wide ranging, applying not only to most areas of economic policy but also to aspects of governance and political processes. Fourth, at least in principle, the conditions are enforced, in the sense that failure to meet the conditions to a satisfactory extent typically means that funding is not released. Taken together, these capture the meaning of conditionality as a *mechanism* to leverage policy reform.

The aim of this chapter is to draw a distinction between conditionality, as defined above, and policy dialogue as alternative ways in which external agents, in the present case bilateral and multilateral donors, can influence policy transfer. Policy transfer here refers to informing and promoting policy learning in developing (aid-recipient) countries. This chapter depicts conditionality as the traditional approach to policy transfer—donors, to a greater or lesser degree, require recipients to adopt and implement specified policies. Policy dialogue is treated as a form of partnership, where donors engage with recipients to aim to convince them to adopt particular policies. Whereas conditionality has an element of coercion, policy dialogue is firmly rooted in persuasion. This chapter argues that dialogue is a more promising and effective means of policy transfer, while noting that conditions can play a role in supporting dialogue and policy learning.

Limits of Conditionality

Differences regarding the importance of policy reform for aid effectiveness tend to relate to the details rather than the principles. There can be broad agreement that some countries have rather bad or inappropriate policies, and that other countries have rather good or appropriate policies. Arguably, most developing countries are in between—they have some good policies, some not so good policies, and many more or less reasonable policies that are only being implemented slowly, and perhaps half-heartedly. It does matter which policy area one is considering. For example, in the case of macroeconomic stabilization there is broad agreement, at least among economists, of what is required (for example, Boughton 2003): control or stability in domestic credit expansion, money supply, budget deficits, and monitoring inflation, the exchange rate, and real interest rate. There is rather less agreement on what actually is the correct target or equilibrium value (for example, for inflation or the exchange rate) and how quickly and severely one should try to get back to that value during a period of disequilibrium. In contrast, in policy areas such as privatization or poverty reduction there is less agreement on what should be done and often considerable disagreement on the details.

The simple point is that economics is not a sufficiently exact science for one to be confident about what is the optimal policy on any issue—donors themselves will often have different views on areas of policy. One may be able to identify inappropriate and ineffective policies, but in most areas one is left with a "policy range" rather than a specific policy. This view lies at the heart of many critiques of conditionality, where the criticism is that the conditions imposed overly restrict the policy options—in common parlance, the conditions are too tight. If the conditions are viewed as being too tight, this is likely to undermine the willingness of governments to implement the desired reforms. It has proved easy to demonstrate that conditional lending is an ineffective mechanism to induce reform from unwilling governments, and that tight conditions are an inappropriate mechanism if governments are willing to reform (for example, White and Morrissey 1997).

Conditionality of this form has underpinned policy-based lending for almost two decades. Such conditionality does not work in the sense that attaching conditions to lending is in itself insufficient to ensure that governments will undertake reforms they would not have chosen willingly. Conditionality is, in effect, dictating the policy choices that governments should make and then tying lending to the implementation of those policies. This is not a solid foundation for a development partnership between donors and recipients. Policy ownership by recipients should require that countries choose their own policies, which is not an inherent feature of conditionality.

Morrissey (2004a) assesses the literature evaluating the effectiveness of conditionality. A specific weakness of this literature is that few rigorous comparable studies analyze the chain from conditions to specific policies implemented to actual outcomes observed. Many studies argue, in effect, that not all conditions were fully implemented; therefore, conditionality did not work. This shows scant understanding of the nature of the policy environment (Morrissey 1999): countries with relatively strong economies and developed political systems will tend to have greater scope to implement policy reform than countries with weak economies and under-developed political processes. Alternatively, studies observe that the outcomes (for example, investment, exports, or growth) were not as good as anticipated and infer that conditions were not met. Even if the policies were implemented as required, there are many reasons why the anticipated benefits may not be observed. The one point on which there is agreement is that rarely if ever are all conditions fully implemented within the time period of the aid agreement. In this sense conditionality does not work.

This does not mean that conditionality has had no effect on policies. There is considerable evidence that, over time, countries receiving policy-based lending (subject to conditionality) have improved their policies, and that such improvements in policy are associated with improvements in economic performance (for example, Koeberle 2003; Operations Evaluation Department 2004). As a result of policy-based lending most developing countries have implemented policy reform, but more slowly and less effectively than promoted by conditionality. Morrissey (2004a) illustrates this with the case of trade policy. While trade reforms featured prominently among aid conditions, and strictly evaluated conditionality failed (that is, stipulated reforms were implemented and sustained within the posited time period), many developing countries have implemented trade policy reforms over the past two decades and aid leverage has played an important role. Donors play an important role in policy not by dictating choice but by informing and supporting the policy process.

What researchers have shown is that conditional lending per se is not an effective instrument for ensuring relatively rapid policy reform. Perhaps this should be no surprise because reform, except in cases of severe (political and economic) shock, is an inherently slow process. There are few cases where reform was implemented quickly and dramatically (the "big bang" approach), and these cases were almost all failures. A gradual implementation is the most common case, largely because reform is politically difficult, even if governments are convinced of the economic arguments (Morrissey 1999). Policy dialogue recognizes that the pace of reform must accommodate political and administrative constraints, as elaborated in the next section.

Policy Dialogue

Morrissey and Nelson (2003, 2004) review theories of policy learning and of policy making to explore how external agents can most effectively influence the process of policy transfer. In the most simple model, policy makers engage in pure learning by doing; policy choices are based solely on information relating to the history of the policy they have experienced and policy makers have no information on alternative policies (because these have not been implemented). In this context, there is no role for external agents. A second model allows a country to observe the decisions of others. Such social learning provides information on alternatives, so policy makers can observe the policies chosen by others. If others are observed to stick to a policy that is different from a country's policy, and the others appear to be performing well, the country may come to believe that the other policy is better. This change in beliefs induces learning and policy reform. For example, Kenya's willingness to prepare a Poverty Reduction Strategy Paper (PRSP) was influenced by the perceived success of Uganda's adoption of a PRSP (Morrissey 2004b). External agents, such as donors, can influence policy choice by contributing to the learning process. For example, donors could provide information on policies that have "worked" in other countries or could support analysis of the effects of policies being implemented. The international financial institutions, in particular, have a strong research capacity and are therefore better able than individual developing countries to distill and disseminate lessons from policy experiences.

A third model, hierarchical social learning, allows an explicit role for external agents in proposing a particular policy. If external agents have an effective enforcement mechanism, this leads to governments implementing the policies advocated. In the case where external agents advocate essentially the same policies to all countries (the "one-size-fits-all" critique of conditionality), this causes policy convergence. This outcome is inferior to social learning for two reasons. First, convergence arises from effective enforcement mechanisms, not convergence of beliefs. Second, this convergence reduces "policy experimentation," with an information loss for all observers. Only if the policy advocated by external agents is the best option (for all countries) will it lead to choice of the optimal policy. Even if external agents (donors) do not have an effective enforcement mechanism, they can influence policy choices in various ways.

Table 25.1 identifies various stages in the policy process and indicates the ways in which donors can engage to exert influence at each stage. Governments, or policy makers, will have objectives regarding what they want to achieve (depending on their perceived interest) and beliefs regarding which policies best meet their objectives. The willingness of governments to implement reforms (to alter their policy choice) will depend on beliefs regarding the effect of any given policy (described as priors regarding the policy) and the range of policy options. In other words, stages A and B of the process refer to willingness to reform. Donors can influence willingness to reform in

TABLE 25.1 Donor Influences on Policy Processes

Policy Stages	Donor Engagement
A. Priors	Beliefs regarding the effects and efficacy of policies
	Placing specific concerns high on the agenda
B. Options	Provide and interpret information on policy options
	Policy advice and knowledge transfer
C. Design	Technical assistance on elements of policy design
D. Capacity	Support for policy choice and implementation strategies
	Taking responsibility for unpopular policies
	Providing evidence to build support or counter opposition
E. Commitment	Financial support for adopting policies
	Building policy-making capability
F. Administration	Technical support and assistance

Source: Morrissey 2004a.

a number of ways. They can give information on the probable effects of alternative policies, affecting both priors and options, especially if they provide information on the effects of policy choices in other countries (knowledge transfer). By expressing their own views, preferably supported by analysis of evidence, donors can influence the policy agenda, and thereby influence choice. Note that such actions by donors do not require conditions.

Donors may also wish to influence policy makers' objectives, to encourage them to alter what they consider to be the interests of the country. This effort may often involve influencing political processes, such as through process conditionality. For example, the requirement for consultation and participation in the design of PRSPs affects the process of policy making and places the interests of the poor onto the policy agenda (see Booth 2003). Imposing process conditions is problematic because clearly donors are impinging on politics rather than specifically on policy. Within a policy dialogue approach, one could encourage policy makers to consider different objectives by including assessments of policy impacts on different groups in society.

Much of the discussion of policy reform in developing countries has been concerned with the concepts of ownership and commitment. Ownership is often seen as necessary if policies are to be implemented successfully and sustained. What this means is not always clear. Morrissey (1999) adopts a strict definition: a government truly owns a policy reform if it has the capacity to analyze options and to choose and implement the preferred policy. True ownership requires that the policy choice originates with the government. Under this strict definition, donor leverage and influence undermine ownership, but true ownership is not necessary to ensure sustained policy reform. All that is necessary for a genuine attempt at reform is that the government chooses the policy because it believes it is the right policy. It does not really matter if the government arrives at this belief because it conducted an analysis or because it was persuaded by information provided by donors (or other agencies, including independent researchers). The central issue is choice, not ownership. Donors should provide information and options—they may even indicate their preferences—but governments should then be allowed to choose. If donors agree with the free choice (which need not mean exactly the donors' preferred policy), policy conditionality is not required (but donors could have fundamentally influenced the choice).

Perhaps the more interesting case is if donors do not agree with the choice. Here, theory and evidence suggest that conditions will be ineffective (White and Morrissey 1997). An appropriate donor response would be to reduce the amount of aid released. In this context, donors should indicate which policies they consider important or immediate and which they consider less important. While a major part of the aid commitment may relate to an overall program of budget support, much aid will be linked to particular reform areas. Only in extreme cases would donors wish to terminate aid support completely. In principle, for any specific policy area aid disbursement can be linked to implementation of reforms in an agreed direction. If governments are not moving in that direction, disbursement is not triggered. In practice, all parties have an interest in disbursing aid once the money has been committed (this is the main reason why the threat required to enforce conditionality is not credible).

If donors took a long-term view, aid commitments could be triggered by policy choices (in the right direction) with disbursements phased to support implementation.

The other stages of the policy process (stages C–F in table 25.1) relate to ability to implement reforms, and donor influence and support are even more important here. Governments may have made the "approved" policy choice, but may lack the political and administrative ability to design and implement the policy effectively. Even if governments "made" the policy choice because it was required by conditions, failure to implement is often due to administrative and capacity weakness rather than to an unwillingness to reform (Morrissey 1999). Donors can assist with technical and financial support. It is worth noting that if a government has chosen the policy (is willing to reform), it will be receptive to donor assistance in implementation. Indeed, many governments argue persuasively that they need technical assistance (for example, in implementing standards and regulatory commitments under the World Trade Organization). As illustrated in table 25.1, donors can support implementation at a number of stages in the policy process. Technical assistance with design and administration is the most important and effective form of support. Supporting political capacity (for example, persuading the opposition or civil society) needs to be undertaken cautiously because it can appear to be political interference.

Ultimately, if the aid relationship is to be one of development partnership, donors should aim to support policy making and analysis capacity in the country. The aim is not to tell governments what policies to implement, but rather to help them to identify the effects of implementing alternative policies so that they can exercise policy choice. This is a clear and desirable move away from attaching conditions to aid—the support is for policy making rather than for implementing specific policies. Governments will choose the policies they believe are in their self-interest, so if donors want to influence the direction of reform they should influence beliefs. If the government then chooses the policy, donors should "put their money where their mouth is" and offer aid support, for implementation of the policy and perhaps program support more generally. Arguably, donors should go further: if donors believe in the policy they should be willing to compensate governments that implement the policy even if the outcome is unfavorable (Morrissey and Nelson 2004). Viewing donor influences on the policy process in this way serves to show why conditionality has been ineffective.

There is a danger if donors are influential and give "standard" policy recommendations to all governments, so that all countries are following almost identical policy prescriptions. This will encourage policy herding, reduce the information gain from policy experimentation, and reduce the chance that countries will be given the "optimal" policy advice (Morrissey and Nelson 2003). Unless donors can be certain that they are providing each country with the correct policy recommendation, countries should be allowed to experiment. Policy experimentation benefits all because it provides more information on what appears to work or fail under different circumstances. Thus, rather than imposing conditions, donors should provide information and advice but encourage governments to make policy choices. If these choices are in the right direction, then support for implementation should be provided. Ultimately, donors should support policy-making capacity in countries.

Dialogue and Policy-Based Lending

Although policy-based lending only accounts for a small proportion of World Bank lending, mostly to middle-income countries, this understates the importance of policy commitments in the donor-recipient relationship. Bilateral donors typically require that a recipient has an agreement (in effect, an agreed policy strategy) with the international financial institutions before they will provide program aid. For this reason, conditionality has had a more pervasive influence on donor-recipient relations, and on recipient policy choices, than would be indicated by simply looking at policy-based lending as a share of total aid. If a policy dialogue approach is adopted, would the donor-recipient aid-policy relationship look very different? On the face of it, the answer might be no—donors would still be hoping to exert some influence on recipient policies, and implicitly or explicitly there would still be conditions attached to aid.

The real differences would be matters of emphasis, although a properly developed dialogue would be quite different from conditionality. Greater emphasis would be placed on donors to provide evidence-based policy advice if they are to alter beliefs. Thus, if donors recommend a particular policy reform, or rather for every policy they recommend, they should support this with evidence on how the policy has worked elsewhere, reinforced with analysis of how the policy would impact the country. Good policy advice requires clarity and confidence in the policy message, implying that alternatives should be considered. If a clear policy stance cannot be advocated with confidence, it is unlikely to be convincing and will not alter beliefs. Furthermore, it is important that local policy analysis, government and independent, is part of the process. For many countries, especially the poorer ones, local analytical capacity is weak, and donor support for building capacity is an important part of the relationship. This is also vital for local consultation processes, because effective participation requires policy analysis capacity.

If conditionality is interpreted as "select this policy if you want the money," it is evident from the foregoing that policy dialogue would be quite different. Current knowledge on the impact of many policies is quite limited. For example, while there is evidence that spending on social sectors tends to improve aggregate welfare (for example, spending on health is associated with lower infant mortality) and can improve the welfare of the poor, there is less confidence regarding which growth policies are likely to be propoor (Morrissey 2004b). If policy dialogue implies that agreed reforms are restricted to those for which there is solid evidence, the pace of reform will tend to be slow. Furthermore, because agreement is required and local conditions and alternatives will be considered, flexibility and "policy space" will be important.

In practice, there is little new in this—donors and (most) recipients already have, to some degree, a dialogue on the policy options that are subsequently included in the aid-policy agreement. However, if more and clearer policy analysis is required so that the government makes an informed choice, and the onus is on the government to choose rather than the donor to stipulate, aid agreements may be linked to quite specific policy areas. For example, it may prove easier to reach mutual agreement on macroeconomic and trade policies than, for example, on privatization or policies toward capital inflows. Policy dialogue will be associated with slower and less extensive reform objectives than typically embodied in conditionality. Furthermore, genuine policy dialogue implies greater local input; consequently, the policy details are more likely to be tailored to the local environment. One implication is that a policy dialogue approach promotes ownership. Once the government makes its policy choice, it is up to the donor to decide if it is willing to support this choice with aid resources. If so, an agreement can be reached (in respect perhaps of the specific policy area). If not, dialogue continues and may, in some cases, break down (at least for particular donor-recipient pairs on specific policy issues). The implications for donor coordination are considered at the end of this section.

Policy Actions or Conditions?

The policy dialogue approach does not imply that there is no role for conditions in policy-based lending. Conditions associated with monitoring the use of aid, while justified, are not of concern here (for example, donors providing budget support may want to impose conditions restricting the areas in which the money can be spent). However, there may be certain policy actions that the donor requires, even if only to demonstrate commitment to moving in the required direction of policy reform. If the government is convinced these policy actions are appropriate and is in fact committed, then there is no need to specify them as conditions (it may actually be counterproductive to do so). The actions could be listed as required policy actions, with the implication that when the agreement (or the release of tranches of funding) is reviewed their implementation will be given high priority. There are circumstances when it can be mutually beneficial to specify conditions, if the government wants to signal its commitment or lock in reforms. While the primary objective is to provide evidence to alter beliefs and convince governments that the policy reform is beneficial and desirable, attaching policy conditions may reinforce the government's policy choice, especially in cases where strong opposition is anticipated.

Aid agreements in general, and policy-based lending in particular, involve an implicit or explicit contract. As part of this contract, it is reasonable that certain actions or objectives are specified. The issue is whether they are specified as conditions (required actions) or agreed/desired actions. While we would generally favor the use of policy actions rather than conditions, it should be acknowledged that conditions can feature in policy-based lending agreements resulting from dialogue. Such conditions should be of the general form of ensuring that a particular policy direction is followed, and should not be overly restrictive (given that the intention is to reinforce agreed policy, rather than impose policy). The aim is to get policy moving in the direction that is shown to be best for the country.

Three guidelines for conditions are recommended below. The first guideline follows from the tendency of policy dialogue to result in agreements (aid contracts) relating to specific policy areas.

(1) Conditions should be specific, clearly stated, and relatively easy to monitor. The most important criterion is that any conditions relate to policy inputs—actions taken

that are in the control of the policy makers and where the actions themselves can be observed. This is important for a number of reasons. First, the policy input is the action undertaken by the government—it describes what it does. Second, it is relatively easy to monitor actions and assess if the policy input was implemented. Third, concentrating on policy inputs rather than on target outcomes avoids assessment of implementation being contaminated by factors other than government action that determines outcomes. The fundamental objection to conditions based on outcomes is that it is never possible ex post to attribute with certainty the causes of an outcome. Consider an example. In the context of restoring macroeconomic stability, reducing the budget deficit may be an objective. Under the conditionality approach, a target deficit (as a ratio to gross domestic product) could be specified. If this is a condition, the problem is that it relates to an outcome, and even if a "correct" policy input was made, the target may not be met. For example, a government may reduce spending but if, due to external factors, tax revenue fell below target then the deficit reduction would not be achieved. A better type of condition could relate to the policy input, such as measures to reduce spending or to increase tax revenue. Implementing the required policy input implies meeting the condition. If the output (deficit) target is achieved, there is no problem. If the target is not achieved, then it is necessary to determine why. Was it due to external shocks or events, or was the policy input inappropriate or not actually implemented? If an output target is not achieved, one cannot be certain that failure on behalf of the government was the reason. This problem does not arise in the case of policy inputs, giving rise to the second guideline.

(2) **Conditions should relate to observable and verifiable policy inputs.** Donors often like to specify conditions in terms of outcomes or results, because this demonstrates that the objective is being achieved. Although this forms part of the dialogue (in effect the donors are claiming that by adopting specific policies the desired results will be achieved), outcomes should not be made conditions for the attribution problem outlined above. Whether a particular policy yields the desired outcome will depend on a variety of factors in addition to the policy actions taken, especially shocks and unexpected events. The importance of shocks differs across countries. Typically, the poorest countries are also the most vulnerable to adverse shocks (for example, terms-of-trade declines or bad weather); thus, the countries with the weakest policy environment are also those with the weakest link from policy inputs to outcomes. The importance of shocks also differs across policy areas. For example, macroeconomic outcomes are affected by terms-of-trade shocks, whereas health outcomes are affected by outbreaks of disease. For this reason it is not sensible to have assessments in one policy area conditional on performance in another area. Different policy areas should be treated separately, that is, conditions should be independent across policy areas. This leads to the third guideline.

(3) **Conditions in individual policy areas should be defined and assessed independently.** In practice, policy-based lending will relate to a variety of policy areas, and in some cases the effects are related. Continuing our example, while one target may be to reduce the budget deficit, another may be to liberalize the trade regime. Trade liberalization typically involves tariff reductions, which may be revenue reducing. In this case, implementing conditions in one policy area may undermine achieving targets in

another policy area. If conditions are interdependent, governments could end up being penalized (for not meeting outcome targets) even if they implement appropriate policy inputs. Of course, if the analysis underlying the policy recommendations were carefully conducted, such complementarities would be identified during the dialogue. Care should be taken to identify cases in which cross-policy conditions are complementary versus those where they may conflict.

Adopting these guidelines for specifying conditions, and policy actions more generally, in an agreement resulting from dialogue can facilitate improved donor coordination. Separating policy areas and placing the onus on donors to "make the case" for the policies they will support offers the possibility for different donors to focus on different policy areas. This could be particularly relevant if donors wish to concentrate on particular sectors, such as health, education, or private sector development. If donors are in agreement, among themselves and with the country, on the broad policy direction, or on policies in particular sectors, a case can be made for them to pool their resources (for example, Kanbur, Sandler, and Morrison 1999).

Conclusions: Engagement in Different Policy Environments

The core argument of this chapter is that the most effective way to influence the process of policy reform is to promote and support policy learning. Policy dialogue to encourage transfer of "proven" policies is the best way to alter a government's beliefs about which policies it should implement. Altering beliefs is the most effective way to promote sustained policy reform. Conditionality is not inherently a means of altering beliefs; therefore, it is not an optimal instrument of policy transfer. Nevertheless, appropriate conditions on policy inputs specified for each area of policy can reinforce policy transfer.

These general principles apply to all recipients. Among developing countries, some are more willing and able to implement reform than others, but this does not mean one needs a different approach to policy dialogue in each case. Where governments are committed to policy reform, and have the capacity (political and institutional) to implement a reform program, the aims can be quite ambitious. Where governments have a weak policy environment (Morrissey 1999), because they have weak political or institutional capacity to implement reforms, the reform agenda should be less ambitious. One could start with relatively simple reforms in a few areas, because it is typically easier to demonstrate the potential benefits of relatively simple reforms. Successful implementation of simple reforms will help to alter beliefs and build momentum for further reform.

There are likely to be some cases where the policy environment is so weak that even policy dialogue is difficult to establish, such as with failed states or evidently authoritarian regimes. The problem posed by these cases should not be depicted as an inherent weakness in policy dialogue, because conditionality is unlikely to be effective in these cases either. Difficult environments, where donors cannot even engage in dialogue, should be considered on a case-by-case basis, and any aid intervention would be quite limited. Initially, it may be more sensible to focus on projects or sectors rather than engaging on policy. These cases are the exception, however, and dialogue, albeit over a limited policy range, is feasible even in many of the poorest countries.

References

Booth, D. ed. 2003. *Fighting Poverty in Africa: Are PRSPs Making a Difference?* London: Overseas Development Institute.

Boughton, J. 2003. "Who's in Charge? Ownership and Conditionality in IMF-Supported Programs," IMF Working Paper WP/03/191, International Monetary Fund, Washington, DC.

Kanbur, R., T. Sandler, with K. Morrison. 1999. *The Future of Development Assistance: Common Pools and International Public Goods.* Policy Essay No. 25. Washington, DC: Overseas Development Council.

Koeberle, S. 2003. "Should Policy-Based Lending Still Involve Conditionality?" *The World Bank Research Observer* 18 (2): 249–73.

Morrissey, O. 1999. "Political Economy Dimensions of Economic Policy Reform." In *Evaluating Economic Liberalisation*, ed. M. McGillivray and O. Morrissey, 83–102. London: Macmillan.

———. 2004a. "Conditionality and Aid Effectiveness Re-Evaluated," *The World Economy* 27 (2): 153–71.

———. 2004b. "Making Debt-Relief Conditionality Pro-Poor." In *Debt Relief for Poor Countries*, ed. T. Addison, H. Hansen, and F. Tarp, 267–88. Palgrave/WIDER.

Morrissey, O., and D. Nelson. 2003. "The WTO and Transfer of Policy Knowledge on Trade and Competition." In *Growth and Development in the Global Economy*, ed. H. Bloch, 235–51. Cheltenham: Edward Elgar.

———. 2004. "The Role of the World Bank in the Transfer of Policy Knowledge on Trade Liberalisation." In *The Political Economy of Policy Reform*, ed. D. Nelson. Elsevier.

Operations Evaluation Department. 2004. *2003 Annual Review of Development Effectiveness: The Effectiveness of Bank Support for Policy Reform.* Washington, DC: World Bank.

White, H., and O. Morrissey. 1997. "Conditionality When Donor and Recipient Preferences Vary." *Journal of International Development* 9 (4): 497–505.

26

Partnerships in Policy-Based Lending

PATRICK WATT
ActionAid International

There is a problem in the rather loose way in which partnership is used in the development discourse. It is an overused and underanalyzed piece of terminology without an operationally useful definition out there. The United Nations International Conference on Financing for Development, held in Monterrey, Mexico, in 2002, really set in motion much of the thinking about partnership and the need for partnership. The consensus report from that conference states that achieving the Millennium Development Goals will require a new partnership and that effective partnership has to do with leadership and ownership of development plans. But this definition does not really help us a great deal. This chapter attempts to define "partnerships" in more detail and to discuss what sorts of conditionality would be appropriate or inappropriate under a partnership approach.

Defining Partnerships

There are three fundamental aspects of partnerships. First, it is clear that one cannot really have a partnership unless there are some basic shared objectives and there is agreement on certain shared goals. Second, there needs to be a degree of mutual accountability, and it is difficult to achieve that accountability unless there is transparency, and that accountability has to flow two ways. Third, there needs to be some shared learning and an openness to a two-way exchange of knowledge and learning—a kind of iterative process by which one identifies shared objectives.

It may be helpful to eliminate some relationships that are not actually partnerships. Consider the following cases: teacher/pupil relationship—it is clear that the teacher has the knowledge and the pupil is expected to receive the knowledge; parent/child—one does not have a partnership with a two-year-old; and charitable giver/deserving poor. There are elements of all these relationships in a lot of what goes on in terms of donor/recipient practice.

We need to recognize that the balance of power between the donor and recipient is critical, and much of the talk about conditionality is actually talk of power. The balance of power depends heavily on both parties' options and needs, so partnerships are quite unlikely where a country cannot afford not to take money from the donors, and the donors can afford to walk away. An example of this situation might be Malawi, where the new government has signaled clearly that its number one priority is to resume lending with the international financial institutions. A contrasting example might be that of India, where the Indian government decided recently that it was only going to stick with donors that were really bringing in significant benefits to the Indian government, and it was going to boot out the rest of them unless they shifted their funding to nongovernmental organizations.

Conditions Appropriate for Partnerships

Going back to the three aspects of partnership, starting with shared objectives, there obviously needs to be jointly agreed-upon policy targets. But if those targets are really nationally owned (even if they are not homegrown, as Oliver Morrissey suggests in chapter 25 they need not be), then are they actually conditions? Is conditionality a useful nomenclature for those kinds of shared objectives?

In terms of mutual accountability, it is recognized that any funding relationship requires a degree of financial accountability and requires some fiduciary conditions that allow money to be accounted for. ActionAid finances many local nongovernmental organizations in countries in Africa and Asia and Latin America, and it expects some minimum fiduciary accountability. When one employs fiduciary conditions, following on from what has been noted in earlier chapters, it is extremely important to reinforce the accountability between recipient governments and the population. Thus, conditionality around budget transparency might be quite a good way of satisfying certain basic fiduciary accountability concerns on the part of the donor, but at the same time enabling populations to better hold their own governments to account.

Going down the shared learning route, we really need to see some significant changes in donor practice around policy advice and technical assistance. The current knowledge gap approach, which assumes that donors have the knowledge and countries need to receive it, does not really accommodate iterative two-way policy dialogue, which is what is needed in a genuine partnership.

Shifting from Donorship to Ownership

It is clear that conditionality—where it is understood to mean policy leverage—has failed. But at the same time there are still some mixed signals coming from donor agencies. For example, we are told policy conditionality does not really work, but at the same time we hear that strategically deployed conditions can tip the balance and lock in reforms. We also hear that aid only works in a sound policy environment, but the policy environment also has to be owned. This is not a helpful guide to action if we have a country owning an unsound policy environment. And the prevailing donor view is that in weak policy environments, knowledge gaps need more attention than finance gaps.

While we have certainly moved away from coercion, we are still with a suasion model, and the dominant approach of donors on the ground is still seeing aid money as a reform inducement. That carries with it some underlying assumptions. We need to be clear about what we are assuming when a donor comes into a country and applies the principle that aid is there to induce reform. As long as aid is about improving policy, donors have to remain in the reform vanguard. If a country presents the donors with a development strategy that simply contains things that the country would have done anyway in the absence of the donors, then donors cannot accept that strategy at face value as long as their job is to add reforms at the margins.

Adding Reforms at the Margins

Even in reform-minded countries—countries that are regarded by the World Bank and the International Monetary Fund as reform exemplars—task managers often are still adding conditions at the margins that they can identify as "their" reforms. Much of this has to do with the self-definition of donors, as to what they understand their purpose is in the country. Some of the underlying assumptions behind this behavior are that donors know better or know better than the recipient; that the donors' policy course is somehow more constant than that of recipients and is less prone to interruption or diversion; and that donors are in some way insulated from political pressures in a way that recipient countries are not. Finally, and one particularly hears this in the United Kingdom, is the assumption that donors have the interests of the poor at heart in a way that recipient governments do not.

Not all of these assumptions necessarily are in play with a particular donor at a particular time. Nonetheless, these assumptions are quite prevalent and underpin a lot of donor practice. There are many reasons to question these assumptions; however, we need to recognize that the aid for reform model is not about partnership—it is instead a deeply paternalistic approach to delivering aid. It may be an approach that works, but it is not partnership. It is also intensely political, because from what has already been discussed in earlier chapters, it is clear that ownership does not mean universal agreement.

Actually, ownership really is about donors intervening and identifying a critical mass of reformers whom they believe they can work with—it is about tipping the balance. Once donors start doing that, and once they start intervening in internal domestic policy debates, they get heavily involved in politics. This needs to be recognized.

Toward a True Partnership Approach

What would be some of the implications of a move to a true partnership approach? With a true partnership approach, there would be an *end to highly specific economic policy conditions*, namely, policy conditions that are leverage conditions, designed to elicit policy reforms that donors believe would not otherwise be undertaken.

There needs to be an *end to one-size-fits-all conditions* in areas other than economic policy as well. With a genuine partnership approach there will inevitably be much more heterogeneity emerging in terms of the routes the policy dialogue takes and the sorts of reforms the donors have to support.

There should be *no more micromanagement*—with partnerships there is trust. Trust will enable countries to get on with managing programs themselves. No more micromanagement means an end to strategic placement of technical advisers in finance and planning ministries to control the budget process.

There has to be much *greater transparency about how compliance is judged,* which is difficult at the moment. It is hard to foster partnership when judgments about compliance and noncompliance seem to be made for opaque reasons, in a way that allows political considerations to intrude.

If we are serious about partnership then we have to *be serious about mutual accountability,* and that means donors being held to account in quite an active way for the quality of their development assistance. Maybe a forum such as a consultative group could be used to hold donors to account for the quality of their aid, the degree of coordination, the degree of predictability, and the extent to which donors are actually delivering the money they have committed to deliver.

Holding donors to account could go even wider and touch on issues such as trade policy, for example, and could actually start looking at some of the issues concerning the coherence of development assistance. For instance, are the steps donors are undertaking through their aid programs being in any way contradicted or undermined by what they are doing in other areas?

Finally, this chapter advocates a more orthodox approach than that offered by Tony Killick (see chapter 7) on the issue of the involvement of parliaments, particularly as we see increasing democratization in lower-income countries. We must *respect domestic decision-making processes.* Ultimately, donors have to be prepared to work through domestic decision-making processes and allow those domestic processes to have some effective sanction over what donors would like to see happen.

27

Part 5 Discussion Summary

Initial observations concerned the importance of shared objectives between donor and recipient, policy dialogue, and the notion that the nature of conditions should be independent, not overly complex, and monitorable. It was noted that policy dialogue can be difficult to carry out in a certain category of countries—Malawi was cited as an example. This is an important group of countries because they are heavily aid dependent and contain a significant number of poor people—and these countries are extremely important to the achievement of the previously established goals for poverty reduction.

The Role of Partnership

The primary theme was the role of partnership, which is critical in discussions of conditionality, donor harmonization, and the issue of capacity to undertake the analytical work and prepare/implement changes by borrowing countries. There was also brief discussion on the notion of insurance with respect to lending programs.

A number of participants raised questions about the real meaning of partnership and how the level of appropriate partnership could or should vary depending on the particular situation, for example, with a strongly performing country, a weakly performing country with no clear vision, or a country in crisis.

The participant from Tanzania suggested that for middle- or lower-income countries where there is strong support for reforms even before a Poverty Reduction Strategy Paper is undertaken, this differentiation should be taken into account in the course of policy dialogues as well as in the determination of the role of conditionality. Tanzania, Uganda, and Bolivia were cited as examples. There was general agreement that, in the case of a weak performer with no clear vision for reform, it would be difficult to establish a level of partnership approaching parity in the policy discussions because it is clear that a certain reform agenda would have to be undertaken before donors would be comfortable providing funding to such countries. A representative from ActionAid suggested that in the case of Low-Income Countries

Under Stress, an alternative aid model is needed in which partnership is developed over a period of time. In the short term, he suggested that mutual accountability would be difficult to achieve. At the same time, it was noted that this group of countries should be the real focus of the Poverty Reduction Strategy.

In the case of a crisis intervention, the representative from the International Monetary Fund suggested that the measures necessary would be clear not only to the International Monetary Fund but also to the government in crisis, and that the extent of partnership in such circumstances may not extend beyond policy discussions with the treasury or ministry of finance. He further suggested that it is primarily in noncrisis cases that shared objectives are critical for any program to ultimately be successful.

The question was raised as to the point when partnership loses its meaning; leaning toward ownership fundamentalism, whereby the donors would be pushed to respect the recipients' rights to make every single choice, would then result in unilateral determination from the recipient end. The representative from ActionAid responded that the issue is really being able to relinquish a certain degree of control while at the same time persisting with funding; if one is not prepared to actually fund a compromise, then there can be no partnership. It was suggested that at some point a decision must be made if there is a trade-off between helping the poor through albeit more rapid implementation of policy or respecting country ownership.

The level of partnership is in part determined by the level of conditionality and conditions under discussion, and the question was raised as to the distinction between the two. The participant from the United Kingdom suggested that there is a clear distinction between the two. Lenders and donors are entitled to conditions either regarding the use of the funds being provided or, in other instances, related to policies, and it is important to clearly distinguish between conditions that can be part of a dialogue and an agreement, and conditionality as a mechanism that is trying to impose policy reform. It is the latter—the mechanism—that one is trying to move away from, and while there can be some conditions, it is important that the entire lending program does not hinge on them.

The issue of donor harmonization represents partnership on a different level. At stake here is the coordination of conditions/conditionality among donors. One participant suggested that with respect to the determination of policy conditions, any three teams may come up with three different sets of conditions. Consequently, the coordination efforts between donors are made more complicated, and the benefit seen by the borrower is greatly diminished. For there to be an effective level of partnership, there needs to be consistency across donors with respect to policy design and implementation and the design and interpretation of policy conditions. The speaker from the United Kingdom suggested a common pool for donor aid, which could apply to budget support and policy-based lending, noting that such coordination could significantly simplify the process. The conference chair observed that, on the issue of harmonization, as an outsider it would be his perception that there is neither consensus nor a model, and that it will be an important challenge for the donor community to change this perception.

Capacity and Insurance

Other issues raised by participants included the notion of capacity and insurance. The representative from Tanzania pointed out that the capacity of borrowing countries is often underestimated. Although perceptions about a country's capacity to implement reforms may be accurate, donors often underestimate their clients' capacities to conduct the supporting analytical work and strategy development work prior to policy discussions. This issue is still problematic in the sense that little attention has been given to the donor's capacity with respect to knowledge of the recipient country's environment.

There was discussion about the impact of the Millennium Change Agreement. The consensus was that it is still a work in progress and that it will require some time before an assessment can be made as to the extent to which this initiative has addressed the problems being discussed at the forum.

Finally, there was a minor discussion on the notion of insurance, that is, a type of guarantee provided by the donor country to the recipient in the event of significant problems arising from actions/policies implemented that were founded on bad advice. This issue was raised by the participant from Vietnam, who also suggested that in some instances the programs implemented on the policy advice of international financial institutions had led to the wholesale wiping out of the results of reform measures previously undertaken. As a result, a number of these countries have refused to take any more donor advice. This then begs the question to what extent the donors should be held accountable. The participant from the United Kingdom concurred with the point that donors have traditionally not been willing to say mea culpa. It was acknowledged, however, that some progress has been made with respect to accountability.

Part VI
Conclusions

28

Concluding Remarks

MASOOD AHMED
Department for International Development

Conditionality: Part of a Cycle

There is a need to think about conditionality as part of a cycle, which also includes policy dialogue and capacity building. Conditionality is most effective when it follows a period of policy dialogue, during which people discuss the relevant set of issues, as well as speak to the needed design to compensate for the current constraints in domestic capacity. Capacity building is linked to a country's ability to monitor and implement its reforms, and this should be addressed in the future.

Not enough is done about country capacity, in either the multilateral or the bilateral institutions. We sometimes treat these stages as independent product lines. Internally we need to join up better on these issues.

Partner to a Country-Owned Agenda

We are now at a point where we have to replace the series of bilateral processes on policy dialogue and on conditionality between individual donor/lenders and recipient countries with how we all fit into a common country-based, largely country-led process of setting policy priorities and then agreeing within a longer-term strategy for that country what the benchmark of priority actions is for the next year or two. In essence this means all of us have to become more involved in the in-country process in discussing what those benchmarks are. This will minimize the scope for donors setting indicators and benchmarks outside the country process.

A model of such a new cooperation process is Mozambique, where a common country framework now exists, within which 12 donors have agreed to provide budget support. It seems that it is a model that should increasingly be the norm in countries where the donors have dialogue. It also means that there might be a set of questions about how individual donors operate, although it is rather difficult to do this without having a strong, empowered domestic government presence in those countries. It is even more difficult to do this if donors are working to their own cycles and constrained by their own governance structures in doing so.

New Strategy Needed for Low-Income Countries Under Stress and Weak and Failing States

Most of the proposals put forward are more applicable to countries in which there is a country-led process and a partnership than to the Low-Income Countries Under Stress and weak and failing states. We have all found different acronyms, but we do not yet have a working model. In these countries, however, work is under way to bring something together by the end of this year. We need more coherence on how we want to work with the 450 million people who live in these countries and who account for a disproportionate share of the off-track Millennium Development Goals. If we get this wrong, we face the risk of a failure of dreadful proportions.

Has Aid Led to a New Sort of Moral Hazard?

Another difficult issue is the link between predictability and performance, on which we need to do more work. It is worrisome that as we scale up aid for the Millennium Development Goals, we are going to be providing increasing amounts of funding to help countries take on commitments that amount to fixed and recurrent cost commitments to hire teachers, hire health workers, or provide HIV treatment. These are not commitments that a country can take on for a 10-year period and be worried every year as to what happens to the volume of aid flows coming in, depending on their performance or on exogenous shocks, and we do not have a good model to deal with this yet.

One possible way forward would be to expand the definition of humanitarian assistance to include progressively more things and protect them from performance targets. But approaching the dilemma this way increases the risk of eventually not having much aid outside of the protected envelope. A common approach from the International Monetary Fund, the World Bank, and the United Nations would be much appreciated on this issue.

How Much Should the Quality of Political Governance Matter?

We need to do more work on political governance and its link to disbursements. It is a key problem for bilaterals, so as we move toward providing bilateral support in the form of budgets, we cannot ignore political governance issues. At the same time, however, it is troublesome to link disbursements of aid in a kind of mechanical way to performance. In some instances, the analytics could drive in one direction, while the reality of political accountability in a given country would drive in another.

What Is the Donor's Place?

It is perfectly legitimate for donors to be actively engaged as stakeholders in the discussions concerning priorities, whether on policies or on choices to bring best practice from other countries into that process; in other words, to be part of the dialogue in countries. If one is providing a substantial share of a donor country's taxpayer money, if one is providing 40 percent of the recurrent budget in some cases, it is not right for the donors to be disengaged from the domestic debate.

Who Carries the Costs and Blame of Failure?

Moving from a policy debate to setting conditionality needs to be done with a lot of care, recognizing the fact that much of our knowledge about policy choices and inputs is imperfect, and we bear a disproportionately lower share of the cost of errors than do policy makers in developing countries. It is important to recognize that this is going to be an art rather than a science, meaning we cannot give detailed prescriptions, explicitly stating how far a country should go on an issue and not on others. It is difficult to tell ex ante when a group of reforms is going to be successful and when we might get it wrong.

Going forward, we need a little more humility and a little more recognition of the unequal sharing of the costs of failure. Public scrutiny of the advice we give, of the choices we encourage, is a strong deterrent. We should be strongly in favor of as much transparency ex ante through the process and ex post as one can get, in countries and at the institutional level, because when our performance is analyzed by others inside and outside, we have a strong incentive to be more careful in the future.

TONY KILLICK
Overseas Development Institute

The Debate on Conditionality Has Moved On

Many of the earlier controversies were a dialogue of the deaf, or at least seemed not really to be getting anywhere. The main lesson from this meeting is that the debate now seems to be moving on, the center of gravity of the discussion has shifted, and there now seems to be a wider acceptance of the limitations of 1990s-style approaches. Even Mark Allen of the International Monetary Fund said that the evidence is "overwhelming" that conditionality used as policy leverage is not effective. James Adams of the World Bank said there is no consensus among donors about a new model. That is right and the reason for it is that we are in transition. We have lost the old model, or rather we have lost faith in the old model, but we are not yet sure of how we are going to move forward with an alternative.

Have the Practices of International Financial Institutions Changed on the Ground?

All reasonable people want to make decisions on the basis of evidence, but is this reflected in practice on the ground? Is it reflected in what happens in borrowing countries, particularly in aid-dependent, low-income countries? While field work was being performed, in this area 18 months or so ago, there were still a lot of reports of "business as usual" on the part of the international financial institutions, particularly the International Monetary Fund. To what extent is any enlightenment being experienced in low-income countries?

For example, there has been much discussion about ownership and the importance of domestic country authorship of programs, but ownership to an important extent is about *process,* and we have not discussed what is happening to the negotiation processes of the international financial institutions and other donors. Have they changed those processes much, in ways that would be supportive of country ownership?

Have Staff Incentives Changed in the International Financial Institutions?

To what extent have staff incentives within the international financial institutions changed? Formerly there were incentives in favor of preparing loans with many conditions written in, because that made the individual task manager look tough and promoted him/her up the scale. Has that changed?

What Are Our Options on Conditionality Going Forward?

There is now a rich variety of ways in which bilateral and multilateral institutions can move away from 1990s-style conditionality. Chapter 19 by Gilles Hervio on the European Commission experiment was of particular interest from that point of view. We all recognize that finding satisfactory alternatives to old-style conditionality is not easy. The great thing about old-style conditionality was that it appeared to give an assurance that money would be well spent. That assurance turned out to be false, but nevertheless it seemed to provide a greater guarantee than some of the alternatives currently under discussion. To what extent are the Boards of the international financial institutions, and the major shareholders in particular, embarking on the kind of a debate this conference has provided? Or are they still in the mode of requiring conditionality bangs for their bucks, as was the case not long ago?

Caution Urged on Process Conditionality

In the course of looking for alternatives to 1990s-style conditionality some support has been expressed for the notion of process conditionality. But, as Willem Buiter pointed out in chapter 1, process conditionality is actually political conditionality. Some of this is relatively benign and uncontroversial, but some of it gets seriously involved in the domestic politics and institutions of the countries in question. There is absolutely no reason to expect that more demanding forms of process (political) conditionality will be more effective than economic policy conditionality. Empirical studies on political conditionality tell us that the proportion of success of this form of conditionality is, if anything, even lower than in the case of economic policy conditionality.

GOBIND NANKANI
World Bank

Moving Forward: What Have We Learned?

We have heard a lot about the importance of country circumstances, the importance of political economy factors, and the need for more flexibility and humility. All of these themes resonate strongly with some ongoing reflective work in the World Bank on what lessons we have learned from our experiences in the 1990s, particularly with respect to growth, but also with respect to the whole question of partnerships between countries and development partners.

Our research at the World Bank finds retrospectively that there is a vast variety of outcomes relating to country experiences, even though the policy approaches have been similar. This disconnect between policy approaches and outcomes really raised the question as to what the development paradigm ought to be.

Key Lessons from Introspective Analysis

First, there is a much stronger need for country-specific analyses. There have been such a wide variety of policies and institutional approaches that have led to successful outcomes in countries as varied as Botswana, China, India, Mauritius, and Tunisia that we cannot speak about a unique paradigm.

Second, if one takes the issue of country specificity seriously, one also has to recognize that principles such as macrostability, openness, and making good use of state discretion are all critical, but how they are implemented is very much a function of country-specific circumstances. To arrive at policy recommendations one really must do a lot more analytical work—it cannot be based on simple prescriptions.

Last, the issue of humility is applicable in the sense that country-specific analysis is a two-way street. It is a process in which development partners learn as much as they bring technical expertise and cross-country experience to the table.

Evolution of Economic and Sector Work

There is a strong relationship between prior economic and sector analysis and outcomes of specific projects or loans in which the World Bank has been involved. One must recognize that economic and sector work should be done in a much more careful way going forward, in a much more country-based way than has been done in the past.

Taking the examples of Brazil and China, a domestic drive for knowledge has led those countries to work with the World Bank on many specific policy questions, forcing the Bank's economists to work on country-specific institutions in order to provide advice that is far more relevant to the individual circumstances of Brazil and China.

The analytical work has to be done as much as possible with country research and policy institutes, and the strictures with which these analyses by development partners are looked at by country authorities has to be much, much more focused than in the past.

Country Capacity as a Barrier

A country's capacity, particularly in the Low-Income Countries Under Stress, is often a significant barrier to development and partnership with institutions such as the World Bank. We do not have concrete answers as of yet, but there are some good examples, for instance the experience in Tanzania and in Uganda in the 1990s, in which country-led teams organized the quality and level of activity with donors into highly successful outcomes on the developmental front.

Cultural Change Is Needed

It is important to recognize that the resolutions we have discussed will require a lot of cultural change within the international financial institutions, in countries themselves, as well as in bilateral agencies if any of this is going to have an impact. The issue of cultural change within the World Bank is critical. We cannot continue with the same line of questioning that we have in the past concerning what reforms we are buying with this loan or another. With respect to donors there is a question as to how this discussion will actually affect their behavior. In particular, how will it affect the International Development Association negotiations in the future? We simply cannot have as much of a focus on flags and on narrow attribution as has been the case in the past.

Looking to a New Dimension in the Donor and Client Country Relationship

From the country perspective, if donors are going to be emphasizing country specificity in the future, it comes with an important new set of responsibilities. Client countries have to take charge of their relationship with their development partners, and countries such as Mozambique, Tanzania, and Uganda have shown the way.

Index

Note: Boxes, figures, and tables are indicated by b, f, and t following page numbers.